SADDLE TRAMP
IN THE
HIGHLANDS

By the same author

Saddle Tramp in the Lake District

Contents

Illustrations

Acknowledgements

No expedition, whether it is to climb high mountains, cross Polar wastes or simply explore Scotland on horseback, could achieve its objective without the generosity and support of individuals or organisations. I am deeply grateful to Gordon Larkins of Chaplin's Bookshop, Keswick, for helping my dream to become a reality.

A special thanks also to Warren Elsby, librarian of Keswick Library; Tommy Birkett; Robert Izzard; Brian Burscough; Mike Taylforth; Brian Williams; the National Library of Scotland, Edinburgh; the Mitchell Library, Glasgow; Feinman and Krasilovsky, New York, for permission to quote from *A Race of Men That Don't Fit In* by Robert Service; HMSO Edinburgh for permission to quote from *The Control of Midges*, 1946 and 1948, and *Knoydart Estate*, 1948.

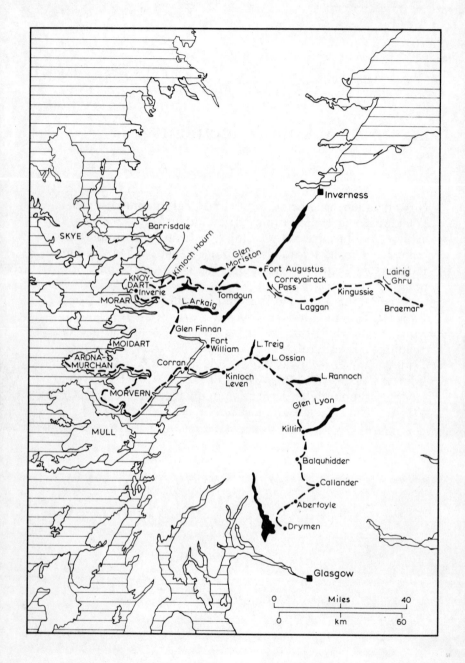

Based with permission on the Ordnance Survey. Crown Copyright.

1

Welcome to the *Real* Scotland

'The Highlands and Islands begin as far South as the tip of the Kintyre Peninsula. The area stretches northwards to the far highlands of Sutherland, to Caithness, and encompasses the scattered islands of Orkney and Shetland, while to the West, off the coast, lie the jewel-like islands of the Inner and Outer Hebrides. Seen at their best in Spring and Autumn or early Summer, these wide-flung landscapes hold an astonishing range of visual attractions.'

'What rubbish!' I muttered to myself, hurling the expensively produced glossy tourist brochure to the back of the tent.

It had been a long, tiring day and I lay back in my sleeping bag, listening to the music of the river gurgling and splashing over the stones. It was hot and humid and around the hills above Loch Ard thunderclouds rumbled a challenge to each other. Before I left home a well-meaning acquaintance had thrust a sheaf of tourist literature into my hands. 'We found them most useful during our motor tour last year,' he said eagerly.

Not wanting to hurt his feelings, I had stuffed them into a saddlebag. Now, having nothing else to read, I had been browsing through them. A large brochure crammed with glossy colour photographs with not a drop of rain or a midge in sight waxed lyrical about Scotland's 'delights', but neatly ducked out by adding that it could not be held responsible for any inaccuracies.

The thunder rumbled closer as I settled to go to sleep and rain spattered against the flysheet. Suddenly a brilliant flash of lightning lit up the forest and crackled over the great dome of Ben Lomond. It was the neon sign of the ancient clans, and as the deluge on the tent increased, the message was clear. 'Welcome to the *real* Scotland.'

When John Knox toured the Highlands in 1786 he wrote in his journal, 'Many hundred thousand acres of land might be occupied in the growth of timber, which at present be wild and useless to the proprietors.' Well over a hundred years were to go by before anyone realised it was a sound piece of advice and even then it took a World War to convince the politicians that if we continued to squander our timber resources it would not be long before there was hardly a tree left standing in the country. In 1919 a hurriedly formed Forestry Commission was told to acquire land and plant trees with all speed and many landowners grasped the opportunity to get rid of large tracts of wet and unprofitable hillside, where even sheep were hard pressed to survive. Having commenced its activities in Cumberland, the Forestry Commission soon fixed its eye on the wilds of Scotland and, in 1928, acquired a large chunk of land in the area of Loch Ard. As time went by more bits were added to it, until it extended from Loch Venacher in the Trossachs over the summit of Ben Lomond and reached down to the shore of Loch Lomond at Rowardennan. Altogether the area totalled 42,000 acres, though 10,000 acres, mainly in the vicinity of Ben Lomond, were not planted. In 1952 this vast forest, comprising Loch Ard, Achray and Buchanan Forests, was named Queen Elizabeth Forest Park to commemorate the coronation of Her Majesty Queen Elizabeth II (though some still argue she is Queen Elizabeth I of Scotland). Because of its proximity to Glasgow and the industrial districts of central Scotland, the Forest Park draws thousands of visitors each year. But on a warm June afternoon, as my two ponies, Thor and Lucy, strode out along the forest track, kicking sand into the air with their hooves as they went, there was not a soul to be seen.

The warm scent of spruce hung heavy in the air as we followed the track in and out of the trees. At intervals laburnum trees, weighed down with long pendulous blossom, overpowered the spruce with a heavy, musky aroma that had me breathing deeply to retain the pleasure for as long as I could. On either side of the track the long brown grass was limp and lifeless in the heat, but here and there sheltered banks or patches of moist ground glistened with clumps of golden primroses. There was not a drop of water to be found in the dried-up watercourses and both ponies sucked noisily at their teeth to create saliva. Mile after mile we plodded through the hot forest and, with each mile, the pace of Thor and Lucy became slower and slower, until I was forced to stop in the shelter of a clump of trees and rest them for half an hour. While the ponies dozed I hunted round for water, but every stream bed and drain was bleached and cracked like a desert gorge. The map showed a track leading through the forest to a little hamlet called Balleich, just by Aberfoyle, and it seemed an ideal place to camp for the night before heading across the Menteith Hills.

As the welcome shelter of the trees thinned out on the edge of the forest we were at the mercy of a burning orb, beating down from a cloudless sky. It was useless to urge the ponies on, their strength had been drained away and they walked painfully slowly, like clockwork toys gradually winding down. A cluster of timber houses surrounded by a clump of shady trees came into sight and I began to wonder what sort of reception we would get. There was no sign of life as we passed the houses, so I hitched Thor and Lucy to a tree and scouted around for water. As in the forest, the stream beds were dried-up and I was about to try my luck at the houses when, to my astonishment, an ice cream van suddenly appeared round a bend in the road. Waving frantically for it to stop, I bought three large cornets with chocolate sticks on top. Thor grabbed his and swallowed it in one gulp, but Lucy, who is more ladylike, licked hers slowly, crunching the chocolate stick between slurps. Thor watched me enviously as I rested against a tree to eat my ice cream, but I was determined not to buy the greedy oaf another one.

Looking across at the houses, I noticed a Forestry Commission van parked in a driveway and I walked across to ask if there was a field I could camp in for the night. A man working on an outboard motor in the garage watched me suspiciously as I approached. 'Is there anyone locally who would let me camp and graze the ponies for the night?' I enquired.

Without speaking, he shook his head indicating a firm No.
'Could I look for a place in the forest?' I ventured.

He reacted as if he had been shot. Flinging the wrench he
had been using into a tool box, he stalked towards me angrily,
'The Forestry Commission does not allow camping in the
forest,' he said officiously, 'nor are you permitted to graze
animals.'

I was really too hot and tired to argue, so I asked if there
was a farm locally.

'There's plenty of farms hereabouts,' he replied, 'but they
don't take campers.'

It was obvious I was not going to get much help from him
and I was turning to go when he suddenly said, 'Hey, wait a
minute. Are you the Forest Ranger who was mentioned in the
Slasher?' (*Slasher* is the Forestry Commission's newspaper and
an article had appeared in it about my intended journey
through Scotland.) I admitted I was and immediately his
attitude changed.

'That's different,' he said, 'you're one of us. Wait here while
I make a phone call and see what I can fix up.' He returned a
few minutes later beaming all over his face and announced
that Peter Martin, one of his Rangers, had some land and I
was welcome to stay there, but it was at Kinlochard, five and a
half miles away. I gulped at the prospect of having to press the
ponies on for another five and a half miles, and in the opposite
direction to my route, but there was no choice.

My new-found friend introduced himself as Eric Howell,
the Chief Forester in charge of the Forest Park and, as we
talked, his wife appeared and invited me into the house for tea.
I accepted gladly, but first I borrowed a couple of buckets
from Eric and took them full of water, down to Thor and
Lucy. You could almost hear the hissing of steam as they
plunged their hot muzzles into the cool liquid and they held
them there for a long time before they started to drink. In the
kitchen of the house it was a relief to be out of the heat and my
throat was so dry I drank several cups of tea before I managed
to taste one. Eric was a keen angler and his wife feasted me
royally on fresh sea trout, followed by home-made cakes and
buns. In the company of a Forester, it is not long before the
conversation turns to trees and the everyday problems of

forestry and, while his wife cleared away the dishes, Eric talked about the difficulties of establishing a forest in an area composed mainly of poor soil, bogs and rock.

I was reluctant to drag myself away from the cool kitchen, but time was ticking on and I still had a long way to travel to Peter Martin's field at Kinlochard. Thor and Lucy were dozing peacefully under the trees when I went out and they made it quite clear that they were not a bit happy about having to set off again. Eric Howell advised me to follow a road through the forest, along the shore of Loch Ard, but to get to it I would have to go through Aberfoyle, then by the main road for a mile or so, to a place called Milton. Waving goodbye to the Howells, I urged Thor on down the forest track and out onto a surfaced road. As we approached an estate of houses on the edge of Aberfoyle, the clatter of the ponies' hooves on the tarmac brought people to their doors to stare curiously after us. Two little boys on bicycles, who were racing each other along the pavement, skidded to a halt and started an argument about what breed of pony Thor and Lucy were. A freckle-faced redhead dropped his bike to the ground and peered under Thor's belly.

'They're Icelandics,' he exclaimed, as if he had seen 'Made in Iceland' stamped on Thor's underside.

'Och, away man,' retorted his pal, with an air of one who knew his horses, 'Icelandics is white, so polar bears canny see 'em.'

I never did get a chance to put them right because a fool in a car came up behind us and hooted loudly. Thor took fright and shot across the road with me hanging on for dear life, trying to stop Lucy bolting in the opposite direction. Fortunately a gate leading into a field was open and once they were in the safety of open space, the pair of them wheezed to a halt and stood trembling. I jumped off Thor in a fury, to go after the motorist, but he had gone.

The roar of a fairground in full swing on a car park in Aberfoyle made Thor snort again, so I slid out of the saddle and led him along the road to Milton. A constant stream of cars and coaches roared past within inches of the packs fastened to Lucy's side and I breathed a sigh of relief when I reached the quiet by-road that dropped down to the attractive cluster of houses at Milton and crossed over a little hump-backed bridge, spanning the infant River Forth. Ahead a man came out of a house and watched as we approached.

'Are those Fell ponies?' he asked when we reached him. I groaned to myself. Was I ever going to reach my campsite that night? I said that they were pure Fell and immediately he made a tour of inspection, looking at Thor's teeth, running a hand down his legs, then standing back to compare Thor with Lucy.

'The mare's a lot lighter than the gelding,' he said, tilting his head on one side in the way that horse-owners do when they are casting a critical eye over someone else's nag.

'Are you sure she's hundred per cent Fell?'

I was tired and weary and wanted to get on and here was a man, not only holding me up, but questioning poor Lucy's pedigree. I was tempted to reply 'Of course I'm bloody sure!' and ride off, but I hesitated. After all, he was only being friendly. Had I been in a better frame of mind, I would have shared his enthusiasm, but evening was coming on and I had a long way to go still.

'Before you go, come and see my Connemara,' said the man, almost pleading with me. What could I do but accept his offer.

Tying Thor and Lucy to a tree, I followed him into the garden of a very nice house and round the back to a block of superb stables. He flung back the bolt of a loosebox and pulled the door open with a flourish, like the unveiling of a priceless painting.

'What do you think of him?' he asked, almost in a whisper.

The bell of caution rang somewhere in the back of my mind, reminding me of an occasion some years before when I was staying at the house of a man who was a connoisseur of wine. In my honour, he had opened a bottle of very rare wine and reverently handed me a glass.

'Tell me what you think of it,' he had said, almost in tears.

More used to drinking out of pint glasses, I had downed it in a couple of gulps and said, 'It's not bad. Do you mind if I have another?' I was never asked back.

When I looked at the Connemara pony it was a bit like

tasting that wine. I had never seen a Connemara in the flesh in my life and was not quite sure what I should be looking for. A very beautiful animal it certainly was, but comparing this immaculate, well-groomed animal with my unkempt and well-worked Fell ponies gave me a complex and, hoping I had said the right things about the Irish beauty, I thanked the man for letting me look at it and left hurriedly to collect Thor and Lucy and continue on my way.

'Enjoy your ride along the loch side,' he shouted after me, 'it's the most beautiful sight in Scotland.'

Beyond the houses the track narrowed and wended its way through a plantation of spruce and pine to the edge of Loch Ard. There was not a breath of wind and the flat, calm surface of the water, reflecting the pale blue, cloudless sky, looked like a fabulous jewel held in a clasp of emerald green. At a point where the path almost touched the water, an elderly man sat holding a rod, quietly fishing, and as I went by I said I was sorry if the ponies had frightened away the fish. He laughed and said, 'Ye needn't bother yersel aboot that. A'm no wanting to catch anything anyway. A'm just sitting here getting used to the peace.'

He went on to explain that he had just retired from the centre of Glasgow to the area, and had not realised what it was like to live away from the noise of traffic.

'How do you get on with the locals?' I asked him.

'Och, they're no bad,' he replied, 'but you have to remember, this is Rob Roy's country. He was looked upon as being something of a Robin Hood character, but if you read between the lines, he was just an unscrupulous thief and a rogue. But he's still a hero with the locals and, given half a chance, they'd carry on his traditions.'

The path turned away from the edge of the loch and went deep into the forest and I was stumped by tracks going off in all directions. The Ordnance Survey have never been able to keep up with the Forestry Commission's road-building activities, so very few forest roads are shown, even on the large-scale maps. I reasoned that if I turned right each time I came to a junction I would head towards the edge of the loch and it would keep me going in the right direction. It worked well for a couple of junctions and each time I neared the edge of the loch I found another track to take me towards Kinlochard. I was full of confidence when I turned right the third time, but after an hour of wandering through the trees with not even a glimpse of the loch, and the ponies so weary they could hardly stand up, I realised I was lost. I climbed as high as I dared up a tall spruce, hoping to get my bearings, but all I could see in every direction was a green carpet of trees. Back on the ground I discovered that Lucy was so tired she had stretched out on the track, pack and all, and I had to prod her with a sharp stick before she would stand up. As the sun dipped lower in the West it cast long black shadows through the sombre trees, which seemed to accentuate the silence of that great forest. Every snapping of a twig or rustle in the undergrowth set my nerves on edge as I hauled the worn-out ponies back along every agonising mile to the road junction where I had turned off.

I had resigned myself to having to spend the night in the forest, but there was not so much as a blade of grass or level piece of ground anywhere to pitch the tent or tether Thor and Lucy. In the occasional open space where trees had been felled, the foresters had left branches in vast tangled heaps and it would have been very dangerous to take ponies over such rough ground. Arriving once more at the road junction, I hunted around in the gloom for any indication of the direction of Kinlochard and almost shouted with relief when I discovered a battered board nailed to a tree that told me to carry straight on. It may have boosted my morale, but it had little effect on Thor and particularly poor, tired Lucy, carrying the unrelenting weight of the packs. Thor kept stopping every hundred yards or so and I had to dig my heels in hard to keep him going. Suddenly, ahead I saw a shimmer of silver through the trees. At first I thought it was weariness playing tricks with my eyes, but, as we drew nearer, I could see water. It was the edge of the loch and beyond I could make out the shapes of houses at Kinlochard. I sang every song I knew as we trundled slowly along, the ponies twitching their ears nervously, wondering what all the noise was about. As we descended towards Kinlochard the shapes of the houses faded into the velvet evening and twinkling beacons of light in the windows guided me through the trees. The forest road merged with a stony track that gave way to a tarmac road encircling the small estate of forestry workers' houses. We had arrived. Leaving Thor and Lucy chewing furiously at a patch of grass, I found Peter Martin's house and rapped on the door. A woman opened it cautiously and I explained who I was.

'Oh dear,' she said, 'Peter thought you weren't coming and he's gone out. But he said if you did come you were to take your ponies to his field.'

At first my heart sank when she told me that Peter was out, but I cheered up when she said I could use the field. 'That's great,' I said, 'where is the field?'

'Oh, it's two and a half miles back up the track you have just come down.'

I sat in the dark outside Peter's house for half an hour or so, trying to summon up sufficient strength to face the two and a half mile climb back into the forest. How was I going to break it to Thor and Lucy? They would be convinced they were in the hands of a raving lunatic. To soften the blow, I gave them a packet of peppermints and a chocolate bar each and it brightened them up. A quick check with the torch to see that the pack saddle was not chafing Lucy's back and we set off to retrace our steps. About half a mile above Kinlochard I heard a car approaching and wondered if it might be Peter. It was not, but the man at the wheel knew about me and said that Peter was in the forest looking for me. I thanked him and pushed the reluctant Thor on again, into the darkness. As we reached the edge of the forest I could see the lights of a car moving through the trees. It came towards me and stopped and a voice shouted, 'Are you Bob Orrell?'

'Yes,' I shouted back.

'Thank God for that. I thought you had got lost. I'm Peter Martin. Follow me.'

Starting the engine, he turned the car round, then drove slowly in front while we did our best to keep up. He opened a gate into a field and showed me a good place to camp by the edge of a river. After helping to unload the ponies and pitch the tent, Peter said he was longing to talk about ponies with me, but it was now nearly midnight and he had to be up early the following day to go to a horse sale at Stirling and was booked to take a German tourist deer stalking in the evening.

He said I could stay as long as I liked and if I was still around in a couple of days time we would have a good 'blether'. As he spoke, a tremendous flash of lightning lit up the forest around us like broad daylight and was immediately followed by an ear-splitting crack of thunder.

'I must be off. There's going to be one hell of a storm,' said Peter and flicking on a torch he ran for his car. I dived into the tent and was in my sleeping bag before the first drops of rain hammered on the canvas. Every muscle in my body ached but, snug in my sleeping bag with the rain beating down on the tent, I was gloriously happy to be back in Scotland.

2

Over the Menteith Hills
to Loch Venachar

Rain battering on the flysheet woke me at about eight o'clock and when I opened the tent door it was a dismal sight. Thick grey cloud swirled among the trees, leaving the branches heavy with water that cascaded into the sodden grass below. The shallow river that had chattered and gurgled softly by the tent during the night was now ugly and swollen, a chocolate-brown, foam-flecked torrent that angrily swept all before it in a maelstrom of tree trunks, fence posts and bloated carcases of drowned sheep.

I filled the pre-heating bowl of the Primus stove and when I applied a match to it the acrid tang of hot methylated spirit filled the tent. I lay back in my sleeping bag and watched the blue flame flicker round the vaporising tubes of the burner, heating them to a cherry red that quickly turned the paraffin into a hissing flame under a pan of coffee. My muscles still ached and my backside felt as if the saddle had been lined with sandpaper. As I sipped coffee I decided to stay another night in Peter's field, though the decision was hardly a momentous one. The voice in my head which usually puts up a lively argument when I want to take things easy was strangely silent that morning.

Towards noon, the rain stopped and a bright sun pierced the clouds and began chasing them off in the direction of Ben Lomond. The grass around the tent steamed like a Turkish bath as the sun became hotter and soon the ground was so dry it was difficult to believe that only an hour before it had been saturated in water. The river returned to its normal, gurgling self and once more birds twittered amongst the branches. Clad only in my underpants, I splashed in the river, gasping

as the icy water rose around my nether regions. Thor and
Lucy were contentedly munching grass at the far end of the
field. I climbed out of the water and lay by the tent, letting the
rays of the sun laser-beam their way into my aching joints. I
did not relish the prospect of riding back through the forest to
Aberfoyle the next day and, spreading the maps out in the
sun, I looked for an alternative route. There appeared to be a
way over the hills to Crianlarich, to join a drove road leading
to the Kingshouse Inn at the head of Glencoe, then by the
Devil's Staircase route to Kinlochleven. It seemed an
attractive alternative at first glance, but when I realised I
would have to miss out crossing Rannoch Moor, I decided
against it. I had always wanted to cross Rannoch Moor but
had never got round to it. On this journey it was a must.

I had not eaten a thing since tea at the Howells the previous
day, yet had no appetite. Deciding I needed some exercise, I
jogged down through the forest to Kinlochard. In daylight it
was quite an attractive little place and I was amazed to find
that almost every house seemed to own at least one horse.

As I walked back through the forest, the sound of bagpipes
floated through the trees and I stopped to listen. I happen to
like the music of the pipes, but there are many in the South
who insist that they are best heard from a distance and, if you
live in London, then Scotland is about the right distance. The
first time I ever handled a real set of Scottish bagpipes was at
Armadale in Skye, in the early 1950s. I had come across from
Mallaig on the motor vessel *Blaven*, in the company of a pipe
band on their way to play at the Portree Games. It is doubtful
if they ever made it, though. They were so drunk they could
hardly stand and were carried ashore and dumped on the
quayside, in a tangle of kilts, bonnets and hairy legs. One
giant of a man, who lay flat on his back, proving beyond all
doubt that no self-respecting Highlander wears anything
under his kilt, kept shouting, 'Donald, where's ma pipes?
Donald, where's ma pipes?'

But Donald was too busy being sick into the harbour to take
any notice. I remembered seeing a set of pipes lying in the
scuppers of the *Blaven* and, jumping back on board, I picked
them up, It was a superb set, with the black chanter and
drones mounted in ornate silver and ivory.

'When we get to Portree I'll buy you a good dram, laddie,' said the grateful piper and, clasping the pipes to his bosom like a mother holding a baby, he fell fast asleep.

I never forgot those pipes and it inspired me to buy a chanter and learn to play it. At the time I was rather sweet on a girl whose father was a piper, but unfortunately the fire of love cooled before I had mastered the basic notes. The girl's mother came from a well-to-do English family and liked the world to know that she had married beneath her station. One day I called at the house to find father doing his best to escape the incessant verbal onslaught with a bottle of 'White Horse'.

He grasped me by the shoulder to save himself from falling over, 'Dinna get yoursel' tied to a woman, sonny,' he mumbled, 'they make life hell on earth.' Picking up his pipes he began to tune up, when the door burst open and mother stood on the threshold.

'I've had about enough of your caterwauling noise,' she yelled 'and I'm going to stay with mother.'

Father took the chanter out of his mouth and the pipes squealed to a halt. 'Well on ye go then, ye auld witch,' he roared, 'ye'll find yer broomstick leaning against the back door.'

Mother's mouth moved as she screamed something back at him, but her voice was lost as the pipes wailed into life with 'The Road to the Isles'.

By an odd coincidence, it was the same tune that the hidden piper was playing as I walked along the track and I quickened my pace to keep in step with the march. The sound of the pipes had faded away by the time I reached my campsite, but it had not only stirred my legs, it had also livened up my appetite. I felt quite hungry. With a mug of hot soup in one hand and a lump of cheese in the other, I sat outside the tent and watched, fascinated, as a huge red deer stag brought a bunch of his girlfriends down for a bathing party on the far side of the river. The hinds paddled in the shallows, having a fine old time, but the stag rushed up and down on the river bank like a youth too shy to take his trousers off in front of girls.

During the night the wind brought the rain clouds back and

water beating on the tent woke me at five o'clock. I lay wondering if I would be able to leave that morning and fell asleep thinking about it. At eight o'clock I made a mug of coffee and opened the tent door to get some air. The rain had stopped and shafts of light from a weak sun flashed through the trees, illuminating hundreds of cobwebs, spread like exquisite silver lattice-work across the branches of the spruce. It promised to be a lovely day and a surge of excitement went through me at the thought of setting out once more.

Peter Martin arrived as I was saddling Thor and Lucy and we sat on the grass and talked. A stalker all his life, Peter was worried about the way estates were being bought by outsiders and sometimes sold off in bits and pieces.

'It's destroying the whole country,' he exclaimed angrily, 'and there doesn't seem to be a politician, Scots or English, who gives a damn about it.' He went on, 'Most of these new owners only want cheap land, they aren't interested in preserving Scotland's traditions and they certainly don't care a hoot about the way local folk used to look to the estates for employment.'

Some years ago he had worked for a lady who owned an estate near Kinlochard. She was typical of the old type of laird, who really looked after her employees. 'Mind you,' said Peter, 'she was an old tyrant in many ways. She used to inspect every deer carcase and if it hadn't been shot cleanly through the neck she wanted to know why. There aren't many about like her now though,' he continued. 'She didn't just look on the deer as a source of money. She looked after the herd like a farmer looks after his cattle and only the weakest were allowed to be culled.'

While Peter and I were talking a peculiar squawling sound came out of the forest. It sounded like a tawny owl at first, but when it rose to a shriek it was obvious something was in pain, so we dashed across, thinking an animal was being attacked. As we neared the fence dividing the field from the forest the noise stopped and there was not a sign of life anywhere. Then I saw it. In the thick grass growing through the fence and with its head wedged fast in the wire mesh, lay a roe deer calf, about a week old. Mum was frantically rushing up and down the fence calling to her youngster, but when she saw us she raced off into the forest. Peter knelt down and very gently eased the tiny head back through the wire and lifted the calf up to inspect it. Fortunately it was none the worse for the ordeal and bawled lustily for its mother. Judging by the noise she was making, she was not far away and when Peter lifted the calf over the fence it scampered away to join her.

It was almost noon by the time Peter left to go stalking, and I led Thor and Lucy out of the field and on to the forest track. A mile or so outside Aberfoyle we were forced to join the busy A81 trunk road and for another mile we jockeyed for position amongst a convoy of cars and coaches whose drivers thought it very clever to blare their horns as they drove past the ponies. From the windows of the coaches, a steady stream of beer cans, bottles, food cartons, cigarette packets and smouldering butts of cigarettes were hurled into the grass, and sometimes over us, as they hurtled by. I can only hope that there is someone in Parliament with sufficient concern for Scotland's future to recognise that the country's existing wild areas are a priceless asset to be defended at all costs from the speculators, who see not mountain lochs and beauty, but a gigantic cash register. Those who seek to drive motor roads through the mountain passes of the Cairngorms and the wild areas of the Western Highlands ought to be boiled in a large vat of North Sea oil and the planners who approve such profanity should be fed to the lobsters in the Minch.

The edge of Achray Forest came into sight beyond Aberfoyle golf course and it was a blessed relief to leave the road and ride into the quiet of the trees. A signpost told me it was six miles to Callander via the Menteith Hills and I followed a well-marked track, climbing up through the trees. Thor snorted as the sound of a tractor engine starting up ahead of us echoed across the hillside and, rounding a bend, I found our way blocked by a winch hauling tree trunks out of the forest and stacking them in a huge heap at the side of the track. The operator very kindly stopped the engine to let us through, but even then Thor crept by on tiptoe, with eyes rolling as if he expected the machine to leap out and eat him. One good thing about his fear, it kept him going uphill at a smart pace and soon we reached the edge of the forest and a gate in the boundary fence. Through the gate we were on the

Menteith Hills, but although the soft path that led gradually upwards was a great deal easier on the ponies' feet, Lucy kept stopping and eventually refused to budge. It dawned on me that we had hardly stopped for a rest since we had left Kinlochard and it was her way of reminding me that even the best ponies cannot keep going forever. I said I was sorry and gave her a piece of chocolate to keep her going.

Higher up the hill I called a halt in an isolated clump of trees and, unloading Lucy, I gave her back a good massage, then left her to graze. There was a good stream nearby and along with the ponies I submerged my face in the cool water, before lying back against a tree to inhale the dry odour of peat that hung heavy in the hot air.

Both Thor and Lucy were a lot livelier after their rest and we made good time across the hills and descended towards Loch Venachar. On the side of the hill great tracts of land had been ploughed up for afforestation and it rather spoilt the look of the place. Fortunately someone had had the good sense to keep the plough well away from the drove road and, I suppose, one day the path will go through a forest instead of across open land. It was late in the afternoon when I reached the road by the edge of Loch Venachar and although I had hoped to camp in Strathyre Forest that night, there was nothing to be gained by rushing. Here was a nice area of flat grass for my tent, plenty of grazing for the ponies and a good stream for water. What more could man and beast want?

As the sun went down, threatening clouds gathered on the summit of Ben Ledi above the loch, and it looked as if a storm was brewing. It was still quite warm and I sat on a log at the edge of the loch watching the ever-changing patterns of light ripple across the water like burnished gold, gradually turning to silver, then to grey and finally to ebony as the black clouds drifted across the setting sun and day became night. A zephyr of wind sped across the loch, splashing water against the rocks along the shore and rattling the leaves of the birch and alder. The first drops of rain heralding a downpour thudded into my face as I stumbled through the darkness to the secure womb of the tent. Though the rain poured down with monsoon proportions, it did not last long and gradually the storm crossed the hills towards Aberfoyle.

Early next morning, I sat outside the tent with a mug of coffee and watched the sun warm the glen. There was not a trace of cloud in the sky and Loch Venachar, which had looked dark and threatening on the previous evening, was now blue and inviting. The road on the other side of the loch was already well filled with motor coaches carrying loads of pilgrims to Brig o'Turk and Loch Katrine, to retrace the wanderings of the poet Wordsworth and his sister Dorothy, or to bring alive Sir Walter Scott's poem 'Lady of the Lake', which tells the story of a medieval Scottish king who set out from Stirling Castle with an army of followers to hunt deer in the Trossachs. It was certainly no ordinary hunt and the pace wore out the riders, until only one was left.

'T'were long to tell what steeds gave o'er
As swept the hunt through Cambusmore
What reins were tightened in despair
When rose Ben Ledi's ridge in air;
Who flagged upon Bochastle's Heath
Who shunned to stem the flooded Teith.

Few were the stragglers following far,
That reached the Lake of Vennachar;
And when the Brig o'Turk was won
The headmost horseman rode alone.'

As I looked at the line of coaches, I could imagine the passengers leafing through their guidebooks and perhaps making the same mistake in pronouncing Katrine as a lady friend of mine did some years ago. She was on the pier waiting for the steamer and reading aloud from a guidebook when a fierce Highlander thrust his beard into her face and said, 'Madam, the name of the loch does not rhyme with latrine. We do not pee in it, we drink it.'

3

Helpful Motorcyclists and Highland Funerals

After breakfast I struck camp and let the ponies jog gently along the side of Loch Venachar until we joined the crowded Callander to Trossachs road. Even on a short lead-rope, Lucy had a habit of walking to one side of Thor, rather than behind him, and it was nerve-wracking leading them in traffic. Coach after coach thundered by and it never seemed to occur to the drivers to slow down just a little as they passed us. The situation was no better when we reached Kilmahog and the Callander to Lochearnhead road, which, if anything, was busier with traffic. Adding to the tide of coaches and cars were convoys of commercial travellers, driving like bats out of hell in their Ford Cortinas, jackets swinging on coathangers in the rear windows, pink shirts newly pressed. All were heading for the West Highland tourist honey pots to fill order books for 'genuine Scottish rock, lettered right through', or 'a present from Oban', probably manufactured in a plastics factory on the outskirts of London; or tartan dolls, tartan badges and a whole host of 'local crafts' more likely to originate in Hong Kong or Eastern Europe than Scotland.

Leaving Kilmahog, the road had been blasted through rock in the Pass of Leny and workmen were erecting barriers to prevent vehicles going to a watery end in the picturesque waterfalls below. Traffic was being controlled by a man operating a Stop-Go sign and I was about to join a long queue of cars waiting to go through when the man signalled me forward and through. The impatient motorists were furious and sounded their horns in annoyance, but our kind friend held them back and waited until we had got safely through the roadworks before unleashing the snarling horde. I waved my thanks and left the road to cross a wooden bridge into Strathyre Forest at the foot of Loch Lubnaig.

Before 1964 you could have enjoyed one of the most delightful railway journeys in Scotland on a line that ran from Oban to Callander. For breath-taking scenery it rivalled any of the Scottish railways and the line that ran down Glen Ogle and along the western bank of Loch Lubnaig was, to me anyway, a most exciting and spectacular journey. But then came Dr Beeching with his axe and, one by one, he severed the lifelines that kept the rural areas alive and filled the roads with juggernauts. Even then, the politicians missed the most obvious use for these derelict highways and allowed them to decay or be sold off into private ownership. What ideal routes they would have made for cyclists, walkers and horse riders and the stations could easily have been converted into hostel accommodation. But no, the wise men in organisations like the Countryside Commission prefer to concentrate their attention on developing and publicising long-distance paths through wild country, rather than encourage people to read maps and find their own way about. When attention is focused on walks like the West Highland Way, they become fashionable and soon there will be a deep furrow worn between Glasgow and Fort William.

In Strathyre Forest the Forestry Commission have put one section of the old railway line to good use: they have surfaced it and provided an access road to their holiday cabin complex on the shore of the loch. Eric Howell at Aberfoyle had advised me to telephone the Head Forester when I reached the holiday cabins and he would tell me where I could camp, but there was no sign of a telephone kiosk.

It was very hot and humid and the loch glistened temptingly through the trees as I rode down to the water's edge and let the ponies have a long drink. The strange sight of a pony carrying a pack attracted a crowd of youngsters, who came down with their mothers in tow to offer Thor and Lucy sweets and pat them on the nose. One of the mothers sidled up to me and said in a loud whisper, 'Hey mister, are you a filum star, 'cos if you are my wee girl would like your autograph,' and she brandished one of those small, plastic-covered books with different coloured pages and 'Autographs' embossed in gold on the front. I was about to confess modestly that I had, in fact, appeared on television with my ponies on several occasions, when her 'wee girl', a well-endowed sixteen-year-old with peroxided hair and a cleavage extending to her navel, peered at me and shrilled, 'He looks kinda old to me Mother. If he's no famous don't let him write in my book. Get him to put his name on the back of this fag packet, somebody may have heard of him.' I smiled sweetly at her mother and wrote 'John Wayne' across an empty packet of Players No. 6.

The ponies had discovered a patch of juicy grass and looked content to stay there, so I left them and went to find a telephone. I got through to the Forest Office at Strathyre and the forester said he had a campsite fixed up for me and I was to see the lady in charge of the holiday cabins. There was just one small snag; she lived a mile and a half back down the road we had just come along. I went back to the grass patch to collect Thor and Lucy, but it was deserted. In and out of the holiday cabins I searched, thinking that I would find them being offered titbits on someone's doorstep, but there was not a sign anywhere and I began to get worried. Lucy still had the packs on her back and Thor was carrying my money, maps, cameras, everything. While I was trying to decide in which direction to search for them, a man on a motorbike came along the road and stopped.

'I've just passed two ponies down the road,' he said, 'are you looking for them?'

'Looking for them!' I replied, brimming over with anger. 'I could bang their stupid heads together.'

'Jump on the back,' said the man, 'we'll soon catch up with them,' and with me clinging to his waist he gave the machine full throttle and roared away as if he had only one more point to get to win the title of World Champion Motorcyclist. The slipstream over his shoulder made it difficult to see ahead, but in the distance I could vaguely make out the fleeing Lucy, followed by the ever-faithful Thor.

Without any warning, the motorcyclist braked hard, twisted his handlebars and skidded to a halt, broadside across the road. It was a neat manoeuvre, calculated to halt the runaway ponies, but I was unable to appreciate it for a while because centrifugal force catapulted me off the pillion seat and down a bank into a ditch oozing with black slime. The ensuing dialogue is best left unrecorded, but the motorcyclist did help me to catch the ponies. He was full of apologies when he pulled me out of the ditch and he did hold Thor while I climbed into the saddle, so really I should not have called him what I did.

I arrived at the camp warden's house, tired, sore, irritable and ponging very strongly of decaying vegetable matter, only to find that she had gone out. It was the last straw and I cursed and swore under my breath. 'Will I ever find a place to get my head down for the night?'

While I was fuming a lady came out of the house next door and asked if she could help.

'The forester has given me permission to pitch my tent in the Scout Camp field,' I said. 'Have you any idea where it is?'

'Och yes,' she said pleasantly, 'just gang awa' up the brae to the edge of the burn, ye'll see it there.'

Ganging awa' up the brae involved turning round once more and going back half a mile along the road. I was beginning to feel like a shuttlecock. Arriving at the campsite, I was disturbed to find that there was no fence round it. I tried shortening the hobbles even further and, to make it more difficult for Lucy to wander, I tied a rope from the hobbles to her head collar. It did not seem to make much difference, but there was no time to do anything about it. Thunder had been rumbling in the distance and a heavy shower broke as I was pitching the tent. Throwing the bags inside, I dived in after them and crouched under the canvas as the deluge poured down. I lit the Primus and had just got a brew of coffee going when I heard a vehicle stop by the tent.

'Anybody in there?' shouted a female voice.

'Yes,' I shouted back, 'what's the trouble?'

'I've just passed your ponies miles down the road. Would you like a lift to catch them up?'

Cursing loudly, I pulled on my boots and anorak, abandoned my coffee and dashed across in the rain to a blue van.

'I'm Pauline Harvey from Stank House, just by the campsite,' explained my new friend as we drove down the road. 'You're welcome to put the ponies in one of our outbuildings if it would help.'

I thanked her for her offer, but pointed out that they needed to graze and wondered if there was a paddock I could put them in. She said Mrs Whiteman, the lady in charge of the holiday chalets, had a paddock next to her house and might let me put them in it for the night. Mrs Whiteman was at home when I called and she was most helpful. Her son produced a bucket of water and soon the wandering ponies were safely locked behind a fence. At least I would be able to sleep soundly.

The night was still and quiet but the dawn broke cold and grey and torrential rain poured down as I was having breakfast. Thunder rumbled ominously around the hills, as though the gods guarding the towering summits of Ben Ledi and Ben Vorlich were assembling their armies ready for the fray. There was no wind, but wave after wave of heavy rain falling from low black clouds swept across the loch swelling the streams and cracking the branches of giant conifers with the force of the deluge. Within seconds, the ground by the tent was churned into a mass of thick mud and the thought of sitting in the saddle with solid water pouring down my neck was enough to make me stay another day. After a couple of hours the gods controlling the storm stopped for a lunch break and to fill the watertanks, so I took the opportunity to dash down to ask Mrs Whiteman if I could leave the ponies in the paddock for another night. They had all but devoured every blade of grass, but she said it would be all right. The rain came on again when I returned to the tent, but a few bright patches in the sky hinted at better things to come. I hate being cooped up all day so, pulling on my waterproofs, I put a bar of chocolate, an apple, map and compass in a small rucksack and set off to climb Ben Ledi.

Despite the rain it was fairly warm and the sweat poured off me as I clambered up a steep path through the forest. Above the treeline the way crossed a large expanse of saturated heather that flung up clouds of penetrating spray as my boots ploughed through it. Great banks of cloud obscured the summit of the Ben but as the air in the valley became warmer it rose and dispersed the cloud into long plumes that drifted like ghostly grey figures among the crags. On the final ridge the visibility was very poor so I abandoned the idea of reaching the summit and worked out a compass bearing that would take me to Lochan nan Corp (Loch of the Corpse) on the north side of Ben Ledi.

According to local legend, the loch owes its macabre name to a tragedy which happened many years ago when a funeral party was carrying a body over the hill from Glen Finglas for burial at St Brides Church, on the shore of Loch Lubnaig. It was winter-time, with thick snow covering the ground, and the surface of the loch was frozen over. Whether the funeral party could not see the ice-covered loch under the snow, or they were so full of whisky they did not know what they were doing, we will never know. Whatever the reason, the frozen surface of the loch collapsed under the party and they were all drowned. Most of those lost were from the Clan Kessanach and it is said that after the disaster their numbers dwindled almost to the point of extinction.

It may sound irreverent to suggest that the funeral party was so much the worse for drink that those carrying the body did not know where they were, yet some of the stories told about early Highland funerals are hair-raising. Smollett describes a typical scene in his book *Humphrey Clinker*, written in 1770: 'Yesterday we were invited to the funeral of an old lady ... and found ourselves in the midst of fifty people who were regaled with a sumptuous feast ... the guests did such honour to the entertainment that many of them could not stand when we were reminded of the business on which we had met ... Then we returned to the castle, resumed the bottle and by midnight there was not a sober person in the family, females excepted. The squire and I were, with some difficulty, permitted to retire with the landlord in the evening, but our entertainer was a little chagrined at our retreat; and afterwards seemed to think it a disparagement to his family that not above a hundred gallons of whisky had been drunk upon such a solemn occasion.'

There are stories of bodies being left on the hillside and the funeral party having to go back to retrieve them, sometimes losing them altogether. One funeral that must have been a rare sight was Lord Lovat's in 1631. It is recorded that five thousand armed men attended the sumptuous funeral celebrations. Unlike the custom in Cumberland and Westmorland, deceased Highlanders were not conveyed in a coffin strapped to the back of a horse, but on a litter of poles carried by clansmen. At the time Smollett wrote his account of a Highland funeral, Bishop Forbes was also observing the customs of the country. 'They have an excellent way of carrying a corpse,' he wrote, 'which is upon two long poles, the ends of which are laid upon men's shoulders, the poles being so long as to receive two men if necessary, without incommoding each other, or being too near the corpse, which is placed on a bier or frame in the middle of the poles. Thus by a change of hands, they can carry a corpse a long way without any fatigue, as indeed in some places they have to carry their dead many miles.'

When I eventually reached Lochan nan Corp it was difficult to make it out in the mist and I almost walked into it. Knowing the story of the tragedy added to the eeriness of the place and I was glad to get away from the sombre atmosphere and descend to the edge of the forest.

After a day visiting corpse-filled lochs, I was in a melancholy mood and felt in need of more exciting company than the tourist brochures. They were still in my saddlebag and were the only reading matter I had with me. When Mike Harvey called and asked me if I would like to spend the evening with them I did not need any coaxing. I took half a bottle of whisky with me, which helped to remove some of the depression and Mike's supply got rid of the rest. A farmer friend of the Harveys arrived and I asked him if it was possible to follow the old railway line to Balquhidder. He scratched his head and thought about it for a minute or two.

'Well,' he said finally, 'I think the best thing to do is to follow it for about five miles or so, then strike across to Laggan Farm and go through the yard onto a nice quiet road. Trouble is though, it's private land and you'll need permission to get through.'

With that he asked Mike if he could use his phone and, minutes later, he came back with the news that the owners would leave the gates unlocked for me. I was feeling very tired and, as I was hoping to leave early next morning, I thanked the Harveys for their kindness and went to my sleeping bag.

Lucy learns about hobbles, helped by the author's mother

'Get your clenches tight' — blacksmith, Peter Long, shows how it's done

The start of the journey —
Queen Elizabeth Forest Park,
Drymen

Ready to go back to mother
— Peter Martin with a roe
deer calf

4

Rob Roy Country

At six o'clock the next morning the rain made such a racket, battering on the tent, it made sleep impossible. How I longed to stay in my warm sleeping bag, but I could not hang around any longer. Thor and Lucy had demolished every blade of grass in Mrs Whiteman's little paddock and there was nothing left for them to eat. My socks were still wet from the previous day's downpour and, as there did not seem much point in putting on dry ones to put into wet boots, I pulled them on and jumped up and down to get the circulation going. Swathed in my waterproof suit, I sloshed down to the paddock and brought the ponies back to load up. Packing gear in the rain was a dreary business and it was ten o'clock before I hammered the sodden flysheet into its bag and lashed everything onto the pack saddle.

A constant stream of water ran off my hood, onto Thor's head and down his face, to drip off his nose to the ground, as we squelched along the old railway line following the edge of Loch Lubnaig. The rails and sleepers had long since been removed and a thick carpet of grass covered the chippings, providing a comfortable surface for the ponies to walk on. Here and there birch and alder, left unchecked, had grown rapidly and bent over to form a natural arch that in time will extend to make a tunnel. Rabbits, playing in the grass, stopped their games to watch us approach, then, with cotton tails bobbing, raced into the safety of the hedgerows. A stoat, who had also been watching the rabbits, stood up on his hind legs to see what had caused his dinner to depart in such a hurry. He did not seem at all bothered by our presence and, after watching us quizzically, he dropped on all fours and followed the rabbits into the undergrowth.

Tremendous crags towered above the loch, cascading water down glistening expanses of rock to the stone culverts, beautifully built by the railway engineers of long ago to direct the flood water under the line and empty it into Loch Lubnaig. Even in the rain, the scenery was glorious, but the steady downpour dampened any enthusiasm for stopping to gaze at the view and we plodded on towards Laggan. Near the farm a hurdle barred the way, but, as promised, it was unlocked and here I left the railway and struck across several meadows to emerge on a good track by the farmhouse.

Beyond Laggan the road was surfaced and we clip-clopped along by Kipp Farm to the fringe of Strathyre village and an estate of modern bungalows. A well-known song describes it as 'bonny Strathyre', but it is more 'noisy Strathyre' these days, with the almost constant roar of motor vehicles and heavy lorries pouring along the A84. I was glad I was on the peaceful side of the river. In a sheltered glade, half a mile or so out of Strathyre, I stopped for an hour and let the ponies graze. The rain eased to a drizzle, then stopped altogether, and I was able to peel off down to a sweater and hang my waterproofs over a branch to dry. Studying the map I had about five miles to go to Balquhidder, where Mike Harvey had obtained permission for me to camp at a farm owned by a Mr Ferguson at Auchleskine. While the ponies grazed I got the Primus out, made a pot of coffee and sat back against a tree, watching the sun battling to penetrate the low cloud. To my delight it won and bathed the whole of the glen in a warm glow that had the birds singing their heads off on the tree tops. The clouds rolled away like a curtain at the start of a play, revealing a magnificent backdrop; only in this theatre there were no artificial trees, make-believe mountains or painted water: they were real, alive and breath-takingly beautiful.

The ponies, having fed and rested, were keen to go and even Thor strode out at a fine pace, as we followed the road by Bailefuill to the tiny hamlet of Balquhidder. The farm of Auchleskine, where I was to camp, was about a mile east of Balquhidder and I was looking forward to meeting Mr Ferguson, whose ancestors had farmed in Balquhidder for generations. According to Mike Harvey, the family had some interesting documents about Rob Roy MacGregor. Mr

Ferguson's greeting was not exactly effusive, but he was friendly and showed me a paddock for the ponies. He said that instead of pitching my tent, I could sleep in the barn, a huge, open-sided building with rather a lot of fresh air blowing through it. He forgot to mention that he was in the process of shifting several tons of very ripe cow muck out of it and when I prepared my dinner later that evening the aroma of the waste products of Aberdeen Angus bullocks somewhat overpowered my chicken supreme. Mr Ferguson did not seem very keen to talk and I felt rather disappointed that I was not invited to the house to hear about the family's connection with Rob Roy. I hoped it was only because he was wary of strangers and that he might be more forthcoming the following day.

The Clan MacGregor, or Clan Alpin as they were originally known, are thought to be one of the oldest clans in existence and they must certainly be one of the most persecuted. It was into this clan, with its history steeped in human blood, that the most famous and colourful folk-hero of all time was born, on 7th March, 1671. Rob Roy MacGregor.

Rob Roy took part in the Jacobite rebellions of 1715 and 1719 and, as can be expected, he was in the forefront of the fighting. But in 1734 he fought his last battle. Though old and losing his sight, he fought a duel with a young Stewart of Invernathyle and was wounded in the arm. The wound would not heal and his family realised he was dying. As he lay in his bed a visitor came to see him, some say his hated enemy, MacLaren of Wester Invernenty. Rather than let his enemy boast that he had seen Rob Roy weak and unarmed, he made his wife dress him in full Highland dress, complete with weapons, before the visitor was allowed to enter the room. After MacLaren had gone Rob sat up in bed with his plaid around him and his sword in his hand, reciting Ossian: 'The winds shall whistle in my grey hair and not wake me. The sons of future years shall pass away – another race shall rise, for the people are like the waves of the ocean; like the leaves of woody Morvern, they pass away in the rustling blast and other leaves lift up their green heads on high.'

On 28th December 1734, in his eightieth year, the great warrior Rob Roy MacGregor departed from a turbulent Scotland, over the great horizon to join his ancestor, Alpine

MacAchai, King of Scotland in 787, 'for the woods, the waters and Clan Alpine are the oldest things in Albyn'.

It was cold and draughty in the barn at Auchleskine and I slept with all my clothes on, wedged between a few bales of straw. At first light I made a cup of coffee and watched a grey dawn creep below a thick bank of cloud that hung low over the hills, wetting the glen with a fine drizzle. At six o'clock the drizzle increased to heavy rain and the clouds almost touched the roof of the barn. Despite the weather, I was keen to be on my way, but I waited around, hoping Mr Ferguson would appear so I could ask him about his family history. To pass the time I gave Thor's saddle and bridle, the pack saddle and my boots a thorough coating of leather oil. The alternate doses of heat and water they had been subjected to since I left Drymen had rendered the saddle and bridle dry and brittle and as I brushed the oil into the leather it soaked it up like blotting paper. It had gone nine o'clock when Mr Ferguson eventually appeared in the yard and although I tried to talk about local history I got no further than being informed that the Fergusons had lived in Balquhidder for many hundreds of years and had farmed at Auchleskine since 1715. In the end I gave up and, having thanked Mr Ferguson for letting me stay, loaded the ponies and set off. One useful piece of information I did glean from our brief conversation was that the Forestry Commission had erected a stile instead of a gate across a right of way by Balquhidder Church. This would mean a three quarter mile detour to get back on to a path up Kirkton Glen that would take me over to Glen Dochart. A forester I spoke to in the Commission's office in Strathyre had assured me it was a good route and was used by a pony trekking centre at Aberfoyle.

When I reached the forest track at the foot of the Kirkton Glen I was annoyed to discover the way blocked by a chain secured with a padlock. Not only had the Forestry Commission blocked the right of way at Balquhidder, it seemed they were determined to stop access to it from any direction. Fortunately, I happened to be carrying a key that fitted most of the Commission locks, but it would be hard luck on anyone travelling that way who had not got one. I let the ponies make their own pace up a steep, winding track until, crossing a concrete bridge high up in the forest, we joined the old drove road. In a deep gorge below the track the river roared and thundered over the rocks and I steered the ponies well away from the edge. The rain continued to come down like stair-rods, but the air, trapped in the narrow glen by low cloud, was tolerably warm.

Thor and Lucy ambled on for an hour or so until we came to a road junction and a sign 'To Glen Dochart', pointing to a narrow path through the trees. I rested a while to eat a chocolate bar and let the ponies chew on the sparse grass, then set off along the path, only to find after a few hundred yards that it was blocked by fallen trees. Cursing, I went back to the forest road and continued to follow it upwards, hoping that it would eventually end at a gate at the top of the forest. After we had been going for half an hour I looked at the compass and realised we were heading in the wrong direction. Swinging the ponies round I rode back to the Glen Dochart path and went ahead on foot to see if there was a way through the tangled heaps of fallen trees. My daughters would have whooped with delight and thundered their ponies over the obstacles, but flabby Thor and laden Lucy, standing patiently in the rain, looked unlikely to perform any spectacular leaps. I hacked away at the branches with my sheath knife, showering myself with spray as I wrenched and heaved the springy sitka to one side. Thor sniffed cautiously at the gap, but would not be tempted and I was forced to lift his front legs over, one by one, push against his great backside to move him forward, then lift his hind legs over. There were dozens of trees to negotiate and progress was painfully slow. Happily, Lucy clambered over without any fuss and, at long last, the edge of the forest appeared through the rain and there in the fence was a gate. Sweat poured off me with the effort of negotiating the fallen trees and, under my waterproof suit, my shirt was like a wet dishcloth.

On the hill outside the forest, the thick clouds closed around us and I had great difficulty in finding the path in the blinding rain. I kept stumbling into bogs that filled my boots with water, or finding myself in a maze of boulders impassable for the ponies. Up and up we struggled, through the murk, when suddenly what looked like a large hut appeared ahead. Desperate for a place to shelter and get my bearings, I drove Thor and Lucy forward, only to discover it was a huge boulder. It was disappointing, but at least it gave me some shelter and, studying the map, I was able to judge roughly where I was. Somewhere ahead, in the mist, was Lochan an Eireannaich, nestling in a hollow at a height of just under two thousand feet. I set a compass course for it and led the ponies forward. A few evil looking patches of bog caused a problem or two, but to my relief the lochan loomed out of the rain-soaked mist, bang on course.

I was horribly thirsty and sucked an orange while Thor and Lucy enjoyed a new diet of blaeberries. Lucy found them very much to her liking and had to be dragged away before we could continue. Visibility was still very poor but a good stony path headed in the right direction and I followed its descent alongside a stream running out of the lochan. The mist thinned, then cleared away altogether as I stepped below the clouds to look down on an awesome sight. The distance between where I was standing and the road running through Glen Dochart was about four miles and every one of those miles was a quagmire of bog and rock.

For three hours we floundered from one bog to another, making long detours and searching frantically for a path to take us through this nightmare. When we reached firm ground at the foot of the hill the ponies and I were absolutely exhausted.

The map showed the path passing under a bridge on the old Oban to Callander line, and I headed towards it only to encounter a locked gate barring our way. Climbing up the railway embankment, I scouted around until I found an old gate. It was heavily wired up but I was able to move it and get the ponies through into a field, and here I was in for another shock. What appeared to be easy meadow land was, in fact, a sea of spongy ground and I became thoroughly lost in a maze of deep, wide drains and trembling areas of moss. All the time, the rain lashed down and Thor and Lucy were utterly miserable. The good old peppermints came to the rescue and I coaxed the pair of them to leap across the ditches towards dry ground and finally onto a safe, stony track.

While I had been trying to find a way through the maze of ditches, I was aware of two figures watching me intently from the yard of Ledcharrie Farm. As we drew near I could make out the cold expressions on the faces of two men and I felt I was in for a roasting. I was pouring out apologies as I walked towards them, but the older of the pair smiled and said, 'Dinna fret yerself, laddie, thaes din nae harm.'

I explained where I was from and what I was doing and we talked for a while in the shelter of a barn. He told me that although a man who ran a pony trekking holiday did come over from Balquhidder two or three times a year, there was no public right of way through Ledcharrie Farm. When I checked D.G. Moir's excellent book *Scottish Hill Tracks* some time later, I read that the route is shown as a road on Roy's map of 1755 and was named 'Larig Earne'. If this is the case, then it is time the padlock on the gate was thrown into the river.

Crossing the busy Killin to Dalmally road, I joined a quiet back road, clattered over the rain-spattered River Dochart by a picturesque bridge and continued down Glen Dochart, on the north side of the river. I was extremely tired, wet and cold, and longed to find a place to pitch camp, but each tempting little glade had a fierce sign that growled 'No Camping' and chased us on.

At Auchlyne, faces watched us from the windows of cottages clustered round the 'Big House'. In response to my wave, the nod from a man behind the windows of 'Keepers Cottage' quite clearly carried the message 'I am returning your greeting out of courtesy, but keep moving.' A long line of fox brushes hanging on a fence served as a warning to trespassers.

Two miles or so beyond Auchlyne there was a little farm set below the road, at Bovain, and I turned into the yard and went across to the door. Scottish country dance music was blaring out of a radio, but it was switched off with a loud click when I knocked. An old man opened the door and I asked if I could camp and graze the ponies.

'You are traffelling with ponies, are you?' he said, in a

strong Highland accent, 'Well now, that is just wonderful to see.' He came out into the rain and looked at Thor and Lucy. 'Man, there was many a stag I brought down on the backs of fine beasts like them,' he said wistfully, 'Yes, you can stay. I'll see you in the morning.'

And with that he hurried back to the house and switched on the wireless. Strains of Jimmy Shand and his band followed us as I led the ponies into a small paddock. I was so weary I could hardly think and, having pitched the tent, I made a cup of coffee laced with whisky. I was only half way through it when I fell fast asleep, still clothed in my waterproofs, wet boots and all.

I woke, cold and stiff, at six o'clock and lay for a minute or two while my clouded brain worked out why I was still wearing all my clothes. The stove soon warmed the tent and I changed into dry clothes and warmed my inner core with a mug of coffee. A heavy dew glistened on the fields around the farm, but already the sun was evaporating it into wisps of white mist and it promised to be a warm day. I heard the farmer stamping round the yard in his hob-nailed boots and I went over to talk to him. He told me he was seventy-six and was shortly giving up the farm and retiring to Killin.

'What will happen to the farm then?' I asked.

'Och well now, I am sure I don't know,' he replied. 'The estate at Auchlyne own it, but I don't think they will put another tenant in.' He kicked the mud off his boots against a wall. 'Maybe the place will become a holiday house,' he said quietly. 'I'm a Campbell myself, but this used to be the seat of the MacNabs and I wonder what they would think of it.'

5

Through Glen Dochart
to Glen Lyon

The road was quiet and I enjoyed the ride along the bank of
the river, watching the water sparkling in the sun as the rapids
swirled and tumbled over the rocks. What a contrast to the
previous day.

On the outskirts of Killin, a new estate of fancy houses,
complete with street lamps, looked out of place against a
background of hills, but perhaps I am too much of a
traditionalist. The narrow road dropped down between the
houses of old Killin to a yard and a building that had once
been the village smithy. A jig for making iron wheel hoops was
still lying against the wall. I was adjusting the packs when a
battered shooting brake packed with dogs and fishing rods
squealed to a halt. A large, kilted Highlander clambered out,
grasping a half empty bottle of whisky at arm's length. 'Hae a
drink laddie. Ah've heard all aboot ye,' he boomed,
hiccuping loudly and drenching me in whisky, as he tripped
over one of the dogs and nearly dropped the bottle. 'Ye black
heathen bitch!' he yelled at the cringing labrador. 'Ah bloody
near dropped ma dram, get yersel back in the car.' With that,
he placed a large brogue under the poor dog's rear end and
shot it into the front seat. 'Now laddie, drink yer fill,' he said,
shoving the bottle into my hands and swaying backwards and
forwards like a tree in a gale, as I obligingly gulped a mouthful
of the fiery liquid.

Grabbing the bottle from me, he drained it dry and fell back
into the car. 'If you come to Glen Lyon, you must come and
see me,' he shouted through a pall of black exhaust smoke as
he drove off. 'We'll hae a guid dram together.'

I was determined to avoid that part of Glen Lyon like the

plague and, looking at the map, I found a road going from Edramurchy, on the side of Loch Tay, over the hill by Lochan na Lairige to Bridge of Balgie. I disliked the prospect of fourteen miles of motor road, but it was worth it to avoid being trapped in a drunken orgy. I prefer my whisky by the glass, not the bottle.

It was very hot as I left Killin and its smart hotels behind. We were quite a tourist attraction for a while, with hotel guests flocking out of the bars and lounges to stare and wave. The price of just one of the cars drawn up by the hotel entrances would have paid for several horseback journeys round Scotland and the rest of Britain, but I did not envy them one bit. It was a lovely day, I had two good ponies and the excitement of wondering where tomorrow would find us. The owners of those cars would meet the same type of people in similar bars and lounges no matter where they went.

The road was chock-a-block with traffic and I had to keep Lucy on a very short rope to prevent her from wandering too far. For the life of me I cannot understand why some people on motoring holidays drive as if they are in the RAC rally. How can the drivers possibly see the countryside they have come so far to enjoy? As for having a relaxing break from normal everyday life, they may as well spend a week hurtling round in dodgem cars on a fairground.

There were six very tedious miles to cover before turning off for Glen Lyon and the ponies were tramping along steadily when a man came out of a house at Tomocrocher and invited me in for lunch. My throat was dry with dust and exhaust fumes and I was glad to accept his offer. With the ponies safely penned in with the hens, I found myself in a cool kitchen enjoying a huge salad. My kind hosts were Robert and Penelope Gibson, who ran a small-holding very much in the tradition of self-sufficiency, shearing their Jacob sheep and spinning the wool. Robert was a qualified forester but had given up forestry to restore antique furniture. They had passed me in their car while I was riding along the road and said I looked hot and in need of a cool drink. I spent a very pleasant and relaxing hour or two in their company and I was most reluctant to leave. Thor and Lucy were not keen to leave either. They were quite content to continue chomping at the hens' food, much to the alarm of the hens, and they sulked while I loaded up. We were about to leave when Robert suddenly realised that there were two cattle grids on the Glen Lyon road and the gates alongside them were padlocked and a local farmer had the only key. Penelope went away to phone him, but he came back to say he was out.

'Never mind,' said Robert, 'I'll take some boards up in the van and put them over the grids.'

His son David helped him and they drove off to wait for me. It took quite a while to reach them, the road was steep and narrow and zigzagged up the hillside in a series of hairpin bends. I had to keep stopping to let cars go by. Robert and David had the grid covered in boards when we arrived and the ponies walked across without faltering. The van roared away to the next grid, about a mile up the hill and again the Gibsons had a long wait before we arrived and crossed the boards. I was very grateful to Robert for the help; he had gone to a lot of trouble to save me wasting a day and it meant I had a good chance of reaching Glen Lyon that evening. With a hoot and a wave they drove off back to Tomocrocher and I let the ponies graze while I sat in the sun and looked down on the vast expanse of Loch Tay.

Dragging myself away from the view, I gathered the ponies and continued the climb towards the skyline and the huge man-made dam that prevents the waters of Lochan na Lairige pouring down the hillside into Loch Tay. On the way we passed the National Trust for Scotland's Ben Lawers Visitor Centre, a rather odd-looking, crescent-shaped building, containing a display showing how the land locally was formed and providing motoring visitors with a glimpse of the countryside they would not see through the windows of their cars. Above the dam the gradient flattened out and we jogged along steadily in the warm sun. What a joy it was to ride along in a shirt, instead of being swathed in sweaters and waterproofs. There were lots of tempting places where I would have liked to camp, but it was open country and I had visions of wandering Lucy disappearing during the night.

On and on we went, along the road high above the loch, passing a large cairn marking the boundary of the land owned by the National Trust, and descending towards mysterious

Glen Lyon, by the side of the swift-flowing stream of Allt Bail a' Mhuilinn. To my delight I saw a sheep pen by the side of the road, but when I rode over to it I found that every rail was rotten and ready to collapse in a heap of dust. Both ponies were dog-tired but although it was now after seven o'clock and still five miles to go to Bridge of Balgie, I had no option but to press on.

A small boy and girl were playing outside a cottage by Bridge of Balgie and they rushed over to give Thor and Lucy a piece of apple. I asked if they knew of a farm where I could camp and the boy said his father was a shepherd and if I would wait for a 'wee minute' he would go and get him. Father was a typical Highland shepherd, taking life and people as they came, and he asked me in for a dram. He told me that the estate he worked for was up for sale and he was a bit worried about his job. Since it was only for one night, he said I could camp at Kerromore Farmhouse, about half a mile away, which was empty and awaiting a new owner. The children, who told me their names were Alistair and Dana MacDougall, waited eagerly to show me the way and were thrilled when I let them ride on Thor. It was a humid evening and the midges were uncomfortably active, so I quickly turned the ponies loose and dived into the tent for a late meal of biscuits and cheese.

I slept extremely well and it was a missel-thrush, chirping away at the top of his voice, that woke me next morning. It was almost nine o'clock and a bright sun was busy mopping up the dew in the attractive tree-lined meadows surrounding the farmhouse. Thor's great bulk was stretched out in the grass, but the ever-hungry Lucy was taking the opportunity to cram her belly with rich grass. When I went up to the farmhouse to have a wash at a tap in the yard, I was saddened to see such a beautiful house and outbuildings falling into decay. You can see the same neglect all over Scotland, where landowners seem to prefer their property to crumble into a heap of rubble rather than put a tenant in. Many of them blame the Agricultural Tenancy Act but, judging by the observations made by Robert Southey during his tour of Scotland in 1819, the situation is not a new one. He wrote,

'Some fifty land leviathans may be said to possess the Highlands ... A few of these are desirous of improving their own estates by bettering the conditions of their tenants. But the greater number are fools at heart, with neither understanding nor virtue, nor good nature to form such a wish. Their object is to increase their revenue, and they care not by what means this is accomplished.'

On the way through Bridge of Balgie I called at the little post office to buy some stamps. I was sitting outside, writing in my notebook, when a man in a well-worn tweed suit came over to talk to me.

'Are you writing the history of the glen?' he asked, with a broad smile on his face. I laughed and replied that it would make a very thick book.

'That it would, my friend, that it would,' he said and went on, 'the trouble with the history book writers is that they've no humour and they miss most of the best tales. I don't live in the glen now, but I was born here and when I was a lad we had a minister who was a nice enough man, but a bit slow on the uptake, as they say. Well, one day, one of these tourist fellers came to the glen looking for the site of the house where the Roman Governor, Pontius Pilate, was supposed to have been born, and somebody said he should go and ask the minister. So away he goes and bangs on the minister's door. "Can you tell me where the house of Pontius Pilate is?" he enquired.

' "Pontius Pilate?" replied the minister, scratching his head. "Pontius Pilate, well now, it doesn't sound a very Highland name to me."

' "Highland or not, he was supposed to have been born in the glen and surely you must be aware of it," said the visitor, irritably.

' "Och well," said the minister, "he may have been born here, but he was never a member of my congregation." '

The man in the tweed suit roared with laughter at his story. 'Get a few of those tales together,' he called over his shoulder, as he went into the post office. 'They're a hell of a sight more interesting than the ones about those fools in the clans chopping each other's heads off.'

From the map there appeared to be a good track going over to Loch Rannoch from Inverwick, about a mile down the glen, but Thor was in a sour mood and refused to leave before he had mowed the grass round the post office. When I did get him to move, he walked so slowly he almost went backwards and Lucy got so cross she kept nipping his bottom. I stopped and checked his feet, but they were all right and the only reason I could think of for his slow speed was annoyance because I had disturbed his sleep in the grass at the farmhouse. It took ages to reach Inverwick and the start of the track up the Lairig Chalbhath for Rannoch. Thor was certainly having an off day and kept stopping every few yards, wheezing like a punctured bellows. I wondered if he had caught a chill due to the extremes of weather we had been through, but I had no means of taking his temperature. He was obviously feeling the heat of the day and the strain of the rough track, so I jumped off his back, slackened his saddle girth and led him up the steepest bit, to the edge of a very deep gorge lined with birch. With the worst of the climb behind him, he recovered quickly and I enjoyed a leisurely plod along the rim of the gorge, with the added excitement of being able to look down past my left stirrup to the waters of Allt Chalbhath, three or four hundred feet below. For two miles the scenery was spectacular, then the gorge came to an end and the track crossed a wild expanse of moor, before descending gradually towards the edge of Rannoch Forest.

The ride down through the huge trees of the Caledonian pine forest was a delight and soon we reached Dall at the edge of the loch. The map showed a number of dwellings and I hoped one of them was a farm. Through the trees I could see a large building and, forcing my way through a clump of rhododendrons, found I had walked the ponies onto a beautifully kept expanse of grass which led up to an enormous turreted house. At first I thought I was in the grounds of an hotel, but a lad on a bicycle informed me, haughtily, that I was damaging the sacred grass of Rannoch School. His pal was a bit friendlier and I asked him if there was a field belonging to the school where I might be allowed to stay. He raced off on his bike to see his housemaster and returned looking very downcast, with the message that if I wished to camp I should continue to either Carrie or Camghouran. A lot of words raced through my head but not wanting to use them in front of the young lad, I thanked him for his help and set off down the drive to the main gate. Stopping to look at the map, I found that Carrie Farm was nearer but in the wrong direction. I was heading West, so Camghouran it would have to be but, oh dear, it was five miles up the glen.

Both ponies were very tired after the long slog under the hot sun and poor old Thor kept stopping and refusing to go on. But on we had to go and I broke a switch off a tree to keep him moving. I was aching in every muscle by the time we reached the farm gate and I could hardly climb out of the saddle. I trailed all the way to the house only to be told by the lady who answered my knock that Mr MacGibbon, the farmer, had moved to a new house, half a mile up the glen. Wearily, we went back down to the road and along to the new house. A man standing in the yard looked rather stern, but when I poured out my story he softened and said we could stay. His wife sent their son to open the gates and we crossed the fields to the edge of the loch. At the sight of thick grass, Lucy could hardly keep still to allow me to take the bags and saddle off her; but old Thor found a shady patch under a tree, stretched himself out and fell fast asleep. I pitched camp in a superb position on the edge of the loch and all the time thunder was rumbling in the distance and flashes of lightning played around the hilltops.

After dinner I spread the map out in the tent to plan the next day's route. From here on I was entering very wild country, where I would be a long way from help if anything went wrong. I wanted to follow the historic Road to the Isles, across Rannoch Moor, and eventually reach Ben Nevis, but I was still plagued by the thought of being stranded if Lucy wandered off. I decided I must reach Loch Ossian, in the middle of Rannoch Moor, in one day, but when I measured the distance it was over twenty miles from my campsite. It would be too much for the ponies after the strain of the past few days, so I went up to the house to ask Mr MacGibbon if I could stay another night to give Thor and Lucy a rest. A tremendous clap of thunder echoed across the loch as I reached the door, followed by torrential rain, and an hour went by before it eased off sufficiently for me to run for the tent.

The following day the clouds gathered again and thunder rolled around the hills, coming ever closer. In the afternoon a squally wind brought a heavy shower that sent me rushing for the tent, bundling sleeping bag, notebook and cameras before me. The shower increased to a downpour and I was cursing myself for not filling the billycan with water when young Frank MacGibbon arrived with a message from his mother that I was to go up to the house for tea. She had put on a grand meal and I was tucking into steak and potatoes when there was a tremendous flash of lightning followed by an almighty crack of thunder and all the lights in the house went out. We finished the meal by the light of candles and afterwards moved into a comfortable sitting-room hung with photographs of Clydesdale horses pulling ploughs or decorated with rosettes at shows. Mr MacGibbon reminisced about the time when, as a lad in Forfar, he worked as a ploughman. The day started at five-thirty in the morning, when the horses were fed and groomed, and they had to be yoked to the plough and working by seven o'clock. Each man worked two horses and usually took a great pride in his harness. Working hames (the metal parts of a horse collar) were painted black, but when they went off the farm to deliver sacks of potatoes to the railway station, they used another set that were kept sparkling with emery paper.

'We were hired for six months at a time,' said Mr MacGibbon, 'and everything we owned was kept in two wooden chests, one for your clothes and the other for food. One of the first things you did when you were hired by a new farm was to hitch up a cart and go back to the farm you'd just left, for your boxes.'

Laughingly, I said if he had enjoyed working with horses, why was there a tractor sitting in the yard.

He smiled and replied, 'Well, we had good times, certainly, but it was very hard work and it's something I'd rather look back on.'

Storm approaching over Loch Venachar

'I hope we're not lost' — Lucy looks on while the author studies the map by Loch Lubnaig

Resting in the rain on the way to Glen Dochart

Progress blocked by fallen trees — Kirkton Glen, Balquhidder

6

The Road to the Isles

The next morning was dull and overcast, with a chilly nip in
the air. I left Camghouran and rode steadily along the tree-
lined road by the edge of the loch. Fresh from their rest, the
ponies were in good form and Thor strode out like a two-year-
old. A little wooden post office with a corrugated iron roof
caught my eye at Bridge of Gour and I bought some chocolate
just to have a look inside. It was a delightful, old-world
interior, with a vintage wooden telephone kiosk built into the
counter. The post mistress was very friendly and we chatted
for a few minutes about the weather and the difficulties of
keeping small shops going in remote areas like Rannoch.
Outside, the ponies were making holes in her garden hedge
and I had to leave hurriedly and haul them away from it. A
few yards down the road an old man was leaning on a gate.
When I reached him he asked, in a strong Highland accent,
where I was making for. When I said across Rannoch Moor,
to Loch Ossian, he frowned and wagged his finger at me,
'Then you must be careful,' he warned, 'because if you step
into the bog on either side of the path, you will never see your
ponies or yourself again.'

I promised I would be careful and carried on, feeling a bit
worried about a mass of black cloud gathering ahead of me
and wondering what I was letting myself in for.

The road swung to the right, to cross a beautifully built
stone bridge over the River Gour. On the left, half hidden
among the trees, was Rannoch Barracks, where a garrison of
English redcoats was stationed after the 1745 uprising. It had
been converted into a house and very attractive it looked, with
swans drifting on the quiet river in front of it. Beyond the
barracks, the road followed the winding course of the river and

I let the ponies rest for a while and graze along the river bank. A large rucksack with legs suddenly appeared round a bend in the road and Thor snorted and tried to run away. It turned out to be an elderly chap in shorts, bent double under an enormous pack, boots hung round his neck, limping along in a pair of gym shoes. I said 'Good morning' but he ignored me and stared vacantly ahead, muttering 'Ah canna go on. Ah canno go on.'

I felt I ought to have gone after him, but he was close to habitation and there was plenty of help around if he needed it.

The sky looked very threatening as we climbed above the bleak expanse of Loch Eigheach and it was surprisingly cold for the time of year. Near the end of the loch I left the road and joined the most famous highway in the whole of Scotland, the Road to the Isles. Practically every child at school, all over the British Isles, must at some time have sung:

'Sure by Tummel and Loch Rannoch and Lochaber I will go
By heather tracks with heaven in their wiles;
If it's thinkin' in your inner heart braggart's in my step
You've never smelt the tangle of the Isles.
Oh, the far Coolins are puttin' love on me
As step I with my cromach to the Isles.'

The section of the Road to the Isles I was about to start on crossed Rannoch Moor and was a long way from the Coolins and the Isles. But to the drovers of long ago, returning home after walking their cattle all the way from the West coast to market at Stirling, the track across the moor must have been a welcome change from the steep-sided glens, where danger lurked behind every rock. Even after the Jacobite rebellions when the clans were ordered to surrender their arms the Government acknowledged that without arms the drovers, who often carried large sums of money, would be defenceless against robbers. Licences to carry a gun, sword and pistol were issued to the 'foresters, drovers and dealers in cattle and other merchandise, belonging to the several clans who have surrendered their arms'. The drovers must have been a very tough bunch to have slept out in the open with their cattle, protecting themselves from cold by dipping their plaids in a stream and wrapping it round their bodies. They seem to have survived on little or no food. According to one historian, 'a Highland drover was victualled for his long and toilsome journey with a few handfuls of oatmeal and two or three onions, renewed from time to time, and a ram's horn filled with whisky, which he used regularly but sparingly, every night and morning.' Ewen Dubh, an old man I knew in Glen Moriston, came from a family of drovers and he said that his grandfather used to mix the oatmeal and whisky together in the heel of his shoe and scoop it out with his fingers. Sometimes, he said, the drovers would bleed a cow and mix fresh blood with the oatmeal. The life of a cattle drover must have been sheer hell at times, although even he was probably quite well off compared with the crofter, who had to scratch a bare living from the land. How those drovers managed to get a herd of several hundred cattle across Rannoch Moor without losing half of them is a mystery to me. The track was never more than five feet wide at best and the old man at Bridge of Gour who warned me not to stray from it certainly knew what he was talking about. Black peat bogs stretched as far as the eye could see, on either side, and to have left the safety of the track would have been fatal. Even on the track I had a few hair-raising incidents, trying to coax Thor and Lucy across sections that had been torn away by winter storms. Sometimes culverts carrying the streams under the track had fallen in and I had to jump the ponies across. They often landed up to their knees in the water-logged surface on the other side, within a hair's-breadth of breaking a leg. From the tops of hillocks, herds of red deer watched curiously as we made slow progress along the undulating track and I felt like a pioneer crossing the prairie in the days of the Wild West, watched by a band of Indians ready to sweep down and remove my scalp. The mournful sound of a railway engine's siren echoing across the moor, as the Glasgow to Fort William train pulled out of Rannoch Station, added to the feeling of a cowboy movie and I half expected to hear shots as the marauding Indians turned their attention away from me towards a richer prize.

In the vast loneliness of Rannoch Moor it is easy for one's imagination to run riot and if there were bad weather and poor visibility it would require a steady nerve to survive.

The ponies floundered steadily forward and, in the distance, the ruin of Corrour Old Lodge came into sight on the only piece of green in a wilderness of brown and black. Away from the lodge the track climbed steadily on a stony surface, but then levelled out, so that we were back in peat again and the ponies kept sinking into it. Mercifully, the black clouds that had been brooding over the mountains of Glencoe all morning stayed put, watching with a malevolent eye as we ploughed an erratic course across the moor. Through the binoculars I could make out the scattering of small lochs by the isolated speck of Corrour railway halt, away to my left, and I pressed on, eager for a glimpse of Loch Ossian and safety. At five o'clock in the afternoon I caught sight of the loch between the hills and the track started a long descent towards it. More of the loch came into view and I could see the tiny building of Loch Ossian Youth Hostel, sheltered by a clump of trees at the water's edge. It was a tremendous relief to have crossed the moor, but it had one final test for us. A huge ditch barred access to a track at the edge of the loch and not even peppermints would persuade the ponies to jump across it. I struggled for half an hour, trying to move them. Finally, in desperation, I ran up from behind, shouting at the top of my voice and waving a stick. That did the trick, there was hardly an inch between them when they landed on the other side. I said I was sorry for giving them a fright, but I could not hang around all day. They seemed none the worse for their ordeal and crunched contentedly on a chocolate bar as we made our way along the edge of the loch. I pitched camp near the Youth Hostel.

It had been a great adventure and a man called MacCullough, who crossed Rannoch Moor on horseback in the nineteenth century, was not exaggerating when he wrote: 'a ride this was not, by any figure of speech. I cannot even call it a walk as half the space was traversed by jumping over bogs and holes and ditches and pits which were generally as wide as to demand much serious attention. I may fairly say that I jumped half the way to Loch Rannoch.'

The menacing clouds decided that they had left me alone long enough. Easing themselves off the summit of Buchaille Etive Mor, they drifted across the sun, taking the warmth out of the air and sending a nasty wind that whipped spray off the surface of the loch and sucked it upwards in a series of miniature waterspouts. Close by the Youth Hostel there was a large fenced-off paddock with a wooden shelter that accommodated ponies during the stalking season and I quickly turned Lucy and Thor into it.

It was bitterly cold and as I piled boulders around the tent, a grey belt of rain was already advancing up the glen. Before I had the Primus lit the wind was screeching like a thousand tormented souls and a vicious rain squall was doing its best to tear the tent to shreds. Fortunately, my mountain tent was built to withstand such onslaughts and, snug and warm, I filled my stomach with chicken supreme mixed with crumbled oatcakes, and sank into my sleeping bag to listen to the gale.

It raged all night and the noise made sleep impossible. I lit a candle and tried to catch up on my notes, but the furious flapping of the tent canvas disturbed the air inside the tent so much it kept blowing the candle out. The long night ticked by and it seemed an eternity before it was sufficiently light to open the tent door and take a look outside. The scene did little to raise morale. The surface of the loch was white with spume and clumps of uprooted heather were bowling along the track like tumbleweed. I climbed out to check the ponies and was immediately blown clean off my feet and almost rolled into the loch. The trees surrounding the Youth Hostel were bent over like palm trees, cracking ominously. As I crawled on my stomach back to the tent, I felt relieved that I had not camped closer to them. The gale raged for most of the morning, then ceased suddenly as if someone had closed a valve. I dashed across to see how the ponies had weathered the storm and found them standing in the lea of the stable, in exactly the same position as when I left them. The way they snatched a piece of chocolate out of my hand showed they had not eaten either and they were very grumpy.

Walking back by the tiny timber-built Youth Hostel, I stopped to grumble about the weather with a young chap who told me he worked for the Forestry Commission in Corrour Forest, on the shores of the loch. He was cursing because he was planting trees on piece work and the more it rained, the less he earned. While we talked, the Youth Hostel Warden, Tom Rigg, invited us both in to drown our sorrows in a mug of coffee and a cheese sandwich. The common room-cum-kitchen also served as a drying-room and every available nail and piece of string was draped with socks, sweaters, shirts and battered jeans. The Chinese have a saying that the gathering of clouds on a mountain denotes the presence of women, but inside the Youth Hostel there was no need to look at the clouds. On a temporary clothes line, above the stove, hung a pair of voluptuous bloomers and a long row of brightly coloured panties. Tom laughed when he saw me looking at them and explained that they belonged to a group of girl guides, led by a lady who was rather more woman than girl. They had got soaked the previous day, but had bravely gone out again to walk round the loch. As we toasted our feet by the ancient cast-iron stove, Tom told me that the Youth Hostel had been built originally as a coachman's house, at which the owners of Corrour Lodge kept a horse and trap to collect them from Corrour Station when they arrived for the summer season. There was no road and a boat took them up the loch to the Lodge. A private telephone line was installed between the Lodge and the railway station so the train could be stopped if the house party wanted to go to Fort William or Glasgow, or perhaps towards Loch Treig for a day's stalking. Before 1934 Corrour Station was the private property of the estate.

Mike Pearson, the forestry worker, glanced out of the window and saw that the rain had almost stopped. He rammed an oilskin suit and a flask of tea into a rucksack and set off to continue planting trees. To pass the time I wandered along the track to Corrour Station and what a bleak, god-forsaken place it was. It could have been a scene from one of those weird films, where people are spirited away by aliens from outer space. The cluster of buildings on either side of the line stood silent and empty. Doors on outbuildings hung at a crazy angle, on one hinge, as if some monster had burst them open. A domestic washing machine lay on its side, flattened by a mighty fist, wheels and drive belts protruding through a hole, like intestines. Children's dolls, headless and minus arms or legs, lay half-concealed in the stunted grass that struggled for survival among the rotting pales of a fence. It was so quiet it was unnerving. When I looked through the windows of the railwayman's house the rooms were cold and bare, the occupants had been taken. My footsteps seemed to echo across the bleak moor as I crossed the line, boots crunching on the bed of stone chippings supporting the sleepers, and when I opened a door with the sign 'Waiting Room', it was dark and empty. Inside, the sensation of disaster became stronger as I opened door after door, only to find each room deserted. I was on the point of turning and running for the Youth Hostel before I too was seized by the sinister beings, when, forcing open the last door, I gasped with relief. My overworked mind had been playing tricks and I knew human beings were not very far away. I was looking at a filthy, overflowing British Rail toilet, complete with graffiti.

Standing on the bridge that spans the railway line at Corrour Station and looking round at mile upon mile of hostile wasteland, you could be forgiven for thinking that only a maniac would consider building a railway across it. This may well have been the thought that ran through the minds of seven men who set out to walk across Rannoch Moor to Inveroran, a distance of forty miles, on 30th January, 1889. They were all connected with the West Highland Railway Company, which had a very ambitious proposal in mind: to build a railway from Glasgow to Fort William, through some of the wildest and most difficult country in Scotland. The seven men were the most unlikely group of hikers imaginable. The purpose of the walk was not to admire the scenery but to assess whether it was possible to drive a railway over it. The party consisted of Charles Forman, J. Balloch and J. Harrison, from Forman McCall, a Glasgow civil engineering company; Robert McAlpine, head of Robert McAlpine and Sons, the contracting company; John Brett, the factor of Breadalbane Estates; N.B. McKenzie, the Fort William agent for the railway company and Major Martin, the factor of the Poltalloch Estates. It was hardly the best time of year for such a difficult walk and things went wrong from the start.

Having walked from Spean Bridge to the north end of Loch

Treig, they were ferried in a leaky boat up the loch to a lodge owned by Lord Abinger, the company chairman, only to discover there was neither food nor beds waiting for them. They spent the night huddled under blankets, listening to the rain beating on the roof, and one would have thought they would have had the sense to stay where they were. But they pressed on, through the rain and peat bogs until, almost exhausted, they came to the River Gour, near Rannoch Barracks, where they met a keeper employed by Sir Robert Menzies of Rannoch Lodge. The party had arranged to meet Sir Robert to discuss the line of the railway over his land, but he became tired of hanging around and left his keeper to wait for them. With incredible stupidity, they refused the offer of a night's shelter at the lodge and carried on over the moor towards Inveroran, fourteen miles away. Darkness overtook them and, floundering about in the bog, Brett collapsed, unable to go any further. Martin and Harrison stayed with him, while the rest went for help. In the darkness they became separated and Balloch stumbled on to a cottage at Gorton and raised the alarm. Two shepherds living in the cottage went out onto the moor and eventually located the unconscious Brett and his friends, together with Forman and MacKenzie, who were wandering around in the dark. They were taken to a hut, where the shepherds lit a stove and revived them. The next morning they were well enough to walk to Gorton where a cart took them to Inveroran, on the way collecting MacAlpine, who had been lucky enough to reach a remote cottage. That night a blizzard swept across the moor and the next morning the party had to clamber over snowdrifts on their way to the railway station. Had the blizzard arrived twenty-four hours earlier, they would all have perished and the building of the railway may have been abandoned as too hazardous a project. But built it was, and on Saturday 11th August, 1894 a train left Glasgow Queen Street Station for Fort William, filled with gentry and nobility to perform the opening ceremony of the line. Critics argued that a line running mainly through a sparsely populated area would never be able to pay its way, but it is still there. I have made the journey from Glasgow to Fort William many times and it is one hundred miles of the most fascinating railway experience in the British Isles. The full story of its construction should go down as a classic in Scottish history.

The rain came on again as I left Corrour Station and I hurried back to the tent, just in time to dodge a heavy downpour. It passed over quickly and as there was still a lot of the day left I set off to walk to the other end of Loch Ossian, to Corrour Lodge. The grounds of the lodge were of particular interest to me, as an ex-forester. It was there that the technique of planting trees in peat was pioneered by Sir John Stirling-Maxwell.

Around the Lodge were magnificent specimens of Spruce, towering skywards and larger than anything I had seen in the forests of the Lake District. Spread among the trees were shrubs of many different kinds, ablaze with colour and contrasting sharply with the dark green of the conifers and the silver trunks of the birch. The previous winter had been a hard one all over the country and rows of birch saplings had been stripped bare of bark by herds of red deer that had swarmed down from the hills, desperately searching for food. Considering the weather at Corrour and the glutinous acid peat surrounding it, the dyed-in-the-wool foresters of the last century must have thought Sir John was mad when he started planting trees in his elevated wilderness, but his experiments were a success and close by the Lodge I found a plaque, set in a boulder, with the inscription: 'To commemorate Sir John Stirling Maxwell, Bt. 1866-1936, whose pioneer work on the planting of peat at Corrour led to the successful afforestation of large areas of Upland Britain – This memorial was unveiled by his daughter, Mrs Anne Maxwell MacDonald, on the 21st September, 1967, when the Society of Foresters of Great Britain visited Corrour Forest.' It is an achievement the fervent objectors to commercial afforestation may choose to ignore, though they may find another of Sir John's 'firsts' acceptable. He gifted the National Trust for Scotland their first property, Crookston Castle, near Glasgow. On the north side of the loch there were thousands of other monuments to Sir John's work, in the acres of trees planted by the Forestry Commission, but I could hardly see them. Heavy rain reduced the view to a yard in front of my feet as, bent double, I staggered back to my campsite.

In the evening a brave sun tried its best to break through, but the grumpy old men who steered the clouds were suffering another bilious attack and thunder was rumbling round the hills. I went across to the Youth Hostel where a lively singsong was in progress, with the owner of the large bloomers leading her girl guides in a loud and animated rendering of 'Kookaburra sits in an old gum tree'. She had pitched the key so high that the faces of the men who were trying to join in were contorted in the sort of agony associated with five days of constipation. I wedged myself in a corner next to an ancient Glaswegian, who told me that he was a founder member of the Scottish Youth Hostels Association and had spent his life as a riveter in John Brown's Shipyard on Clydebank. He was very bitter about the way Scotland's ship-building industry had crumbled to nothing and blamed the politicians for not looking far enough ahead and modernising shipyards.

'No wonder they Japs can build a ship quicker'n us,' he complained, 'Win ah was made redundant they wiz still using a machine ah learned on win ah joined the yard as a wee apprentice, fifty years before. They Japs must be laughin' up their kilts. I'll tell ye something else,' he went on, before I could get a word in, 'they politishuns think they're bein' clever knockin' all the tenements down in Gleska, but wit they'll niver understand is that they're killin' people's way of life. Whin ah was workin' in the yard we all lived in the tenements. We wiz born in 'em, we wiz raised in 'em, and we wiz happy to die in 'em. Ye canny jus' wipe out a community and start again.'

He got up to make himself a pot of tea and I found myself sitting close to an extremely attractive Australian girl, with honey-blonde hair and a sun tan she assured me went all the way down. I was fondly trying to imagine which pair of nylon frillies, hanging above the stove, might belong to her, when a friendly banter started about the reputation the Scots have for being mean and reluctant to part with their money.

'It's awe rubbish,' said the old Glasgow man, pouring treacle black tea into a chipped enamel mug.

'Well, I heard a good story, a week or two ago,' said a man, sat so quietly behind the stove I had not noticed him. 'It was about a farmer and his wife, somewhere in Aberdeenshire, who had always been tightfisted and would do anything but part with money. Anyway, the old man was taken seriously ill and, lying on his deathbed, he was overcome with conscience and called his family and relations round him. "I owe £10 to the blacksmith," he whispered, hoarsely, "and £50 to the seed merchant." "He's rambling," said his wife, looking alarmed, "don't listen to him." "Then there's £100 to my manservant, for wages owed," mumbled the old man. "£100," shrieked his wife. "Get the minister, quick, the poor man's fading." The old man moaned and his wife sponged his brow. "Donald Fraser owes me £20 for that stirk I sold him," he whispered "and Willy Grant owes me £70 for some sheep he had." "Wait a minute," said his wife, "I think he's rallying." '

The hostellers roared with laughter and even the old Glaswegian had a broad grin on his face.

'Well there must be a grain of truth in it,' said a fresh-faced lad from Inverness, when the laughter had died down. 'Last winter, when we had that very heavy snow, there were a lot of people cut off in isolated areas in Scotland and the RAF Mountain Rescue helicopters were called out to check if they were all right. As one of them flew over the moor, the pilot saw the chimney of a croft sticking up through the snow and, as the helicopter hovered above the chimney, one of the crew shouted down it, "Is there anyone there?" "Yes," came the reply. "Who is it?" "It's the RAF Mountain Rescue," the crewman shouted back. "Well go away," said the voice, "we bought a flag off you last year." '

The sound of hammering on the hostel door broke through the laughter and when Tom the warden pulled it open, the figure of a girl staggered in, absolutely exhausted and dripping with water. Someone thrust a mug of tea into her hands and, between gulps, she explained that she had walked from Rannoch and got caught in the gale near the hostel.

'Gale near the hostel?' I thought to myself. 'What gale?'

When I opened the door I could not believe my eyes. Horizontal rain poured past the door, driven along by a ferocious wind and somewhere out there was my tent. Shouting good night to the crowd in the hostel, I went out into the night and fumbled my way from one tree to another, until the noise of flapping canvas guided me to the tent. An hour later the gale reached such a pitch that the guy lines, holding the flysheet, snapped one by one, like cotton, and the flogging canvas streamed from the tent poles, like a banshee held by one leg. The tent vibrated as if there was an earthquake underneath it and wind-driven rain seeped through the canvas and drenched my sleeping bag with a fine spray. I tried covering it with my waterproofs, but it was a wasted effort. At two o'clock in the morning it seemed that the long service my mountain tent had given me was about to come to an end. The wind was gusting a good force nine when there was a terrific crash and the end of the tent fell down, slapping a great dollop of wet canvas into my face. Flinging it off, I grabbed a torch and a knife and crawled out into the gale, clad only in my underpants. It was impossible to stand up and I worked my way along the side of the tent. In the light of the torch I saw that a branch about three inches thick and eight or ten feet long, had snapped off one of the trees, flown about thirty yards through the air and hit the tent pole, snapping the main guy line. I was lucky it had struck the pole and not me. The guy line was easily knotted together, but the pole was very badly bent. The flysheet had flogged itself into a tangled heap and was doing more harm than good, so I hacked through the remaining guy line holding it and it flew away in the storm. The whole operation only took ten minutes, but having been blasted by the rain, my back and legs felt as if they had been peppered with buckshot. A large pool of water slopped about in the tent, but at least I was out of the wind. Pulling on a sweater and trousers, I crawled into the damp sleeping bag, downed a very large swig of whisky and hoped that the guy lines would hold until it was light enough to sort the mess out.

The wind never let up for a minute, but at six o'clock it stopped raining and, mercifully, the shower bath above my head was turned off. The inside of the tent was like a leaking boat. A soggy box of matches floated about among islands of half-submerged socks and muddy water oozed out of my supply of coffee bags. I climbed out to have a look at Thor and Lucy and was pleased to find that they had had the sense to shelter inside the shed, instead of in the lea, and they rushed out to tell me how hungry they were.

The wind moderated to a breeze, but it was bitterly cold and my fingers were numb by the time I had emptied the tent and spread everything on the grass. I found the flysheet floating in the water at the edge of the loch and waded out to retrieve it. The water was so cold I felt as if my feet had been plunged into molten steel. Tom Rigg said I could dry all my clothes and sleeping bag in the hostel, but the sun was peeping through the clouds and it looked as if the worst of the weather was over and I decided to set off for Loch Treig. I did take him up on his offer of hot water and in the washroom I stripped off and, with a hot flannel, revived the circulation in my legs and feet. Dressed in my last clean shirt, dry trousers and socks, I felt a lot happier and was eager to be on my way. It was approaching noon by the time I had packed the gear and loaded the ponies and, waving goodbye to Tom, I joined the track leading to Loch Treig and we were on our way.

7

An Enchanted Glen

Thor was in such a hurry to get away from Loch Ossian, his feet hardly touched the ground. The surface was much firmer than the track over Rannoch Moor and I was able to relax and enjoy the scenery. About a mile away from the Youth Hostel, the track swung close to the railway line and passengers on the Glasgow to Fort William train crowded to the windows to wave as they went by. A walker approached from the direction of Loch Treig and, as he came nearer, I recognised him as a man who was staying at the Youth Hostel. We chatted for a while and I discovered he was Richard Lister, the author of several books about the journeys of Marco Polo. It was too cold to stand for long and Richard made for the Youth Hostel, while I descended to where the Allt Luib Rhuairidh flowed under a two-arched railway bridge, only to find the way blocked by a heavy wooden hurdle. It took ages to unravel yards of wire and heave the hurdle to one side and I was wiring it back in place when a goods train crossed the bridge, with a tremendous roaring and rumbling. Thor and Lucy looked up for a split second, then bolted like rabbits. Fortunately they galloped along the track in the direction of Loch Treig and I caught up with them half an hour later, contentedly grazing as if nothing had happened.

From Loch Treig I had planned to cut across to Kinlochleven and Tom Rigg said I could save a few miles by going up Glen Iolairean. When I studied it through the binoculars, it looked like a place to avoid at all costs with ponies but, hoping I might find a good path higher up, I set off. Almost as soon as I was in the glen I realised it was a dangerous place to be taking Thor and Lucy. Acres of bog myrtle well-laced with patches of wet peat stretched as far as I could see. What little path there was became progressively worse and soon the ponies were floundering heavily in the morass. I was so intent on finding a way round the peat holes, I failed to notice that the pack saddle had slipped and suddenly Lucy bolted, with it hanging under her belly. Bags and equipment went flying in all directions as she galloped past, one hoof firmly wedged in the tent bag. Thankfully, she stopped a couple of hundred yards ahead, but what a sorry state the bags and harness were in. One side bag was badly ripped and the contents strewn like a paper chase over the glen. The tent bag was almost shredded, but amazingly the tent and flysheet were undamaged. Both the breast strap and the breaching on the pack saddle had snapped and, just to make a proper job of everything, a large container of midge repellent for the ponies had burst open and covered bags, contents, and harness with a sticky ointment.

I gave Lucy a handful of mints to calm her down and a few to Thor, who was threatening to come out in sympathy, then set about gathering my bits and pieces together. A quick repair to bags and harness and we escaped out of that dreadful glen, back to the safety of the track by Loch Treig.

Reaching a deserted farmhouse, I rested the ponies for an hour, but when I got out the Primus to make a brew, I found that Lucy's hoof had flattened an essential piece of the burner unit and I had to straighten it out very carefully with pliers before I managed to boil a billycan of water.

The map showed a path that followed the Abhainn Rath, a wide river that flowed into the loch, to a collection of buildings at Luibeilt, about five miles away. It seemed a good place to camp for the night and I felt sure there would be a paddock or a shed to keep the ponies in. A bank of ominous cloud was gathering over the hills when I collected the ponies and set off. The weather was unsettled and I was anxious to reach Luibeilt and cross the river to the Kinlochleven track before the rain returned and made the river impassable. From the Lodge the river flowed through a little rocky gorge, almost as if a canal had been hewn out of the rock. Above the gorge we were in very wild and beautiful country, with high towering crags on either side and no easy escape if anything went wrong. I was musing about this when I received the fright of my life. A jet fighter, on a low-flying exercise, came from nowhere and flew over us with an ear-splitting roar. Crazy with fright, Thor took off like a thunderbolt and, though I stood up in the stirrups and heaved on the reins as hard as I could, his mad panic gave him strength and I could not hold him. Flinging up clouds of mud and spray, he bolted through a bog and on through a field of boulders. We were heading rapidly for the edge of a high crag above the river and I was powerless to stop him. On the very edge of the cliff it penetrated his skull that it would not do either of us any good to go over the edge and he skidded to a halt a hundred feet above the river. Lucy, who had been racing close behind, saw the drop and swerved away, dragging me out of the saddle, to land heavily on a patch of rock. Blood was seeping through my trousers from a cut knee, my right index finger swelled up like a purple egg and I was shaking with fury and fright as I lay back in the heather to get my breath back, composing a letter to the Air Ministry that overflowed with obscenities. Worried that the plane might come back again, I quickly led Lucy and Thor up the glen to a safe patch of grass by the side of the river. My knee and finger were extremely painful and I longed to stop for the night, but when I looked at the rocks close by and found driftwood wedged in crevices, I realised that at times of flood the river must rise from its normal three feet depth to nearly twenty feet and the patch where I was planning to camp would be under water.

Further along, the river bank was gouged into a maze of deep gullies and I jumped Lucy across, with Thor following at his usual lumbering pace. Safely away from the gullies, a solid path climbed by the side of a series of impressive waterfalls, but it was too good to last and soon we were splashing through a sea of bog. As we squelched the last mile towards Luibeilt House, it was a miracle that the ponies did not break through the expanse of trembling moss and I gave them their heads to find their own way. A shallow ford crossed the river and Thor had an anxious time putting a hoof in the water, until he discovered it was only a foot deep and we crossed without difficulty. The house must have been a very attractive dwelling at some time, but even in such a remote place vandals had reduced it to a windowless ruin. I was overjoyed to find a large, well-fenced paddock, but not more so than Thor and Lucy, who sank into the grass and enjoyed a long roll. My damaged finger was throbbing like an engine and though I tried to reduce the swelling by plunging it into the icy river, this had little effect. The shock took some of the purple out of it, but it still looked like an egg. The air was incredibly cold and I lost no time in pitching the tent and lighting the stove to heat a pan of chicken supreme. I was ravenously hungry and filled up with a large helping of blackberry and apple pie filling. A few biscuits and cheese, followed by a mug of coffee, and I felt a new man. There was only one thing nagging me, it was the thought of crawling into a wet sleeping bag in my only dry shirt, trousers and socks. I solved the problem by wearing my waterproof trousers and coat and kept my boots on, before wriggling into the soggy fabric.

Not having slept a wink the previous night, I was incredibly weary and cocooned in all my clothes and the sleeping bag, I dropped off to sleep very quickly. I had a dreadful nightmare about being in a hospital with my arms pinioned in a strait-jacket and I woke up in a cold sweat. I tried to lift my arm out of the sleeping bag to look at my watch, but I could not move. Almost in a panic, I clawed my way out, but it was not a sleeping bag anymore, it was a cardboard tube. I rubbed my eyes to make sure I was not still asleep, but no, I was very much awake and shaking with cold. Feverishly I hunted for the box of matches and lit a candle. The wick spluttered as I put a match to it and when it flared up I could hardly believe my eyes. The wet sleeping bag was frozen solid and the inside of the tent white with frost. I lit the Primus and as the warm glow spread around the tent, the frost melted away and the cardboard sleeping bag became a soggy tube of fabric again. In the paddock I could hear Thor and Lucy snorting and stamping their feet and I opened the tent door and shone the torch outside. It was crazy, the ground was white with frost and the river covered with a layer of ice; this was in mid June. For a while I thought the strain of the last few days and the lack of sleep was causing hallucinations, but when I stuck my head out into the night air, the intense cold that took my breath away was very real.

Crawling back into the sleeping bag, I battled to keep awake. I had to keep the stove going to stop the inside of the tent freezing up again, and yet I dared not fall asleep in case I suffocated. In the end I could not keep my eyes open any longer, so I put the stove out, pulled a woollen balaclava over my face and tried to ignore the biting cold as it crawled back into the tent like the icy hand of death.

For hours I tossed and turned, trying to get warm, but it was no use and, at six o'clock, I jogged round the paddock to revive my circulation. The entire glen was like a scene from the depths of winter. A blood-red sun was peeping over the rim of the hill, casting pink and yellow light over a white landscape that hissed and crackled as my boots crunched through the frozen grass. Half a dozen deer, covered with hoar frost, stood on the river bank looking puzzled at the sheet of ice that yesterday had been drinking water and a heron skidded like a runaway jumbo jet as it attempted to land on its favourite fishing spot. As the sun rose higher in the cloudless sky, I witnessed the most incredible transformation of a landscape I have ever seen in my life. One minute it was a winter scene, with white frost and an ice-covered river, deer and ponies frozen immobile, then, as I watched, the heat of the sun wiped the canvas clean and repainted a sunlit glen with browns and purples, deer drinking from a glittering river and ponies grazing contentedly on the short grass. Half an hour after being frozen to the marrow, I was having breakfast in the sun. It was uncanny.

Breakfast over, I heaved everything out of the tent and spread my wet clothes, flysheet and sleeping bag over a fence to dry. I set about repairing the broken breaststrap and breeching and patched the torn kitbags. New guy lines were spliced onto the flysheet, the damaged tent poles were hammered straight and, with all the leather work coated with oil, I was ready to face another day. In less than two hours the sleeping bag and flysheet were bone dry and, with everything packed and lashed onto the ponies, I left Luibeilt, wondering if by chance I had camped in an enchanted glen.

8

Chaos on Corran Ferry

The wide track that headed towards Kinlochleven by way of Loch Eilde Mor was a welcome change after the gymnastics of the previous day and Thor and Lucy pottered along enjoying the easy walk. Near the loch the weather performed another of its reversal tricks. The sun disappeared and a biting wind whistled over the water and had me scurrying for my sweater and anorak. At the end of the loch the track climbed steeply up the side of a hill and from the summit there was the most fabulous view of Loch Leven, with the Glencoe hills beyond. Far below, the surface of the loch was white with spindrift, whipped up by a strong wind, yet when we descended a long series of hairpin bends on the sheltered side of the hill, it was overpoweringly hot.

At Mamore Lodge the track ran through the yard of a keeper's house and joined an old military road that wound its way over the hills towards Fort William, climbing steeply at first, then levelling off to a less exhausting gradient. For the first mile I had a magnificent bird's-eye view of the compact little town of Kinlochleven, but the town and loch faded out of sight as the track went deeper into the hills, and away from the wind it was very hot. Like me the ponies had not had much sleep at Luibeilt and they slowed to a snail's pace, stopping to snatch at the roadside grass whenever they thought I was dozing in the saddle. It was a gorgeous day and the scenery was superb, but my one thought was to find a campsite and enjoy a long rest and undisturbed sleep.

The track seemed endless as it dipped and rose, following the contours of the hills, but suddenly the climbing was over and I looked down on a small forest by Loch Luim na Bhra and there, by the boundary fence, was a newly enclosed paddock of about three acres. When I turned the ponies into it they sank to their knees as if giving thanks for their deliverance, then stretched out and within minutes Thor was actually snoring.

It was late afternoon but still deliciously warm and I sat outside the tent to cook my regular meal of chicken supreme. My supply of coffee bags had welded themselves together like a lump of peat after the soaking at Loch Ossian and I had to use tea bags. The packet boasted that the tea was from India, but I am sure that the only connection the tea had with India was that when added to hot water the dark liquid tasted like the River Ganges. Having eaten, I could hardly keep my eyes open and before the sun had dropped behind the hills I was fast asleep in a nice dry sleeping bag.

By the law of averages, I should have had a peaceful night, but a cuckoo perched itself on a tree at the edge of the plantation and launched into a loud and hysterical conversation with its mate farther down the glen. My watch said three o'clock and I burrowed into the sleeping bag to get away from the irritating cuckooing, but it penetrated my head like some fiendish Eastern torture. Bleary-eyed and angry, I crawled out of the tent but it flew away before I could hurl a stone at it. Dawn was well on its way in a cloudless sky and it promised to be another sunny day. Clouds of midges poured through the ventilator of the tent, looking for breakfast, and any further sleep was out of the question. The only way I could get rid of the brutes was to light the Primus and drive them out with heat.

Having slept fully clothed for several days, I felt decidedly grubby and went down to a stream for a strip wash, but the midges put paid to that idea. They descended on me like millions of piranha fish, chewing hungrily at my acres of flab. Making do with a quick splash round the ears, I rushed back to the tent.

At nine thirty I set off and followed General Wade's stony track through the forestry plantation to a tarred road leading to Lundrava Farm. As we approached the farmyard a fierce little terrier stood his ground in the middle of the road, determined not to let us go by. He was joined by another and both of them guarded their patch with such ferocity, snarling and snapping at the ponies' heels, I felt sure there would be an accident. Lucy tolerated them for a while, then began to lash out with both hind legs at one dog, then strike with a foreleg at the other. It was absolute pandemonium, dogs yapping and snarling and rushing in and out of the ponies' legs, Thor and Lucy rearing and bucking. To add to all the din, a woman ran out of a gate, shouting at the top of her voice and trying to grab the dogs. A car drew up and a man and boy joined the fray and that normally peaceful and forgotten little glen echoed with snarls, yelps, curses, shouts and whinnying ponies. Finally, one snarling little bundle of fur was helped through a gate with the toe of the woman's wellington boot and the young lad risked life and limb by diving under Thor and grabbing the other brute by the tail. Order was restored. The farmer, who had watched the antics from the safety of his yard, was almost speechless with laughter.

'By God, man,' he cried, pulling open the gate to let us through, 'it was better than anything on television.'

He was very helpful and, still chuckling to himself at the picture of two tiny dogs whizzing in and out between Thor's and Lucy's feet, he described the best way to cross the hill to Glen Righ Forest.

The rich meadow land close to the farm was too tempting for the ponies and every few yards they stopped to grab a mouthful of grass, as if they were on the point of starvation. It took a lot of pulling and heaving to get them through the meadows onto the open fell, but once they were ankle deep in bog they forgot about eating and we reached the edge of the forest without mishap. I was alarmed to find that there was no gate, but when I looked closely at the fence I found a section of netting had been stretched between two gate posts and it was easily removed and replaced. I rested for a while and drank deeply from the cool stream while the ponies nibbled at the sparse grass among the trees. It was gloriously warm and, lulled by the silence of the forest, I dozed against a rock, while flies droned overhead and wood-pigeons cooed softly to each other among the branches. High in the blue sky a silver jet plane was heading West, carrying a cargo of executives to the

plush hotels of New York. I would not have exchanged places
with them for anything.

The road through the forest ran parallel with a fast-flowing
river, but after two miles we left the conifers behind and rode
out into an area of rough moorland, flanked on one side by a
birch wood. Winding through the yard of an attractive little
farm at Glen Seileach, the road descended in a series of long
hairpins to the village of Inchree and all the way there was a
terrific view down Loch Linnhe and across the mountains of
Ardgour.

From Inchree I had three quarters of a mile of the main Fort
William road to go along and I pulled Lucy in close behind
Thor. A boot lace came undone and flapped round my ankles
and kept tripping me up, but the traffic was so dense I dared
not stop to tie it. Thor came to the rescue by plonking his
great hoof on it and snapping it off short. The side road
leading to the ferry came into sight ahead and with a sigh of
relief I left the roar of traffic and turned off to join the queue of
cars waiting to cross Loch Linnhe to Ardgour.

We attracted a few odd looks from the waiting motorists
and a bearded chap came across to look at the ponies. He only
had time to tell me that he was a Ranger with the Forestry
Commission when the ferry arrived and he had to rush back to
his car. The vehicles trickled slowly onto the boat and it was
so full I hung back to wait for the next one. The skipper waved
me forward, however, and jammed the ponies and me into a
very tight corner between the side of the ferry and a car with a
lady driver. Both ponies shook with fear when the engines of
the ferry roared into life, and I had a feeling of impending
disaster. Without warning, Lucy reared up and tried to jump
over the side and hung with her forelegs on the rail. The
woman, in the car next to us, started to scream and that was
enough for Thor. He reared up and, for one dreadful moment,
I thought his feet would go through the windscreen, but he
turned and tried to follow Lucy over the rail. I clung onto the
lead ropes, but I was being torn apart and Lucy was almost in
the water. The silly woman in the car screamed even louder
and both ponies were mad with fright. I desperately needed
help, but the occupants of the other cars either stared sourly at

me or looked the other way. Lucy was pulling the last few inches of her lead rope through my hand when the forest ranger saw my plight and climbed along the edge of the ferry and grabbed her head collar, hauling her back onto the deck. The ferry was in the strongest part of the tide and had Lucy gone over the side, she would have been swept to certain death. Shouting my thanks, I concentrated on keeping Thor off the car, but he was struggling to get away and still the woman in the car continued to scream. At last the ferry grounded on the Ardgour shore and the cars rolled off, leaving me limp and soaked with sweat, hanging round Thor's neck. One of the crew took Lucy, to allow the ranger to move his car.

'What do they call you?' I shouted as he drove away.

'I'm Paul Willett, from Polloch,' he called back.

'Well thank you, Paul Willett, you're a hero,' I cried and, with a wave, he was gone.

A line of motorists were impatiently waiting to drive on to the ferry, but the skipper held them back while I sorted out a tangle of ropes.

'You had a frightening few minutes, I am thinking,' he said, as I walked Thor down the ramp.

'I never want to go through that again,' I replied. 'I think the woman in the car had an accident!'

'Och yes,' he smiled, with a twinkle in his eye, 'I thought I saw a wee trickle of water coming from under the door as the car went by.'

The crewman walked Lucy to the road for me and I asked him if he knew of a place where I might camp the night.

'Try Captain Bailey, at Inversanda, about six miles down the loch,' he said, 'his wife and daughter are mad about horses and they might let you stay.'

From a phone box by the ferry, I dialled the Bailey's number, but as it was ringing I began to feel apprehensive about how they would react to a tramp with two ponies. I was used to pitching my tent in open country and, not having had a proper wash for nearly a week, the odour of sweat and horses was rather ripe. A female voice answered the telephone.

'Is that Mrs Bailey,' I enquired nervously.

'No, it's her daughter,' said the voice.

I explained that I was travelling with two ponies and wondered if there was a corner of a field where I could pitch my tent and feed the ponies. The reply was instant. 'But of course. Your journey sounds fascinating. I've ridden over a lot of the mountain routes myself. Keep going along the road from the ferry, you'll soon find us.'

The ordeal of the ferry crossing seemed to have sapped the strength of Thor and Lucy and they moved so slowly I wondered if we would reach Inversanda before it went dark. Round the long curve of Sallachan Bay we went, and Thor kept stopping and turning to look at me with an expression that clearly said, 'I'm just about all in. Don't you think it's time we stopped.'

'Keep going, old lad,' I urged, 'not far now.'

About a mile or so from Inversanda, an approaching car flashed its lights and pulled off the road. A woman and an attractive girl in her early twenties got out and introduced themselves as Mrs Bailey and her daughter, Lucinda. We talked about ponies and pack saddles for a short while, then they had to leave to take Lucinda to the ferry on her way back to college in Aberdeen. I let the ponies chew at the grass on the roadside while I took a few photographs of fishing boats steaming down the loch, then set off on the last lap. Rounding a bend, I saw a large white house with a Highland pony racing up and down in a paddock and I knew we had arrived. I turned into the drive and was just climbing off Thor when Mrs Bailey returned in her car and waved me to a group of outbuildings. Within minutes she produced two buckets of oats and Thor and Lucy almost choked in the rush to eat this rare treat. Leaving the ponies to their meal Mrs Bailey took me into the house for tea and scones and, to help away the fatigue, a glass of whisky appeared at my elbow. She said there was no need to pitch my tent as she had an empty cottage in the estate yard and I was welcome to use it.

My pile of scruffy equipment rather lowered the tone of the cottage sitting-room, but it was a welcome change from the tent. Flinging off my mud-stained trousers, filthy shirt and socks, I sank up to my neck in a bath of hot water and lay there for an hour, soaking away the rain, frost and sweat of the past week.

I slept magnificently and woke at eight in the morning to find the sun streaming through the windows. It was a scorcher of a day and, taking cameras and binoculars, I walked up the hill behind the cottage. Thor and Lucy were flat out in the sun so I did not disturb them and climbed high up a knoll to gain a view across the fields to Loch Linnhe and the hills of Glencoe. The rest of the morning was spent cleaning all the harness and saddles and repairing more holes that had appeared in the kitbags. I gratefully accepted Mrs Bailey's offer of the use of her spin drier and, having washed my foul clothes and a black towel that turned out to be yellow, I spread them in the sun to dry.

I had seen little of Captain Bailey, but in the afternoon while I sat outside the cottage writing my notes he came by and stopped to talk. He had spent most of his life in the Royal Navy and had retired to an entirely different way of life, struggling to make a living out of a Highland estate. Apart from a shepherd, he employed no staff and tackled most of the jobs himself, including tramping for miles over the high mountains of Ardgour in the stalking season. Like all sheep farmers in the Highlands, he had suffered a great many losses among his flock from marauding foxes, but instead of sitting back and grumbling about it he went down to the Lake District, where packs of hounds are followed on foot, and spent some time going out with a huntsman to learn the job. He took a pack of hounds back to Inversanda and, for a while, this tough ex-sea captain whose contemporaries would be enjoying their retirement sipping port in London clubs, hunted the hounds himself. I said he must have found it very different controlling a pack of hounds after a ship's company.

'Not at all,' he replied, breezily, 'the principle is just the same. You feed them well and swear at them.'

Certainly Inversanda was run very much on the lines of a ship, with 'a place for everything and everything in its place'. I liked his philosophy towards campers. Tourists heading for Morvern or Ardnamurchan had to pass Inversanda and people often camped on his land without asking permission and created many problems. Other owners would have been quick to turn the inconvenience into a money-spinner, but Captain Bailey created campsites, charged an overnight fee and sent the proceeds to the World Wildlife Fund. In the twelve years he had been taking campers the Fund had benefited by over £1,500. Scotland could do with a few more landowners like him.

In the evening, Mrs Bailey said she had warned the factor's wife at Ardtornish Estate in Morvern I was heading that way and she had said she would look out for me. On the way I had to pass through Kingairloch Estate and when I telephoned the Estate shepherd he said I could go through the grounds of Kingairloch House and follow a path along the cliff top, overlooking Loch Linnhe.

Taking the opportunity to have a change of diet before going back to chicken supreme, I bought some bacon, eggs and sausages from Mrs Bailey and prepared a feast in the cottage. It would have been nice to have had a glass of wine to help it along, but I made do with a large dram of whisky and dropped into bed, at peace with the world.

9

Midges and Mystery in Glensanda

I woke to a truly beautiful morning, with a cotton-wool mist lying over the flat calm surface of the loch and not a wisp of cloud to be seen in the sky. It was great to see Thor and Lucy looking so fit and well and they stood quietly while I brushed the dry mud out of their coats and checked their shoes for stones and loose nails. I was very grateful to the Baileys for giving us such a wonderful rest. The saddles and equipment were in good order; I had caught up on my notes; in the saddlebags were a clean set of clothes, and the weather was perfect.

Waving goodbye to Mrs Bailey, I set off down the road, blissfully happy. A narrow B-class road left the main road and climbed steeply for half a mile to level out at a small loch by the side of the road. Because it was off the beaten track I hoped I would have the road to myself, but numerous motorists had the same idea and I constantly had to pull the ponies onto the verge and let them past. A yellow Saab drew alongside and a cheerful lady wound down the window and said she was Mrs Coyne, the wife of the factor of Ardtornish Estate. She could not stop to talk as she was in a hurry to catch the ferry to get to Fort William, but would ride out to meet me the following day to show me the track to Ardtornish. I pulled over to let her get by, then followed the edge of a pine forest until the road descended gently to the farmstead of Kilmalieu and the rocky shore of Loch Linnhe. It was unbelievably hot and the summits of the hills across the loch stuck up above a bank of heat haze, as though they were detached and floating. Tying the ponies to a signpost, I lay in the short grass between the road and the edge of the water and watched a lobster-fishing boat nosing its way across the loch.

Its bow cut through the blue water that fell in a cascade of silver ripples. Among the worn and pockmarked rocks at the edge of the water a tangled mass of seaweed, plastic bottles, bits of rope and cork trawl-net floats surged backwards and forwards as the tide climbed higher up the rock. A weathered fishbox labelled optimistically 'Return to Aberdeen', had been forced by a gale into a rocky crevice, to lie broken and battered, like a wrecked ship, forever on this foreign shore.

Above Kilmalieu, the towering crags of Maol nan Each dropped steeply into the water and road-builders had blasted a way through the hard rock. From the unsightly mess floating at the edge of the loch it was obvious that the low wall, built to stop unwary travellers falling into the loch, was the perfect height for locals to balance their dustbins on, and hundreds of tons of tin cans, bottles, rotting vegetables, bedsteads, prams and every conceivable item of junk had been dumped on the rocks. It is difficult to understand why people who live in such a picturesque area should defile it in this way, and it is time the local authority put a stop to it before the entire shore is ruined.

At the headland of Rubha an h'Airde Vinnsinn the road turned inland to cross Glen Glamadale river and the strong smell of sheep hung in the hot air from Glamadale Farm, where workers were busy shearing. I rested for a few minutes in the shelter of a group of tall larch, but the river bank was too steep for the ponies to reach the water and they had to make do with sucking what they could from a drain.

The road ahead climbed steeply above the brightly painted houses and tiny church, dotted round the Bay of Camas na Croise, gardens and hedgerows ablaze with white and red rhododendrons and bright yellow gorse. Set against the vivid blue of the water, it was like a scene in the Mediterranean. The road crossed the headland of Ceanna Mor and I looked down on the miniature fiord of Loch a' Choire, cut into the Morvern peninsula like an elongated horseshoe.

At the head of the loch was Kingairloch House and a sign directed me down a private road to the lochside. Close to a crumbling jetty there was a small cottage with a couple sitting outside, sheltering from the heat under a large, brightly

coloured umbrella. Thor's eyes rolled when he saw it and he
tried to do a smart about turn, but the man quickly furled his
circular rainbow and let us by.

'You look hot, would you like a beer?' said the man.

In a flash I had Thor and Lucy tied to a tree and was sitting
next to him before he had time to fill the glass. I was so
parched I hardly tasted the beer, so his wife suggested we went
into the cool of the cottage for cakes and tea. They told me
their name was Hay and they came from Lincoln every year to
the same place for a holiday. All they required was peace and
quiet and said Loch a' Choire was the ideal spot. Thor and
Lucy enjoyed a bucket of water each and, grateful for the rest,
I pressed on round the edge of the loch by Kingairloch House
and Farm to a ruined mill and the start of the path that, on the
map anyway, followed the south side of Loch a' Choire to
Loch Linnhe, then along the cliff top to Glensanda, where I
planned to camp for the night. Among a haggle of ruts and
gullies on the salt marsh, the path was difficult to find, but a
thin line cut through the meadows of South Corry House, then
along the shore to a tiny croft house at Creag Ghlas. From
here the path was non-existent and we floundered in and out
of holes full of slippery seaweed and shallow pools, where tiny
crabs ran for their lives when the ponies' hooves crashed
through the water. The map showed the path crossing a
headland at the point where Loch a' Choire joined Loch
Linnhe, but when I left the ponies to scout ahead, all I could
find was a dried-up watercourse.

Although it was seven o'clock in the evening, the sun still
blazed down from a cloudless sky and sweat dripped off me as
I led the ponies up the steep hillside. Gasping for breath, I
rested at the top but when I looked down on the other side I
found I had climbed too high and what appeared to be the
path ran some distance below. We were forced to descend very
steep heather and the pack saddle slipped forward at the worst
possible time, on the brink of a long drop into the loch. It
rolled underneath Lucy's belly but luckily she kept calm while
I disentangled the harness and led her to the safety of the
path, dragging the packs and saddle behind me. Although it
was certainly a path, I was not convinced I was on the old
pony track and my fears were confirmed when, having

followed the gravelly beach for a short distance it climbed, to disappear in acres of high bracken.

I searched backwards and forwards and up and down, but there was no trace of a path anywhere and the ponies stumbled and snorted as they fell over hidden boulders or slid into holes. Lucy was rapidly becoming exhausted and every few hundred yards she sank to her knees and tried to roll. To have forced a route through the bracken would have been extremely hazardous and I dropped down to what appeared to be an easy route along the shingle beach. It was a mistake: after half a mile the shingle ended and ahead was a mass of boulders covered in slimy seaweed.

Finding a way through it was an absolute nightmare but, with rocky cliffs on one side and the loch on the other side, there was no means of escape. We had to go on and every foot of the way had to be chosen with the utmost care. Unable to get a grip, the iron shoes of the ponies skated off the slimy rock and more than once the animals slipped and crashed to the ground. To add to the worry the tide was advancing up the beach, sending us closer and closer to the cliff, and I began to fear we might be trapped.

We staggered on and were within a hundred yards of safety when Thor decided he could go no further and no amount of shouting would move him. The tide was now rapidly covering the boulders and rising up his legs, but still he would not budge. It was bad enough trying to find a way along the beach when I could see the boulders, but now they were covered with water and the situation was really serious. I slid off a rock into the water beside him and gave him a great whack on his backside and he lumbered forward, slipping and staggering through the water, until with a final dash we reached firm grass by the ruined house of Airigh Shamraidhe. It would have been an ideal place to camp had it not been for loony Lucy's wandering fits, but I dared not risk it. The pack saddle blankets had rolled into an uncomfortable ball and I unloaded to give Lucy's back a rub down and let her graze for half an hour. When he saw the grass Thor made a lightning recovery and spent the entire rest period with his nose to the ground.

The sun had already dipped over the horizon and there were still two and a half miles to go to Glensanda, where the shepherd at Kingairloch had told me there was a good paddock to put the ponies in. Leaving our resting-place, I spurred Thor along a flat expanse of grass and bracken at the edge of a shallow bog, but the easy ground did not last long. The path climbed away from the beach and followed a tortuous route over a long series of bracken-strewn crags. At intervals the path was buried under an avalanche of boulders, swept down the hillside in the winter floods, and a lot of valuable time was wasted finding a way through loose scree and potholes. Darkness was falling when the square tower of Glensanda Castle appeared ahead and, with the last obstacle behind us, we slid down through the bracken to a soft, sandy beach. I gave Thor and Lucy a big hug and a bar of chocolate each and led them quickly round the back of the abandoned farmhouse to a paddock. Before I could turn them loose, however, I had to block numerous gaps in the fence. When I returned to the ponies, I found them submerged under a cloud of midges and poor Lucy was almost frantic. Unsure about the security of the fence, I fastened the hobbles on both the ponies and turned them loose. Lucy went berserk and cantered round the field, trying to get away from the tormenting cloud. Unable to escape, she threw herself into the grass and rolled violently from side to side, then up she got and started the whole process again. I knew she was ravenously hungry, but not once did she stop to eat, as she whirled crazily round the field. Lucy always suffers in the summer: she has a particularly sensitive skin and midges and horseflies always upset her; but I had never seen her react like this and I was very worried. I dared not leave her out so, finding one of the farm buildings was still in good order, I removed her hobbles and led her into the cool interior. Cutting a heap of grass with my knife, I took it to her but she ignored it and stood with her face in a corner. Amazingly, the midges did not seem to bother Thor and he chewed at the grass, quite oblivious of the black cloud swirling above his head.

Having lost Lucy, the fiendish little beasties turned their attention on me and by the time the tent was pitched, my face and arms were covered in itchy lumps. It was almost midnight and I was too exhausted to make a meal or even a hot drink, and made do with a mug of orange. Covering my face and neck with midge cream, I pulled the sleeping bag over my head and tried to sleep, but without success. A warm, humid night made the bag overpoweringly hot and, a few yards away, Lucy stamped impatiently on the stone floor of the old barn. Sweat poured off me, but I dared not open the tent door. Just about dawn, I was startled by a tremendous bellowing outside the tent. I fumbled with the door and looked out into the face of an enormous stag, with his new growth of antlers still in velvet. He was as shocked to see me as I was to see him. He whirled round and, with a tremendous leap, cleared the field fence and was gone.

The morning was dull and humid, perfect for midges, and they were not slow in appreciating it. Inside the tent it was like an oven, and when I opened the ventilators thousands of the little pests poured in and began to chew through the midge cream, looking for me. A friend who camped a lot in Scotland had given me what he described as a 'miracle concoction', manufactured in Hong Kong. The box assured me it was 'a most effective, economical and scientific mosquito-repellent – harmless to human'. Whether the mosquito and the Scottish midge were blood cousins I was not sure, but anything was worth trying.

The device was a green coil, rather like a catherine wheel, the centre of which was attached to a very oriental-looking metal stand. Obeying the instructions on the box, I applied a match to the end of the coil and waited. For a while nothing happened, then a wisp of green smoke spiralled upwards. I half expected a genie to appear armed with an aerosol fly spray, but the smoke merely got thicker and thicker. Soon the inside of the tent was like a kippering plant and I could hardly breathe. It was certainly effective though. The midges took one whiff of the oriental magic and ran screaming for the ventilator. Unfortunately, I could not stand it either and dived through the door. Outside, a large deputation was gathered to let me know what they thought of my smoke treatment, but I did not wait to argue, I fled across the grass to join Lucy in the barn.

As long ago as 1944 the Department of Health for Scotland was concerned enough about the midge to set up a committee of eminent scientists to see what could be done to combat the little pest.

'The midge in Scotland,' wrote Sir Alexander MacGregor, chairman of the Scientific Advisory Committee, 'may not be a carrier of infection, but its biting properties make it a serious source of irritation both to the Scottish people themselves and to the many tourists who visit our beauty spots.'

The Committee's task was to produce a midge repellent and the Scottish Tourist Board entered enthusiastically into the battle by sponsoring the successful formula. Extensive tests were carried out on forestry workers, fishermen, roadworkers and schoolchildren throughout the Highlands, and resulted in an effective cream comprised of kaolin and a chemical with the tongue-twisting name of Dimethylphthalate, or DMP for short.

It will be of little consolation to those allergic to the Scottish midge to learn that there are at least fifteen different species of the biting variety. The nastiest of the breed is *Calicoides impunctatas* and, as the name suggests, it inflicts its misery by puncturing the skin with a proboscis constructed for piercing and sucking. Microscopic though the piercing device may be, it certainly hurts and often causes the skin to remain hot and burning for hours. In severe cases, people with particularly sensitive skin have required hospital treatment.

Though few are prepared to admit it, the Scottish midge is as much a part of the Highlands as the mountains and the lochs. Its reputation is legendary and grown men have been reduced to tears when attacked by the fiendish hordes. Individually, they are minute and insignificant, but collectively they become a powerful monster that has caused farm work to be suspended, schools to be closed, animals to collapse with exhaustion, milk yields in cows to drop alarmingly, forestry workers to rush frantically from the woods and military establishments to be moved or abandoned altogether. With such a weapon available gratis, there is surely no need for governments to waste money developing missiles and other atomic nasties!

When the sun came up I carried the bags over to the barn and, away from the midges, I cooked the last of the sausages I had bought from Mrs Bailey. Lucy was still standing in a corner, but the smell of frying sausages must have sharpened her appetite. Ambling to the door, she looked cautiously from side to side, as if expecting to hear midges whoop with glee and rush towards her. Discovering the paddock was empty, except for Thor, she stepped outside and gulped the grass as fast as she could go. Looking round the barns, I was surprised to find rough bunks made out of beams and stable doors, torn from the outbuildings, and, in the centre of the floor, a fireplace had been built out of stone. Whoever had used the barn was very untidy: half empty food tins and recent copies of a Scottish daily paper were strewn all over the floor and a disturbing find was several spent rifle cartridges lying in some rubbish. There was something faintly ominous about the way the place had been hurriedly abandoned and an icy shiver ran down my spine. Outside in the sun I felt less threatened and I walked down the beach to photograph the ruin of Glensanda Castle, perched high on a rock with a commanding view across Loch Linnhe. Although the roof had long gone, the walls were in remarkably sound condition. I climbed a narrow stone staircase to the entrance, half expecting to be challenged by a fierce clansman waving a dirk under my nose. The interior had that dark, oppressive feeling that seems to surround ancient castles. A crumbling staircase slanted up the wall, leading to a void and certain death on the rocks below. I had a feeling I was being watched by the ghosts of prisoners who had been pushed off the ramparts, or whose bodies had hung from chains to feed the hungry crows. The whole place gave me the creeps and I went down to the beach to sit on the white sand and look across to the long island of Lismore. On my way back to the barn I passed the farmhouse and it was a sorry sight. This once beautiful house with a magnificent view across the loch had obviously been on fire and the holes that had once held windows looked across the meadows like the eyeless sockets of a skull. There was something decidedly spooky about Glensanda and I was very pleased to get away from it.

10

Ardtornish and Highland Humour

It was only eight miles from Glensanda to Ardtornish Estate and with the whole day to reach it I let the ponies amble at their own pace as we made our way inland, following the Glensanda river. It was a wild and desolate little glen and the path marked on the map had long vanished into antiquity and thick heather. Thor floundered heavily into a hidden peat hole and when I jumped off his back to lead Lucy round it, the fool thought he was being abandoned to his fate and panicked. He thrashed about so much he sank up to his chest and I had to heave him out with a rope attached to Lucy's saddle. As the ground became rougher and steeper poor Lucy, who had not rested very much during the night, laboured heavily. To reduce the weight on her back I lashed one of the packs to Thor's saddle and led him up the hill. Some kind soul had marked the line of the path with cairns and I was happily following them when it occurred to me that they were leading me off in the wrong direction. Cursing cairn-builders and my own stupidity, I led the ponies back to the first cairn and, with the aid of a compass, reached the narrow strip of water of Caol Lochan. At the head of Glensanda, the hillside was alive with deer: in one herd alone, I estimated there was well over five hundred. As we approached, they moved away like a brown carpet, speeding across the heather, led by true monarchs of the glen. I followed one enormous stag through my binoculars. Even though his antlers were still in velvet, I could visualise him bellowing from a rock in one of those great paintings by Edward Landseer.

From the loch a good path kept to a narrow ridge, then slanted down a deep gorge to a fence marking the boundary between Kingairloch and Ardtornish Estates. Out of the gorge, the path crossed a wide moor. In the distance, I could see a figure on horseback heading towards me and I recognised Sue Coyne from Ardtornish. We were almost within hailing distance when her pony decided it did not like the look of Thor and Lucy and shot off down a gully, with Sue heaving on the reins, trying to hold him back. When we caught up, Sue had dismounted and was holding firmly to the pony's bridle. Spotting us again, he reared and plunged with such violence there was no holding him and he headed for home at a full gallop. Sue took Lucy's lead rope and led the way through a confusion of bogs to a wide stony track at Loch Tearnait, where she managed to catch her pony as he grazed quietly on a patch of grass.

As we rode the last half mile to the estate yard at Achranich, black clouds scudded in from the West and a chilly breeze rattled the branches of the tall trees scattered round the buildings. There was every sign of a storm approaching and we hurried to the Coynes' house where young Trina and Fiona Coyne showed me a field for Thor and Lucy and helped to carry the bags and saddles to the family caravan, where I was to sleep. I was invited to join the family for a meal and during the evening Sue explained that her husband, Ranald, was away on a sailing holiday, but was due back the following day. She asked me what condition the buildings at Glensanda were in. When I told her about the bunks in the barn, she said that the estate was being troubled with deer poachers who landed by boat on Glensanda beach. At one time they camped in the old farmhouse but then they were chased away and returned later to set fire to the house. Since then other poachers had used the barn. My mind went back to the rifle cartridges I found in the rubbish and I was very thankful that the poachers had not arrived while I was there.

Torrential rain drummed on the caravan roof all night. When I looked through the window it was a miserable sight, with thick mist hanging heavily over the trees and water pouring like a miniature river down the path at the side of the house. After breakfast I spread the maps out on the caravan table to look for a route across the hills to Loch Sunart. Ardtornish Estate was at the head of Loch Aline, another fiord, similar to Loch a' Choire but slightly longer and entered from the Sound of Mull. The map showed several ways I could reach Loch Sunart, but the rain streaming down the caravan windows dampened my enthusiasm and I decided to stay until the weather improved. Sue Coyne called to say she was going to visit a lady who was the custodian of Kinlochaline Castle and would I like to look around it. History in the rain sounded more exciting than twiddling my thumbs in the caravan so, clutching cameras and waterproofs, I jumped into the yellow Saab. Mrs Dolly McMillan, the custodian, lived in a little cottage by the side of the castle and she gave me an information sheet about its history and a huge key to let myself in with.

To be unromantically accurate, it was more of a fortified tower than a castle and was almost identical in shape and size to the one at Glensanda. Turning the key in the lock, I pushed the heavy door open and entered the cold, damp interior. A great deal of restoration work had been carried out to the floors and walls, but the atmosphere of the castle's long history was still there and my echoing footsteps must have disturbed the ghosts as I climbed a flight of steps to a trapdoor leading to the battlements. Outside on the roof the rain was still sluicing down and thick mist and tall trees obscured what might have been a fine view across the loch. It was no day for taking photographs so, closing the trapdoor over me, I clumped down the steps, secured the entrance door and returned the key to Mrs McMillan at Castle Cottage. She was waiting for me with a large pot of tea and a plate of cakes. As we sat by the warm kitchen fire, she talked about the days when she worked as a maid at 'the Big House' at Ardtornish, for Andrew Craig Sellar, a descendant of the notorious Patrick Sellar who evicted hundreds of people from their homes during the Highland Clearances. In Andrew Sellar's day over a hundred people were employed on the estate, including fourteen gardeners. Aware of how cut off his little community was from the outside world, the laird transported his entire staff three times a year to Oban on a shopping spree and at Christmas he laid on a great party, with presents for everyone.

'Some might say we were slaves to the laird,' said Mrs McMillan, 'but even with the big wages they get today, people are no better off. There's many a man and his family who spent all their lives working for one owner and they would not have stayed if they weren't happy.'

We were well into our second pot of tea when her husband, Archie, arrived home from his job as a worker on the estate and driver of the 'school bus', an ancient ex-army Land Rover. He was full of tales about the history of the estate. When Kinlochaline Castle was built by the Clan McInnes, the workers were paid in butter and since then the castle had been known as Casteal an Inne, or Butter Castle. Most of the restoration work had been carried out by Thomas Smith, who owned the estate in 1890, but before that an old woman called Mary Cameron had lived in it after her wooden shack had been blown away in a gale. Compared to her shack, the rooms of the castle must have seemed enormous, but the enterprising lady filled the surplus space with hens and a few cattle. Known locally as Mary Casteal, Castle Mary, she was reputed to be a very tough old character who lived to a great age.

Back in the caravan, I settled back to browse through a book that Mrs Coyne had loaned me to read, *Morvern Transformed*, written by Philip Gaskell, a man who regularly spent his holidays at Ardtornish. It was a fascinating read and the author had obviously done an enormous amount of research into the estate and its owners. The book was spoilt for me, however, when I read his description of Patrick Sellar, the man whose name will be forever etched into Scotland's history for the inhumane way he treated his tenants. Philip Gaskell describes Sellar as being a good man who was truthful and honourable. A kind friend and devoted to his wife and children. Yet one of the first things this 'kind and honourable' person did when he moved from Sutherland to Morvern was to evict forty-four families from their homes. Over two hundred and thirty people were driven from his estate at Acharn, to make room for sheep. When he eventually bought Ardtornish in 1844 part of the agreement was that, before Sellar parted with his cash, the outgoing owner should evict all the crofters from the estate. I wonder how he explained to his own devoted wife and family the suffering he caused the defenceless men, women and children. It is hardly surprising that people like Sellar were hated and despised by local people. Dr MacLachlan, the poet of Morvern, dipped his pen in vitriol when he wrote:

'Our Highland mountain with purple heather
Where Fingal fought and his heroes slumber,
Are white with sheep now, for miles together,
And filled with strangers whom none can number.
The ancient customs and clans are banished,
No more are songs on the breezes swelling,
Our Highland nobles, alas, are vanished,
And worthless upstarts are in their dwelling.'

Having exhausted all my reading material, I spent the rest of the afternoon poring over the maps. Since there was no sign that the weather would improve, I decided that next day I would follow the coast road to Drimnin, then cross the hills to Loch Teacuis.

It was depressing sitting in the caravan listening to the rain drumming on the roof so I was delighted when Archie MacMillan arrived in his school bus with the Coyne children and asked if I would like to go with him that evening to Lochaline village to meet Donny Lawrie, the local postman and an authority on the history of the area. He arranged to pick me up at eight o'clock, which gave me plenty of time to have a meal and go over to the bungalow to ask Sue Coyne if she knew anyone who had a field at Drimnin and would let me camp. A quick telephone call soon had me fixed up to stay in a field owned by the MacDonalds at Drimnin post office.

It was still raining heavily when Archie arrived and his car flung up clouds of spray as we sped along the narrow road to the village. Donny was waiting for us in the bar of the hotel and it turned out to be an hilarious evening. Donny was one of those rare people with an infectious sense of humour that has everyone falling about with laughter. As the evening wore on I cannot remember gathering much information about local history, but Donny had an endless collection of jokes and stories. The one that stuck in my mind, despite the numbing effect of a large intake of 'Cream of the Barley', concerned a bull that was sent out by the Department of Agriculture to one of the Outer Isles to improve the stock of cattle. Among the inevitable sheaf of forms that arrived with the animal, was a large label with instructions to attach it to the bull's left horn 'on completion of its duty' and return it to the mainland. The islanders pointed out that it was an Aberdeen Angus and it had not got any horns. Back came a snooty letter from the bureaucrats, that they should 'Kindly abide by the instructions on form XYZ/123/567B and return the animal described thereon to the proper authority.' The islanders tied the label to the bull's tail and returned it with a note explaining that when the bull arrived its horns had been lost in the post and in order to return it, they had been obliged to attach the label to the handle of the milk pump!

The night was well advanced when Archie and I prepared to leave the cosy bar to return to Ardtornish, but Donny had by no means finished his entertaining.

'Wait you a minute,' he shouted, as we headed for the door. 'I must tell you the story of Angus MacLeod and the incubator.' A hush fell over the room as Donny propped himself against the bar and launched into his story. 'Angus MacLeod was from Skye and he was very keen to get into egg production on his croft, because eggs were fetching a good price in Portree, with all the English visitors wanting eggs with their chips and putting them in those wee chamber pots for their breakfast. But Angus could never get enough eggs because he only had a few hens. His brother, Dougal, in Glasgow, heard about his problem and bought him a big incubator so he could breed a lot of chicks and increase his flock, and sent it to Angus on the island. Time passed and there was no word from Angus, so Dougal went to see if the incubator had arrived. When he reached the croft, the incubator had arrived right enough, but Angus was looking more miserable than ever. "How are you getting on with the incubator, Angus," said Dougal. "Och, the thing's useless," replied Angus, "it's been sitting in that shed for over three months and it hasn't laid a single blutty egg." '

The crowd in the bar howled with laughter and we left, waving goodbye to Donny, although I doubt if he saw us. He was busy reciting Gaelic poetry to an audience of wide-eyed visitors.

On the way home Archie showed me the little collection of houses at Larachbeg where the people from St Kilda were housed when that isolated island off the West coast of Harris was evacuated in 1930. He said that when the St Kildans arrived the Forestry Commission employed most of the men, but they had a difficult time settling into a regular job. They had never seen cars or trains and when the Government provided each man with a bicycle to get to work on there were a few hair-raising incidents before they eventually learnt to ride them.

I was tired and weary when Archie dropped me off at the caravan, but it was an evening I would not have missed for anything.

11

Deer Farming by Loch Teacuis

During the night the heavy rain never eased for a minute and I had very little sleep. By morning a fresh wind had sprung up and rocked the caravan as it drove the rain against the windows. It was hardly the best of days for setting off, but I felt I had to be on my way and, after breakfast, I led Thor and Lucy out of the field to load up. Drenched by rain and buffeted by wind, it took me longer than usual to lash everything into place on Lucy's back and load the saddlebags onto Thor. It had gone ten o'clock when I pushed the reluctant ponies into the downpour and waved goodbye to Sue Coyne. She saved me a long ride along the main road by telephoning the manager of Loch Aline Diatomite Mine and obtaining permission for me to use a track along the edge of the loch. Dolly McMillan waved to me from the window of Castle Cottage as I went by but clinging to the saddle to stop myself from being blown out of it, I only managed a half-hearted reply.

The surfaced road ended at the cottage and a muddy track followed the edge of the loch, beneath a canopy of enormous larch and Scots pine. Miraculously, both the wind and the rain died away and a weak sun broke through, transforming the grey surface of the loch to a pastel blue. Peeling off my dripping waterproofs, I rubbed the saddle dry with a towel, then relaxed and let the ponies find their own pace along the track. After an hour or so the noise of heavy machinery warned me that the mine was ahead and I jumped off Thor's back and led him between a row of noisy conveyor belts which were spewing out the valuable deposit that had lain for millions of years under Morvern's crust. With the mine machinery behind us, Thor began to breathe easier and not walk sideways as if some monster were about to jump out and eat him.

Near the steamer jetty there was a shop and I went in to buy some fruit and groceries. Quite a crowd had gathered by the time I emerged clutching a plastic bag in one hand and half a bottle of whisky in the other. Greedy Thor and his ever-hungry girlfriend were in no hurry to move off. Both of them were swallowing a stream of apples, biscuits, sweets and ice cream like hairy waste disposal machines and no amount of complaining from me was going to make them stop. In the end, I had to cut off the source by confiding to the crowd that Thor was an evil-tempered stallion, who often reared up and kicked out without warning. That did it. The crowd reacted as if Thor had suddenly developed bad breath and left him looking very puzzled when his row of choppers bit into thin air instead of an apple. He gave me one of his odd looks, but if I had told the truth, that the vet's knife had long ago removed his stallion equipment and the only time he lifted his leg high was to scratch his belly, we would never have got away.

Sue Coyne had told me that the route over the hill from Drimnin to Loch Teacuis had a locked gate and that I should call at the Forestry Commission's office at Loch Aline to see if I could borrow a key. The office was empty and a lorry driver was busy directing me to the forester's house when Sue Coyne arrived in her car and said she would go on ahead and tell him I was coming. The ponies plodded up the road to a white cottage with a neat, well-kept garden. I was tying Lucy to the fence when Thor marched straight into the garden and stuck his great feet right in the middle of a flower bed. I could swear he did it out of spite for being parted from his food, but fortunately the forester took it in good part and invited Sue Coyne and me in for a cup of tea. One of his children was having a birthday party later that day so we sampled a few of the cakes and pastries. Having borrowed a gate key from him and been given instructions where to hide it at Loch Teacuis, I set off once more along the road to Drimnin.

The clouds had all but melted from the sky and the Sound, across to the Isle of Mull, sparkled in the sunlight. I had been riding for about half an hour when a white Land Rover overtook me and squealed to a halt. An elderly man got out and, coming towards me with a broad smile on his face, asked if I would like to stop off for lunch at his house, a short distance along the road. He said he had heard about my journey and would like to know what route I was taking.

'By the way,' he called through the Land Rover window as he drove off, 'I'm James Levack, a retired doctor. Second house you come to on the right, you can't miss it. We'll be waiting for you.'

Following James Levack's directions I soon found his cottage, sitting snugly into the side of the hill, with a wonderful panoramic view of the Sound of Mull. He and his wife were waiting at the gate but the sight of a magnificent topsail schooner beating up towards Tobermory had James racing to get his binoculars and we spent some time watching the feverish activity on board as the crew heaved on the sheets to put the ship on another tack. It eventually sailed out of view round a headland and James helped me to unload the ponies and turn them loose in the garden. Mrs Levack produced an excellent lunch of salad, cheese, cake and oatcakes and afterwards I sank into an armchair with a can of lager, keeping a watchful eye on Lucy who was sniffing hungrily at an attractive flowering shrub. As we talked and put the world to rights, the lovely view of the Sound with its glistening water, dark hills and blue sky was suddenly draped in grey and we looked out to find the sky to the West obscured by a towering mass of inky black cloud and a rain squall approaching rapidly across the water. It hit the window of the cottage like a clap of thunder and I watched helplessly as a torrent of water bounced off the saddles and packs lying on the lawn. For Mrs Levack it was the signal to put the kettle on again and James, muttering that he had the right sort of medicine for that kind of weather, went out of the room and returned with a bottle of whisky. The oatcakes and cheese came out again and I was so full I could hardly move. I would have much preferred to stay by the fire, rather than brave the rain, but it was now well into the afternoon and Drimnin was still some way off.

Thanking James and his wife for their hospitality, I pulled on my waterproofs, loaded up Thor and Lucy and continued on my way, huddled in the saddle, hardly able to see through the gale-swept rain. On we went, over the fast-flowing Savary river and by the historic manse of Fuinary, where the Reverend MacLeod composed one of the most poignant of Scottish songs, 'Farewell to Fuinary', before he left to become minister of Campbeltown on the Mull of Kintyre.

'The wind is fair, the day is fine,
And swiftly, swiftly runs the time,
The boat is floating on the tide
That wafts me off from Fuinary.

Farewell ye hills of storm and snow,
The wild resorts of deer and roe,
In peace the heath cock long may crow
Along the banks of Fuinary.'

Leaving Fuinary Forest behind, the road climbed up and down, sometimes close by the water's edge and at others high above it, looking down over lush meadows. On the way we passed Clach na Criche, a natural stone dyke some sixty feet long by about thirty feet high. In the end of the dyke there was a hole, roughly oval in shape and about twelve feet high. According to local folklore, if you wanted a wish granted you must fill your mouth with water from a well about half a mile down the road from Clach na Criche, then walk through the hole three times without touching the sides, keeping the water in your mouth all the time. I did not have any water in my mouth, but there was plenty of the horrible stuff running down my neck and I wished it would stop raining, but the request fell on deaf ears.

It was eight o'clock in the evening when I reached Drimnin and the MacDonalds' bungalow, which adjoined the tiniest post office I have ever seen. I hammered on every door but there was no reply. I stood dismally in the rain, wondering what to do next, when a car arrived and a man jumped out and introduced himself as Alistair MacDonald. He took me to a field in which I could camp and pointed out a cottage owned by Sue Coyne and her husband, where there was a water tap in the garden.

The grass in the field was knee-deep and saturated with

water. While I was hunting for a place to pitch the tent, a man came out of the cottage and said I could sleep in the garden shed if I did not mind putting up with the noise of the generator until they retired to bed. Torrential rain was being driven in from the sea by a strong wind and, thankful to be spared the battle with flogging canvas, I gladly accepted his kind offer. He helped me to carry the bags and saddles into the shed, then very kindly invited me to the house for a meal. His wife braved the elements to dash across from the house with a coat over her head to tell me to bring my wet things to the house and dry them in the boiler room. My kind hosts turned out to be the parents of Ranald Coyne, Sue's husband. Together with three friends they were spending a week at the cottage. After working through a substantial meal, I was placed in a comfortable chair by the fire with a large glass of whisky at my elbow, and I yarned about my adventures since setting off from Drymen.

At ten o'clock I left their pleasant company and crawled into my sleeping bag. The noise from the diesel engine was deafening and I burrowed deep into the bag to try and escape from it. It had gone midnight when the last light was switched off in the cottage and the generator spluttered to a halt and, with a long sigh, went to sleep. I tried to do the same, but the howling of the gale made sleep impossible. All night I tossed and turned on the earth floor of the shed, while the wind whistled through the gaps in the timber wall and spattered me with rain. As the first shafts of light penetrated the clouds, the gale blew itself out and the rain eased off to a drizzle. It was surprisingly warm and the humid atmosphere was perfect for midges. They rose in their millions from the wet grass, hungrily searching for breakfast, and began to seep through the wall cracks and under the door. At eight o'clock I went out to see if the ponies had survived the gale. I need not have worried: it would have taken more than a strong wind and rain to tear them away from a field full of grass and, with heads down, they were making the best of it. Mrs Coyne invited me to join their party for breakfast and, with a plateful of bacon and eggs inside me, I felt better equipped to face the day. When I went outside to retrieve the bags and saddles from the generator shed, I felt that someone had forgotten to tell me that it was 'National Midge Day'. Midges from every part of Scotland had gathered at Drimnin for their annual 'Eat an Englishman' competition. I have never encountered so many and trying to load the ponies was sheer hell. Thor and Lucy jumped and lunged and shook their heads furiously to try and throw them off, but they came in droves, so thick it looked as if low clouds were hanging over us. While I struggled to fasten the bags on the pack saddle they swarmed all over my face and into my eyes and ears and up my nose, biting off chunks of precious me as they went. By the time I was ready to leave, my lips and eyelids were puffed and swollen as if I had done three rounds with a prizefighter.

Waving to the Coynes and their friends, I rode up to the post office to thank the MacDonalds for the use of their field. Alistair gave me directions for Mungosdail Farm and the path over the hill to Loch Teacuis. Leaving the road, Thor picked his way carefully along the rim of a tree-lined gorge carrying the boiling torrent of the Abhainn Mhungasdail down to meet the salty waters of the Sound of Mull. At Mungosdail Farm three young girls peered shyly at me from behind a barn and when I stopped to ask their father the best way through the forestry plantation above the farm, they plucked up courage and sidled out to pat the ponies and offer them clumps of grass. The farmer said to be careful not to miss the path among the young trees and I should look out for a stream, then go up the hill by the side of it.

An unlocked gate led into a large expanse of newly ploughed and planted ground and I rode slowly along the bulldozed road, looking for the stream. I had no difficulty at all in finding one; in fact, due to the heavy rain there were dozens of them, running down almost every furrow, but which was the right one? The forest road contoured round the side of the hill, climbing as it went, and I had a superb view of the sprawling hamlet of Drimnin and across the Sound of Mull to Calva Island and Tobermory Harbour on the Isle of Mull. It could have been from the very hill where I stood that the villagers first sighted the Duke of Cumberland's ships, sent in 1746 to bombard the rebel stronghold of Morvern. Two ships, the *Princess Anne* and *Terror*, were despatched under the command of Captain Robert Duff with orders to lay waste the

Morvern coast. Starting at Drimnin, they attacked every house, barn and building down the coast as far as Ardtornish. It was reported that almost four hundred houses were reduced to rubble and 'several barns well filled with corn, horse, cows, meal and other provisions were destroyed by fire and firearms.' Had it not been for a warning signalled from croft to croft down the Morvern coast, which gave time for defenceless people to flee into the hills with their few possessions, history might have had a grimmer tale to tell.

As I stared across the Sound, Tobermory and Calva Island suddenly disappeared and I realised that a rain squall was approaching. I barely had a chance to pull my waterproofs on when a vicious squall of hailstones swept across the hillside and drove into us with such fury it left me gasping for breath. Thor and Lucy tried to bolt as the stinging hail battered their faces and it took all my strength to hold them back. The wind moderated a little as the squall passed over, but the hail turned to heavy rain and a thick mist reduced visibility to less than a hundred yards. I took the ponies higher up the forest road, but nowhere could I find a stream that had a path running alongside it and after riding for an hour it was obvious that I had missed it. An abandoned trailer loomed out of the mist and I tied the ponies to it while I reconnoitred the ground. The hill on either side of the forest road had been ploughed so that walking even a short distance over it in the mist was incredibly exhausting. I stumbled over ridges and fell into furrows and bogs and all the time the unrelenting rain poured down. Reaching the top of a small hillock, I stopped to get my breath and try to identify my position. There were no prominent features anywhere but at that moment the mist lifted for a few seconds and I was able to get a compass bearing on the southern tip of Calva Island. Plotting it on the map, I discovered that the Forestry Commission had considerably extended the plantation since the map had been published and I had gone some way beyond the point where I should have turned off. The rain increased as I returned to the ponies and an absolute deluge drove into us, helped along again by a strong wind.

It was only after a great deal of searching that I finally came across the start of the path to Loch Teacuis. The only evidence

Catching up with the log — Loch Rannoch

General Wade's barracks — Loch Rannoch

'An oasis in a desert of peat' — Loch Ossian, Rannoch Moor

Resting before crossing Rannoch Moor

Pack-saddle problems by Loch Treig

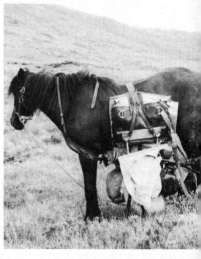

of its existence was a thin strip of unplanted ground between
the furrows. At first it was very difficult to follow its
meandering course through the expanse of thick grass, bog
and peat hags, but on harder ground, higher up the hill, it
became more prominent. A man in the shop in Loch Aline
told me that in dry weather the path was negotiable by Land
Rover, but that must have been before the Forestry
Commission tractor drivers were let loose. Deep drains had
been ploughed right across the path and I had to jump Thor
and Lucy across them. The weather was utterly dismal and
the driving rain had seeped through every button-hole, zip-
fastener and seam it could find so that I was soaked to the
skin. A cold shower was streaming down my back and out of
my boots and there was not a dry patch anywhere on my
body. The wind was gusting so ferociously I dared not sit in
the saddle. Poor Lucy staggered heavily each time the wind
caught the high load on the pack saddle. Gripping Thor's lead
rope, I pulled him up the hill but as we climbed higher the
gale increased to such a degree I had to cover my mouth in
order to breathe. A fence appeared through the mist, then a
gate, and it was a huge relief to know we were heading in the
right direction. The gate was festooned with chains and locked
on both sides in the custom of areas where Forestry
Commission land adjoins a private estate. The key loaned to
me by the forester at Loch Aline opened the Commission's
lock, but I was furious that the gate was locked at all. It was,
after all, an old drove road and a public right of way.

I let the ponies rest while I huddled out of the storm behind
a gatepost and chewed a chocolate bar, but my wet body
cooled rapidly and I began to shiver violently. My mortal
frame was entering a condition described by the medical
moguls as hypothermia, but best known as 'exposure'.
According to the text books I should have been immersed in a
hot bath. It was advice I agreed with wholeheartedly, but for
the moment it was a case of head down and keep going.

'Do you fancy a hot bath, Thor?' I bellowed above the noise
of the gale, as we pushed on up the hill. He snorted as if
replying, 'You bet I do,' but he was only blowing the rain off
his nose.

Sheltering in the lea of Thor's large belly, I worked out a

compass course to take me to Coire Buidhe, roughly in the
direction I wanted to go. The visibility was less than fifty
yards as I led the ponies down the hill, with the rain still
lashing into us, but at least the ground was free from ploughed
furrows and bogs. Suddenly I came onto a good wide path
that zigzagged down the hill. It was the drove road and I
urged Thor forward, hoping to descend quickly and find some
shelter. As suddenly as it had appeared, the path petered out
again, but the mist cleared below and I could see the forest on
the edge of Loch Teacuis and a path leading to a gate. I took a
quick compass bearing on it, although it was not necessary:
below the cloud it was a different world from the Drimnin side
of the hill. The fierce wind ceased and the torrential rain
stopped as if a tap had been turned off and, lo and behold, the
sun came out. Inside the forest the drove road wound down, in
and out of the trees, and here and there the original cobbled
surface showed through the grass between sections of a wall
bordering the road. It must have been a communication route
of considerable importance in its day.

The sun had chased away most of the clouds as we crossed a
concrete bridge over the Barr river and the heat soon dried the
ponies and made them a lot happier. I peeled off my
waterproofs and steam poured off me like smoke as the sun's
rays penetrated my wet clothes. Stopping for a few minutes, I
squeezed most of the water out of my shirt, but there was no
point in opening the bags to get dry clothes as I was nearly at
Rahoy, where I hoped to camp. The forest road followed a
switchback route through the trees to the edge of the very
beautiful and silent Loch Teacuis.

Swarms of midges flew up from the damp grass and made
life very uncomfortable for poor Lucy. Several times she nearly
pulled me out of the saddle by racing ahead to escape the
tormentors, but it was to no avail. Hiding the Forestry
Commission's key under a rock, as requested, I rode by an old
schoolhouse and joined the track to Kinloch Farm.

I was a bit worried about the reception I would get when I
asked if I could camp because I had heard that the farm was
involved in a deer-farming experiment and the Highlands and
Islands Development Board, who owned it, were not keen on
visitors. It was an unusual sight to see deer grazing in fenced-

off meadows, like cows, and Thor rolled his eyes in
amazement when they crowded to the fence to watch us go by.
Lucy ignored these strange creatures with large ears and
puzzled expressions and pressed on towards the farmhouse,
wanting only to be rid of the weight on her back. Tucked in
behind the barn was a large caravan and two girls came out
and invited me in for a cup of tea. They helped me to unload
Lucy and, over tea, they told me they were working on the
farm looking after deer calves. Their job involved having to get
up several times during the night to prepare bottle feeds and
they worked in shifts. When I went to the farmhouse I was
greeted very warmly by Mrs Alexander, the manager's wife,
but she made it quite clear she was not at liberty to answer
any questions about the deer farm and I would have to talk to
her husband. Mike Alexander, the manager, was a cheerful
Aberdonian who made me welcome and said I could stay in
the barn for the night rather than pitch the tent.

12

Through the Black Glen
to Loch Sunart

The sound of a military band playing America's national anthem, 'The Star Spangled Banner', woke me the next morning. For a moment I thought I was dreaming, but then realised it was coming from the caravan occupied by the girls working on the farm. A radio announcer said, 'Today is the Fourth of July, American Independence Day. This is the American Forces Network ...' but a loud click cut him off just as he was about to inform the World where he was broadcasting from. I climbed out of the barn to splash water into my face and take a look at the weather. The sky was dull and overcast, though the air was surprisingly warm and it was a perfect day for continuing my journey. The way to Loch Sunart was by way of Gleann Dubh, the Black Glen, but since there was no proper path through it could only be attempted in dry conditions.

Thanking the Alexanders for their hospitality, I loaded the ponies and followed a narrow track leading away from the farm. A mile beyond Loch Arienas the narrow road joined the Loch Aline to Corran Ferry road and I turned left and crossed a bridge over the River Aline to Claggan. A young man standing in the yard of the schoolhouse watched me curiously as I approached and came out to introduce himself as John Laming and said that he worked as a stalker on Ardtornish Estate. He told me he liked working with ponies but Ardtornish had given up using them for deer stalking and invested in vehicles instead.

'Come and meet my wife, Jeanette, and we'll have a cup of coffee,' he said. Before I could refuse he led Lucy into the old school playground, tied her to the railings, and in no time at all I was seated in the little kitchen with a cup of coffee and a lump of cake in my hand. John talked enthusiastically about his job as a stalker and the shortcomings of the various estates he had worked for and he reminded me greatly of myself when I was his age, working as a deer stalker in Glen Moriston. Brimming over with impetuous youth and totally intolerant of authority. Like so many good women, his wife Jeanette patiently let him follow his impulses, waiting for the day when he found his groove and settled down. John insisted that I stayed the night at his house and, although the day was still young and I wanted to press on, I was reluctant to offend his hospitality. The ponies were put into a field and we returned to find that Jeanette had prepared a huge dinner of roast venison and potatoes.

The following morning John helped me load the ponies then walked with me to the start of the track to Gleann Dubh. A man in a smart blue suit on the Lamings' television set had confidently predicted that the day would be warm and sunny, but his crystal ball must have screened the wrong picture. It was dull and overcast but warm enough to bring out flies, clegs and midges, who danced around us in their thousands. A good track wound through a delightful oak wood, sometimes close to the edge of a precipice above the River Blackwater and, at others, far above it. The wood gave way to open hillside and the track crossed a bridge over the river before continuing round the foot of a hill to an uninhabited house at Crosben. A rickety bridge spanned the river in front of the house and, without even being asked, Thor took one look at it and plunged into the river to wade across.

Beyond Crosben, whatever path may have existed had long been lost in a wilderness of rock and bog and the ponies plunged and staggered an erratic course up the glen. There was one awful moment when Lucy broke through the surface of what appeared to be safe ground and sank up to her knee-caps. Fortunately she did not panic and, having unloaded the packs off her, I managed to heave her onto firm ground. Finding a safe route through that dreadful place was a nightmare and progress was painfully slow. It was hot and humid but the sun the met man had promised lay firmly hidden behind thick cloud covering the sky. Lathered in sweat and covered with mud, we reached a collection of ruined buildings at Lurga, about half way along the glen. I turned the ponies loose before cranking the Primus stove to make a brew. As I sat on a rock sipping a mug of coffee and looking at the old buildings, which appeared to have been an iron ore mine at some time, it occurred to me that if there was not a path leading to it from Crosben, then there might be a path that approached from the other end of the glen. Sure enough, I found a path of sorts, hidden in the grass, and I guided the ponies along it, only to find that every few hundred yards it was swallowed up in a bog. We floundered along through the mire for mile after mile, until the welcome sight of Achagavel Farm and the end of the glen appeared in the distance. With a final thrash through a peat bog, we reached dry ground in the yard of the farm, where I stopped to rest and scrape a layer of mud off the ponies and the saddles. Archie McMillan of Ardtornish told me a tale about a shepherd's son who lived at Achagavel and was keen on a girl who lived at Crosben. He used to walk over and see her every day after he had finished work, then walk back again. Archie did not say if they eventually married, but I hope they did. Gleann Dubh twice a day is just as strong a test of a man's love as braving dragons to rescue a damsel from an ivory tower.

A bitterly cold breeze sprang up as I headed up the track from Achagavel and joined the Lochaline to Corran Ferry road at the summit of a long hill that descended to Loch Sunart. Stopping for a moment to pull my windproof anorak on, I looked back over the bleak, waterlogged Gleann Dubh and tried to picture what it must have been like living in this remote area before roads were built. The nearest town was Fort William, about forty miles away and three or four days journey if cattle were being driven to market. In winter, when the snow came, or the relentless rain deluged the turf roofs of the primitive hovels and turned the hill paths into a quagmire, life for the inhabitants must have been sheer purgatory. The only room in their house was shared with a few cattle that kept the family from starvation. It was an existence of endless poverty and it is said that it was not uncommon for a woman to bear twenty children and not one of them survive to reach their teens. Thomas Kirke visited the Highlands in 1679 and wrote, 'The houses of the commonalty are very mean, mud walled and thatched the best; but the poorer sort lives in such miserable hutts as never eye behold; men, women and children pig together in a poor mousehole of mud, heath and some such like matter.' These days there is a lot of sentimental rubbish sung about the idyllic life in the Highlands, by starry-eyed females or kilted men prancing round in the comfort of a television studio, but theirs is a fantasy Scotland. For the starving crofters in grim places like Gleann Dubh in Morvern, life was hell on earth.

Warm and comfortable inside my anorak, I pulled Thor onto the surfaced road and joined the cars and caravanettes heading downhill towards what, in my view, is the most beautiful loch in Scotland, Loch Sunart. A car passed me, then squealed to a halt and an attractive blonde climbed out and introduced herself as Liz Abbott, the wife of the manager of Laudale Estate. She said I was welcome to graze the ponies for the night at Laudale House by the edge of Sunart. The opportunity to spend the night on the edge of my favourite loch was not to be missed and I gladly accepted. At the foot of the hill I left the convoy of tourists behind and followed a narrow road along the edge of the loch. The tarmac surface ended at the cattle grid and a delightful ride along the edge of the loch brought me into the estate yard. The ponies were turned into a field in front of Laudale House and Liz said that instead of camping I could stay in one of the estate holiday cottages. Her husband Geoff helped me to carry my gear to the cottage then invited me to their house for a drink. As the evening wore on and bottle after bottle of Geoff Abbott's supply of beer clattered to the floor empty, I felt as if my head was floating in the air and every few minutes I had to reach up and pull it down on to my shoulders. At two o'clock in the morning the supply of liquid finally ran out. My head had floated across the room by this time and I was too tired to catch it, so I left it behind and staggered out into the night.

The next morning the effects of the evening's merrymaking were still with me and I woke with a splitting headache. I brewed a mug of tea, but far from making me feel better, the hot, tasteless liquid disturbed the volatile mixture inside my suffering stomach and I ran for the bathroom. Back in bed, I fell asleep and woke at two in the afternoon, ravenously hungry and with only a suggestion of a headache. Although it was fairly late in the day, I decided to leave Laudale and get as close to Strontian as possible so that I could make a good start into Ardnamurchan the following day. Geoff said there was a sheep pen I could put the ponies in for the night near the head of the loch and as it was only five miles away I would have ample time to reach it before evening.

13

Haggis and Floating Churches

Lucy played hard to get when I went to collect the ponies. When she was eventually tied up next to Thor while I saddled up, she whinnied at him as though she was telling him off for allowing himself to be caught so easily. Her legs and body were covered in hundreds of tiny sheep ticks; I have never seen so many on an animal. Strangely enough, only a few weeks before setting out on my journey I had read a report in a farming paper that warned the owners of Scottish estates that, if they got rid of the sheep and did not manage their pasture and hill grazing in the traditional manner, ticks might increase to such a degree as to make the grazing useless.

With an overcast sky and a cool breeze blowing across the loch, it was hardly a typical July day, but a weak sun broke through from time to time and illuminated the landscape long enough for me to take a few photographs. Joining the Corran to Lochaline road again, I had to abandon photography and concentrate on avoiding a stream of holiday-makers' cars. The driver of a shiny new Mercedes who edged up behind Lucy and hooted impatiently that he wanted to pass stood on his brakes and reversed hurriedly when she suddenly lifted her tail and sprayed his chrome plating with a heap of very loose dung. I did not understand what the driver shouted as he drove past, but I rather fear that Lucy may have soured Anglo-German relationships.

The cool breeze had freshened to a strong wind by the time the sheep pen came into sight. Having turned the ponies into a small paddock, I was glad to climb into the tent and thaw out over the stove. As the sun went down, chunks of ragged cloud racing across the sky were an omen of nasty things to come. As I climbed into my sleeping bag the first drops of rain were pattering on the canvas. Apart from the occasional lorry roaring past, the night was fairly quiet; but at six o'clock heavy rain poured onto the tent like a hail of bullets. When I looked out it was a very dreary scene. Visibility was down to a few hundred yards, with wave after wave of rain sweeping across the loch, saturating every stone and blade of grass. There was no point in setting off only to get soaked before I had gone half a mile. I stayed in the comfort of my sleeping bag and enjoyed breakfast in bed. At three o'clock in the afternoon the rain was still bouncing off the loch, so to relieve the monotony I pulled on my waterproofs and walked into Strontian where I ordered tea in the village café-cum-supermarket.

In the early nineteenth century a certain Dr John MacCulloch also arrived in Strontian on a wet day and was grieved to find that the only inn was being rebuilt. His stay was uncomfortable, to say the least, and he complained bitterly that the inn 'was much the same out or in, for it had only half a roof being in fact a barn ... open to the sky. As the rain and wind came with a slant the walls did some good.' Wedged in a corner table in the warm café was luxury compared with what the unfortunate Dr MacCulloch endured and I sipped my tea and watched a tide of humanity flowing through the door to escape the rain. Groups of hikers in vivid orange or red anoraks and trousers dripped pools of water onto the tiled floor as they studied the menu pinned on the wall and laboriously separated wet coins from a sticky mess of congealed chocolate and disintegrating paper mâché, that had once been paper tissues.

'A packet of batter, luvvy,' said a lady with an unmistakable Cockney accent to the young girl behind the grocery counter, and stood looking very puzzled when she was handed a packet of pancake mix instead of a slab of butter. We sometimes forget that once we move off our home territory a regional accent can sound like a foreign language to the unaccustomed ear. Happily, the misunderstanding was sorted out and the lady was about to leave, clutching her packet of butter, when she was almost bowled over by an open umbrella that forced the door inwards and was thrust into the room by an elegantly dressed middle-aged man. He was attempting to shelter a very attractive woman who was clutching a miniature poodle and wore an outfit that would have fitted perfectly on the front page of *Vogue* magazine, but was very much the wrong choice in rain-swept Strontian. As soon as she was over the threshold she thrust the poodle at the man and, pulling out a mirror from her handbag, patted and preened her hair, though from where I was sitting there did not seem to be a single strand of her expensive hair-do out of place. She was not in the best of moods and, shaking with fury, she let her companion and everyone else in the café know about it.

'James,' she stormed, 'I cannot stay in this beastly country a moment longer and I demand that you take me home this instant. Look at my clothes, they're ruined,' and she pointed to a speck of mud on her skirt. 'And poor Too Toos,' she cried, wrenching the overfed poodle out of the man's hands and grasping it to her bosom, 'he's so cold and hungry, aren't you Too Toos?' She rocked the dog like a child for a second or two, then launched into another tirade. 'I thought you said we could take tea here, but you surely don't expect me to sit at those disgusting tables, littered with filth,' she cried, pointing to a spotlessly clean table, a sauce bottle, condiment pots and ash tray neatly grouped in the centre. 'Mother said it was a mistake to come to Scotland for a holiday. She warned us the country was primitive and it always rains and she was right.' Her voice rose hysterically and she stamped her high heels on the tiles. 'It's a frightful, horrible beastly place and I want to go home!'

The man obediently opened the door and, while he did his best to shelter her with the umbrella, she climbed, still complaining, into a large Rolls Royce and was driven away in the rain. Throughout the whole performance the man had never uttered a word. A stunned silence hung over the café and shop for a moment, then as if someone had started a movie projector, the frozen figures sprang into action again as if there had been no interruption.

Even when it is sipped slowly, there is a limit to the length of time you can spend over a cup of tea. Not wanting to outstay my welcome, I bought a few groceries and a haggis and went out into the rain. I sheltered by the edge of the loch and looked across Strontian Bay to a spot that caused the name Strontian to be blazoned across the country's newspapers in the 1840s.

When the Free Church broke away from the Church of Scotland it took virtually all the inhabitants of Ardnamurchan with it and there was a particularly strong congregation round Strontian. The laird, Sir James Riddell, perhaps realising there would only be himself and the minister left to attend the established church, refused permission for the 'Wee Frees' to bui'd a church on his land. If he had it in his head that the lack of a proper place to worship might have brought the straying sheep back to the fold he was sadly mistaken. The breakaway congregation held their services in the open, until one bright soul hit on the idea of having a floating church moored in the tidal waters of the loch and so outside the laird's jurisdiction. The idea was taken up enthusiastically and people were asked to dig deep into their sporrans to provide the cash. Some writers say that the money was used to buy an old ship and convert it, but I have it on the best authority that a specially designed ark-shaped boat, complete with pulpit and pews capable of seating seven hundred people, was built at a shipyard on the Clyde for about £1,400. In 1846 it was towed from Glasgow to Loch Sunart and moored off Strontian and every Sunday morning people came from miles around to attend the service. It is said that the floating church sank one inch into the water for every hundred people in the congregation. Some preachers certainly knew how to attract a congregation. After his service, one wrote, 'Here I preached thrice on the Sabbath, twice in Gaelic and once in English, I was thanked by the office bearers and told that their church had never been so deep in the water before.' On that occasion the church sank six inches. Doubtless the laird would have liked to have seen it sink a lot further, but, even though it once broke adrift in a gale and was driven onto the rocks, it survived. Strontian's floating church served the congregation for twenty-seven years before the laird relented and permission was given for a stone building to be constructed.

Towards evening there was a miraculous change in the weather. The rain stopped, the clouds broke up and shafts of sunlight poured through to warm the saturated hills and send clouds of steam rising from the trees. A stream beside the sheep pen, had risen overnight from a tumbling stream to a boiling mass, and now it flashed and sparkled as the sepia torrent crashed over a staircase of rocks and foamed under the road into the loch. Regrettably the bright spell of weather was short-lived and a bank of cloud advancing across the sky from the West obscured the sun. A cool zephyr flicked the surface of the loch, rustling the birch trees flanking the sheep pen, and drove me into the shelter of the tent. The wizened and rather pathetic-looking haggis purchased in Strontian was boiled on the stove and eaten without any of the elaborate ceremony and tributes usually bestowed on this, the most mysterious of Scottish beasties. The humble haggis has long been the subject of jokes and woe betide a poor innocent who asks a Scotsman 'What is a haggis?' The reply is likely to be a mischievous and highly colourful description of a mythical creature that has short, or long, legs, flies upside down, or round and round, and has four wings, according to how vivid is the imagination of the person telling the tale.

My haggis was a plastic ball about four inches in diameter and probably containing nothing more exciting than a handful of mince mixed with oatmeal and a touch of spice thrown in for good measure. To make a genuine traditional haggis, one Mistress Dodd recommended her prize-winning recipe: 'First clean a sheep's pluck thoroughly. Make incisions in the heart and liver and allow the blood to flow out and parboil the whole, letting the windpipe lie over the side of the pot to permit the discharge of impurities, the water may be changed after a few minutes boiling for fresh water. Half hours boiling will be sufficient, but throw back half the liver to boil till it will grate easily. Take the heart, half a liver and part of the lights, trim away all skins and black-looking parts and mince them together. Mince also a pound of beef suet and four or more onions. Grate the other half of the liver. Have a dozen small onions peeled and scalded to mix with this mince. Have some finely ground oatmeal toasted before the fire till it is light brown and perfectly dry. Less than two cupfuls of meal will do for this quantity of meat. Spread the mince on a board and strew the meal lightly over it, with a high seasoning of pepper, salt and cayenne. Have a haggis bag [sheep's paunch] perfectly clean and see that there be no thin part in it, else your whole labour will be lost by it bursting. Some cooks use two bags one as an outer case. Put in the meat with half a pint of good beef gravy or as much strong broth as will make a thick stew. Be careful not to fill the bag too full, but allow the meat room to swell; add the juice of a lemon or a little good vinegar; press out the air and sew up the bag, prick it with a large needle when it first swells up to prevent bursting. Let it boil slowly for three hours if large.'

I once witnessed this haggis-making ritual and it took a strong stomach to watch, let alone eat the finished product. In the Hebrides in those days slaughter-house regulations were as rare as an Anglican bishop. Standing ankle-deep among slippery heaps of sheeps guts and foul-smelling stomachs, the butcher-cum-crofter-cum-grocer-cum-purveyor of illicit whisky happily chopped the intestines and offal into bits and flung them into an ancient mincing machine driven by a belt from a petrol engine. Despite the total disregard for hygiene, his haggis took some beating for flavour. Together with new potatoes and boiled turnips it was a meal that makes the pre-packed, quality-conditioned supermarket food taste like flavoured putty.

There is no doubt about it though, haggis is very much an acquired taste. Someone once said that it was the belly worship of Robert Burns that raised the haggis to the status of a national dish, but there was one early traveller who was not impressed with traditional Scottish food. In the eighteenth century Tobias Smollett wrote, 'I am not yet Scotchman enough to relish their singed sheeps heads and haggis, which were provided at our request where we dined. The first put me in mind of the history of the Congo, in which I read of negro heads sold publicly in the markets; the last being a mess of minced lights, livers, suet, oatmeal, onions and pepper, enclosed in a sheeps stomach. Had a very sudden effect on mine and the delicate Mrs Tabby changed colour. The Scotch in general are attached to this composition with a sort of national fondness.'

The men from the ministry have reduced the modern strain of haggis to a shadow of its former self and perhaps an early specimen should have pride of place among the spinning wheels, wooden ploughs and other relics of bygone days, in a Scottish folk museum.

14

Onwards to Ardnamurchan Point

It rained all night and I began to wonder if it would ever stop. It took ages to lash the soggy equipment onto the saddles and with the hood of my waterproof jacket pulled over my head, I spurred the ponies through the rain towards the head of the loch. A shepherd waved as we passed his cottage and his wave was a final gesture of the friendliness and hospitality I had found on Morvern. As Thor and Lucy clattered across the bridge over the Carnoch river and turned for Strontian, I wondered how well I would be received in Ardnamurchan. It was a Monday and there was quite a lot of traffic on the road making for Corran Ferry, but we made good progress and soon Strontian dropped behind us as the ponies climbed up the long hill on the road leading to Acharacle. A strong wind sprang up to help the rain find its way into my coat, but I was wearing a towel round my neck and it soaked up the moisture before it could reach my shirt. The driving rain made it difficult to see far ahead and when a Council tractor and mowing machine roared out of the murk it gave Thor and Lucy such a fright they almost jumped back across the loch into Morvern. We must have looked an unhappy sight as the ponies plodded along with me hunched in the saddle, hood pulled over my face like a monk and water running off my boots like miniature waterfalls. Even the motorists seemed aware of our misery and crept cautiously by with shouts of encouragement. The road dipped and wound in and out of bays and inlets on the loch side. Had it not been for the weather, the view would have been terrific, but the wind drove the rain clouds down off the hills and scudded them across the loch.

The squalls lashed into us with such force I pulled the

Waiting to board the ferry — Corran, by Fort William

Looking down on Loch Leven and the Pap of Glencoe

Clach na Criche, Morvern — where wishes can come true

The perfect campsite — Glenborrodale, Ardnamurchan

ponies into the shelter of the trees at the Forestry Commission picnic site at Ardery and waited until the sting had gone out of it. I had just set off again when a red car overtook me and pulled to the side of the road. A girl got out and said she had heard about me and asked where I was making for. I told her about my journey and said I was hoping to camp at Glenborrodale that night and eventually reach Ardnamurchan Point. She listened to me then said, 'Well come and camp the night at Resipole instead, we've got plenty of room for your ponies and we've got a campsite.'

She told me her name was Fiona Sinclair and she helped on the family farm and trekking centre. My watch showed it was only half past one and a bit early in the day for thinking about camping, but she was so nice I did not like to refuse. Following her to Resipole Farm I was not very happy about having to pitch the tent in a field full of caravans, but I found a quiet corner sheltered by trees. The ponies' field was a quarter of a mile down the road from the campsite and when I turned them into it they went wild and tore around at full gallop, like a pair of yearlings.

I left the ponies enjoying a long roll in the wet grass and walked back to the tent to prepare a meal. The rain clouds had moved on over the hills to wash the streets of Fort William. A bright sun beamed down and brought out a swarm of little boys and girls from the caravans, who crowded round and watched while I lit the stove and heated the glutinous mixture of chicken supreme.

'Is that for your horses, mister?' enquired one of the assembly, peering into the pan.

'No, it's my dinner,' I replied, wishing they would all go away and leave me in peace. But I had said the wrong thing.

'Yer dinner!' scoffed a shaven-headed oaf in a punk teeshirt. 'Ma faither feeds his pigs on better stuff than yon.' Turning to his mates he aired the superior knowledge of a ten-year-old. 'Faither says the feed he uses puts lead in the boar's pencil.'

I wished it would start raining again and drive them away, but the fine weather continued and so did the questions.

'Are you a tinker, mister? My dad says you're a tinker and he's going to complain to the farmer and get you moved.'

Before I could say anything the news spread like wildfire.

'He's a tinker, he's a tinker,' they yelled. 'He says he's a tinker. I'm going to tell my mother.' And away they scattered to the bosom of the family caravan like frightened rabbits. Wanting only to mind my own business and get on with my dinner, I was now the centre of attention and mums and dads appeared at windows or stood by caravan doors, glaring in my direction and calling across to each other. I half expected a lynch mob to descend on me, but there must have been something more exciting on their television sets. After a muttered consultation the 'mob', consisting of three of the fathers and a hawk-faced mother who had the look of an executioner, broke up and returned to their caravans, banging the doors after them. I was left to get on with my meal and afterwards, mug of coffee in hand, I leaned against a tree and studied the varying degrees of 'one-upmanship' among the caravan owners. The smallest van on the field was a very modest ten-foot-long painted box which must have been incredibly cramped inside, whereas the largest was an enormous chocolate-coloured bungalow on wheels, the chintz curtains and a smug-looking Daimler parked alongside. Between the smallest and the largest there was a bewildering array of shapes and sizes. Canvas awnings were obligatory, as were large badges and a flag proclaiming to the World an allegiance to the Caravan Club. Those who could not make the effort of walking two hundred yards to the toilet block had a portable 'thunder box' next to their van, modestly concealed behind a canvas screen. Among the wildly extravagant and expensive aids to caravanning displayed for the benefit of the neighbours, there was one that won the prestige stakes by several lengths: a canvas dog kennel with an extension that had 'dog loo' printed on the side. Without exception, every caravan had a television aerial stuck on the roof and some owners were so determined not to miss their favourite soap opera that they had erected portable masts fifteen or twenty feet high. For the life of me I cannot understand families who for their annual holiday travel long distances to remote areas to 'get away from it all', but are so hooked on their daily dose of piped entertainment or other people's misfortunes that they have to take their goggle-box with them.

As I lay against the tree in the early evening a warm sun

slanted across the now calm loch and picked out the pastel shades of the Morvern Hills. A pair of buzzards circled above the field, keeping a watchful eye on a flock of noisy wood-pigeons flitting from tree to tree like a gang of high-spirited lads out on a spree. On a branch above my head a red squirrel raced up and down chattering happily to himself as he waited for a chance to scamper across to a row of waste bins and help himself to an easy meal. Watching the world go by was wonderfully relaxing, but apart from an elderly couple sitting in camp chairs and a few children playing with a ball, there was not another soul to be seen. The signature tune of 'Nationwide' drifted across the field as the pathetic brain-washed television addicts closed their curtains on the sun, the hills and peace and beauty, to wallow in the latest calamity or be mesmerised by the mouthings of the World's leaders. I would have dearly liked to put an axe through every television on the site.

I slept well and woke early, but I was reluctant to leave the comfort of my sleeping bag. After breakfast I went across to a smart new toilet block to have a wash, but the sight of half a dozen flabby gents, stripped to their well-pressed trousers and aertex vests, showering themselves with talcum powder and after-shave, was too much and I made do with a splash under a cold tap outside.

When I left at ten thirty a stiff breeze was blowing off the loch and there was a hint of rain in the air, but at least it kept flies and midges away. There was an exceptional amount of traffic on the road and I constantly had to pull the ponies onto the verge to dodge fast-moving cars and lorries. I had studied the maps very closely for a route over the hills through Ardnamurchan, but the only way was by road and we would have to travel twenty miles of it before we reached the lighthouse on the Point. Thor and Lucy jogged slowly along, climbing and descending as the road turned away from the water's edge and wound through a thickly wooded area to the tiny hamlet of Salen.

When I last saw Salen in the 1950s, it was a thriving little place that boasted a village shop and a garage with petrol pumps. The shop was still there, but the garage and petrol pumps looked dilapidated and abandoned. The view across the small bay was as beautiful as I remembered it. Several motor yachts lying at anchor with dinghies flitting back and forth between them showed that Salen had not been forgotten altogether.

We moved on from Salen to the top of a high promontory formed by the lower slopes of Ben Laga and looked down on Loch Sunart and a marvellous view of Calva Island, with Loch Teacuis glinting in the weak sunlight behind it. In the late afternoon the cool breeze that had been with me since I left Resipole suddenly dropped and the sun emerged from the clouds. Within minutes the air was deliciously warm and, peeling off anorak and sweater, it was sheer bliss to jog along the narrow road flanked by sweet-scented trees and feel the sun on my back.

Fiona Sinclair had told me that a family called Watson at Glenborrodale Farm would probably let me camp for the night so, with the aid of directions from a postman emptying a letter-box in Glenborrodale, I was soon riding up a rough track by a water-powered sawmill, to the house. The Watsons were very helpful and the ponies enjoyed a roll in a large field while I pitched camp on a shelf of level ground above the farm.

The evening was absolutely gorgeous and I ate my ration of chicken supreme sitting in the sun. The panorama below me was spread like a gigantic artist's canvas, with every rock on the great bulk of Ben Resipol in the distance needle sharp, the straw-coloured grasses blending with the darker tones of the heather, as the flanks of the mountain curved down to mingle with the bright greens of the trees at the edge of a pastel-blue loch. It was a blazing kaleidoscope of colour and I stared spellbound until in the setting sun the colours faded into the purple of twilight and the midges came out to chase me into the tent.

The soft cooing of a wood-pigeon sitting on a branch near the tent woke me the next morning and I looked out onto another superb day. A long blanket of cotton-wool cloud covered the loch and drifted round the base of the hills; but the tops were bathed in a dull glow that seeped slowly down like molten copper as the sun climbed above Morvern. Lucy was in no hurry to leave her comfortable field and played hard to get when I went to collect the ponies, but when she saw me feeding Thor with dates she soon trotted over.

The ring of the ponies' shoes on the hard surface of the road echoed through the trees as we followed the narrow path, sometimes close to the seaweed-strewn rocks, where every pebble was visible in the clear water, or high above, looking down on the full beauty of the loch framed by sparkling birch trees.

Beyond Glenborrodale Castle, Thor and Lucy hesitated at the sight of a line of mechanical diggers, lumbering backwards and forwards like giant scorpions as they tore up the earth to widen the road. A man who was busy ramming explosives into a line of holes drilled into the rock waved us on. I led the quaking ponies hurriedly past the diggers, hoping the explosives man would not light the fuse before we were well out of earshot, otherwise Thor and his girlfriend might not stop until they reached America.

The trees gave way to wild, open hillside as the road climbed round Glenmore Bay to the scattered cottages at Glenbeg. We crossed a bridge over the Glenmore river and I was opening a gate next to a cattle grid when a little girl came running out of a nearby house to close it for me.

'Please could you tell me the ponies' names?' she said shyly. When I told her she wrote them laboriously down on a piece of crumpled paper and dashed back into the house before I had a chance to talk to her.

We slogged up a long hill to the top of Ardslignish Point and a wonderful viewpoint overlooking Loch Sunart and the Sound of Mull. It was warm without being uncomfortable and, while the ponies rested and nibbled at the short grass, I lay in the heather and sucked an orange. The view was incredible, so much to look at that it was difficult to take it all in. To my left the islands of Oronsay and Carna floated in the blue water of Loch Sunart, guarding the entrance to Loch Teacuis. In the more violent periods of Highland history they were probably an effective barrier against marauding seafarers trying to sail through the narrows to reach Strontian. Across the Sound, the white speck of Rubha nan Gall Lighthouse stood out against the dark rock of the Mull coast and, close by it, the houses and shops of Tobermory sprawled across the hillside overlooking the bay. Scores of boats were moving in every direction and through the binoculars I could see tugs and yachts, fishing vessels of all shapes and sizes and a grey Royal Navy vessel following soberly in the wake of MacBraynes Outer Isles steamer. Swinging the binoculars to Loch Sunart once more, I saw something that really stirred my heart. Sailing past Oronsay, bound for the open sea, was a gaff-rigged ketch with red tanned sails and a long bowsprit. There must have been more wind on the loch than at my viewpoint for, as the sails filled the boat surged forward through the water and sent a shower of spray into the air. I have always promised myself that one day I will explore the lochs and bays of Western Scotland and there, below me, was my dream boat. A whinny from Lucy brought me back to the job in hand. I went across to her to find that she had wrapped her tether rope round her forelegs and was trussed up like a chicken.

A little way beyond Ardslignish Point the steep slopes of Ben Hiant had forced the road-builders to turn inland from the coast and carve a route like an alpine pass across Beinn Bhuidhe, high above the sheltered Bay of Camas nan Gaell. I was wondering why I had seen very little traffic during the past hour when the noise of an explosion rolled round the hills and I remembered the man ramming explosives into the rocks. The traffic would have been held up, but now the flood gates were open the tide of vehicles would be on its way towards me. I urged Thor forward to be across the pass before the cars came but a sudden movement ahead stopped him in his tracks. It took a lot of heel work to get him moving and as I rode near I saw a cyclist with his bike upside down, mending a damaged tyre; and a very angry cyclist he was too. When I asked him what had happened he replied in a strong Australian accent.

'I'll tell you what happened sport, a god-damned bastard of a Pommie motorist sounded his horn right up my arse and I got such a bloody fright I hit the rocks and split the tyre. Shit, just look at that,' he said, pushing his hand through a long cut in the wall of the tyre. He was a long way from a garage but I told him about the Ranger's cottage near Glenmore and he set off, pushing his bike down the hill, melting the rocks with words I sometimes use myself for describing motorists.

As I neared the thin strip of water of Loch Mudhe, the whine of engines behind me warned that the vehicles held up by the blasting operations were approaching fast and I pulled Thor and Lucy well away from the road into the heather. It was not a moment too soon. I counted over fifty cars, vans and wagons as they thundered by and I could only guess what the Australian cyclist said when he was forced to wait until the convoy had passed him.

At a junction where the road from Achateny in the North of the peninsula joined the Kilchoan road, I stopped to rest the ponies for a few minutes and gaze at the view of the Island of Rhum. I hardly noticed a minibus draw alongside me until a voice said, 'Hullo, do you remember me?' I turned to find the cheerful grin of Gillespie MacMillan, who with his brothers and sisters farmed at Grigadale, near Ardmamurchan Point Lighthouse during the time I was a lighthouse keeper. It was over twenty years since I had seen him, but he had not changed very much. He was in a hurry to be on his way as he was driving the mail bus, but he told me that the family had gone their separate ways, though his elder brother, Malcolm, was still at the farm. Gillespie drove away and we followed after him, down the long hill towards Kilchoan.

I was very stiff and weary by the time the houses on the edge of the village came into sight. Then a lovely whiff of peat smoke took me back to my youth and I forgot how tired I was. There was a patch of grass by the post office and I let the ponies tear at it while I walked up and down to restore the circulation in my legs. A small truck drove by, then screeched to a halt and reversed back to me. Gillespie's brother, Malcolm, climbed out and said he had heard I was on my way to the lighthouse and I could camp and graze the ponies in the first field I came to at Grigadale Farm. Climbing back into his truck he drove off, leaving a cloud of blue smoke hanging in the air before drifting gently over the wall of the church and settling on the close-cropped grass.

Though I was tired and still had six miles to go to reach Grigadale, I wanted to visit an old graveyard some way behind the church, on the hillside. Leaving the ponies securely tied to a signpost, I went through an iron gate and climbed to the ruin of the old church and burial ground. I was interested in one particular grave, for if there was grass on it then a local legend would be destroyed. The story goes that, during the dreadful days of the Highland Clearances, MacColl, the local tacksman or wealthy tenant farmer at Kilchoan, cruelly evicted an old woman from her house and left her without shelter. She cursed him with a dreadful curse and vowed that his soul would rot in hell and that nothing but weeds would ever grow on his grave. It is said that his family and their descendants have tried in vain to get grass to grow over MacColl's bewitched remains and when I saw the grave in 1958 a healthy gooseberry bush was growing out of it, but not a blade of grass. As I approached the high railings surrounding the grave, I could see what appeared to be long grass sprouting over the edge and it looked as if the spell had at last been broken, but when I came closer, what I thought was grass turned out to be nettles. There was no grass anywhere near the grave; the old woman's curse lives on.

Flies and clegs drove the ponies frantic as we set off along the last lap to Grigadale. They tramped wearily on, trying to shake the brutes off their sweating bodies. Down the hill past the Sonachan Hotel we went and climbed slowly up again to Achosnish and the road leading to the farm and the lighthouse. The swarm of clegs increased to such an extent that both Thor and Lucy dripped with blood where they had brushed their attackers off their legs and faces. I had never seen so many clegs and, having feasted on the ponies' blood, their idea of dessert was to have a go at me. More and more arrived and the bites were so painful I could hardly hold Thor's reins. In desperation I soaked a rag in paraffin and dabbed it all over Thor and Lucy and on my arms, neck and face. It smelled awful, but it did the trick. The clegs took one whiff and disappeared.

When we reached the field I was so worn out I could hardly pitch the tent. Rid of their packs, the ponies sank into the cool grass and fell fast asleep. Evening was well advanced and the sun was rapidly dipping towards the sea. I longed to climb into my sleeping bag, but the one thing I remembered above everything else when I was a keeper at Ardnamurchan Lighthouse was the breathtaking sunsets. The way the great orb of molten gold hung above the islands promised an exceptional finish to the day, so grabbing my cameras I walked as fast as I could to the beach. Scrambling over bracken and rock, I looked down on the golden sand and stared in open-mouthed amazement at the sight below. The once deserted beach, where I had lain for hours listening to the oyster-catchers, curlews and squabbling gulls, or watched the red deer browse on the seaweed and baby otters chase each other round the pools; that lovely beach of my memory was now crowded with caravans, tents, yapping dogs and a seething mass of people. I could not believe it, but the noise of revving motor cars and transistor radios was no mirage. Abandoning the sunset, I returned to the tent feeling utterly depressed and wishing I had not come back to Ardnamurchan. I lost interest in preparing a meal and lay in my sleeping bag sipping a mug of Oxo. To add to my melancholy, the fog horn at the lighthouse started to blare out its mournful sound and I looked out of the tent to find the world enveloped in a thick mist.

15

Sick Ponies and Spanish Galleons

During the night the mist cleared away. When I woke the following morning the sky was dull and overcast, but the air was warm enough to strip off at the edge of Loch Grigadale and have a good wash. Clean and refreshed, I went to see how the ponies were enjoying their rest. I ran my hand over their backs, looking for saddle sores, but happily there were none. This confirmed my belief that a good saddle blanket is essential, particularly under a pack saddle, and time spent ensuring there are no creases in it and that the saddles fit comfortably certainly pays dividends. Having checked that shoes were tight, I spent an hour grooming their matted coats and untangling a mass of knots in manes and tails. When I turned them loose they rewarded my efforts by promptly rolling in the mud at the edge of the loch.

I still felt depressed about the sight of the caravans on the beach and my enthusiasm for revisiting the lighthouse cooled considerably. In many ways I suppose it was the wrong attitude to take. After all the tourist trade had increased enormously during the time I had been away, so why should farmers not take advantage of it and let as many people as possible enjoy the beach and the views. That argument would be sound if only people would accept what the wild places have to offer, namely peace and solitude and an opportunity to truly escape from life's treadmill for a while and enjoy a quiet partnership with nature. But they are not content with this. They must have their creature comforts like the television and the transistor radio. They cannot bear to be parted from that mechanical womb, the motor car, so parking areas have to be constructed. Too many bottoms squatting in the heather soon creates a health hazard, so toilet blocks have to be built. In the

end areas of exceptional beauty such as Bay MacNeill, by
Ardnamurchan Lighthouse, are destroyed by the very people
who come to enjoy them.

Towards midday curiosity got the better of me and I walked
up to the lighthouse to see what changes had been made. As I
approached the familiar buildings I had a dreadful lump in
my throat. I had spent one of the happiest periods of my life
working as a lighthouse keeper and the memories flooded
back. A sign on the wall said that visitors were allowed to look
round after 2 pm and to pass the time I explored the pools
among the rocks and photographed bright-coloured lichen
and delicate rock plants. I found a sunny hollow among the
rocks and lay back and looked up at the smooth granite tower
of the lighthouse that had withstood the onslaught of wind
and sea for over one hundred and thirty years. In the days
before lighthouses were built, rounding Ardnamurchan Point
in the dark or poor visibility must have been fearsomely
dangerous.

It was the Sheriff of Orkney who, in 1844, first suggested
that a lighthouse should be built on Ardnamurchan, the most
westerly point on the mainland of the British Isles. It sticks
out into the sea more than twenty miles further than Land's
End. His suggestion received support from the Irish Trading
Association, the Liverpool Trading Association, Lloyds, the
Admiralty, and five Scottish Sheriffs. Building commenced in
1846 under the supervision of the Northern Lighthouse
Board's engineer, Alan Stevenson, who at that time was
already involved in the building of Skerryvore Lighthouse, off
the Island of Tiree. The granite came by sea from a quarry on
Mull and the tower at Ardnamurchan was built in a similar
way to Skerryvore, each curved granite block being dressed by
hand to an accuracy of one eighth of an inch. If that was not
enough, the blocks were dovetailed into each other, creating
immense strength. Not surprisingly, it took many laborious
hours to prepare each one so that three years went by before
the construction was completed and the first light exhibited on
5th October, 1849. The tower is about one hundred and
fourteen feet high and when I was a keeper I had the
unenviable job of climbing onto the dome once a week to oil

the weathercock. Seen from that height, the houses in the yard looked minute. Both the tower and the keepers' houses are magnificent pieces of architecture. It is doubtful whether there are many stonemasons left who could copy it.

At two o'clock I wandered back to the lighthouse yard and met a keeper going on duty. When he heard that I had been stationed at Ardnamurchan and actually lived in the house that he and his wife now occupied, he invited me to join him while he made radio contact with other lighthouses in the area. A group of visitors arrived and asked to be shown round the tower and I followed them up the one hundred and forty stone steps to the lamp room. The lamp had been converted from paraffin to electricity since my day, but I could not as I looked at it see what advantage had been gained. It required a complicated back-up in the event of a lamp failure, whereas the paraffin lamp with its incandescent mantle had operated for years without any problems and must have been considerably cheaper to run. Though the paraffin lamp had been replaced, I was pleased to see that the original clockwork mechanism that revolved the lens round the lamp was still in use. Give a regular squirt of oil, it would last forever, but doubtless the boffins will replace it one day with an electronic gadget costing thousands of pounds and requiring a highly paid technician, sent at great expense, to maintain it. That is considered to be progress.

On my way back to the campsite I saw Malcolm McMillan clipping sheep in one of the steadings and we talked about old times. What I remembered most about Malcolm was his infectious sense of humour and, though time had changed many other things around Grigadale, the mischievous spark was still there. He doubled up with laughter when I reminded him about the bull they once owned. The lively animal was always keen to get on with its function in life, but was frustrated by being unusually short in the leg so that though he mounted the cows, his mechanism would not reach its target. Unwilling to get rid of the bull, the wily McMillans solved the problem by digging a shallow pit and standing the cow in it. There were plenty of calves produced after that.

Malcolm invited me to the house later that evening and

introduced me to his wife. Margaret. The way they had met had a touch of fairytale romance about it. She had been a vet and had come to Grigadale one day to treat Malcolm's cattle. Eventually she gave up her job to help him run the farm.

The following day was Friday 13th and, although I am not normally superstitious, I woke to hear an animal coughing heavily near the tent and I felt uneasy. At first I thought it was a sheep, but there was something horribly familiar about that deep throaty rasp and I went numb when I realised it was Thor. Tearing open the tent door, I was horrified to find Thor and Lucy standing together coughing their hearts out. Pulling on my boots, I climbed out to look at them. Both had runny noses but I could not understand why they should be sparkling fit one day, then sounding as if they were going to peg out the next. My vet had included a few tablets in my first aid kit to give to the ponies in the event of a cough so, cutting a Mars bar in half, I pushed a tablet into each piece and they swallowed the medicine in one gulp. I stayed with them for over an hour, until a cold westerly wind sprang up bringing a belt of driving rain in from the sea, which sent me scampering for the tent.

In the late afternoon I went to check the ponies again. Thor did not cough but Lucy still had a terrible rasp. The rain cleared away so in the evening I climbed Sgurr na Mean, a steep little hill with a fine view across to Rhum. But I felt so miserable I turned back and went to the tent to prepare to leave the next day.

Torrential rain hammered into the tent throughout the night and I looked out next morning on a dismal scene. Thor and Lucy were grazing normally but I was not happy about the sound of their breathing. The rain eased off while I was eating breakfast so I loaded up and called at the farm to say cheerio to Malcolm before setting off along the road to Achosnich, with the intention of crossing the hills to Swordle. It was only a short distance and taken at a gentle pace I hoped the ponies might recover. Lucy plodded along with her head down, looking very miserable. As we started to walk up a short incline, she burst into a fit of coughing so severe I thought she was choking. She almost went down on her knees as she gasped for breath, blowing streams of mucus onto the road. I watched helplessly as wave after wave of coughing racked her body. When Thor started coughing as well I thought he was just coming out in sympathy, but he too was discharging mucus. It was obvious they could not carry on and I led them back to Grigadale to ask Margaret's advice, but she and Malcolm had gone down to the caravan site. Sick with worry, I huddled behind a wall out of the rain, trying not to listen to Lucy gasping for breath. Two hours passed before Malcolm came back and said to put the ponies in the field and he would ask Margaret to look at them. I saw Margaret's car come up from the caravan site, but though several hours went by, she did not appear. By six o'clock in the evening I was desperate, so I ran to a telephone box at Achosnich and phoned my own vet. He said it sounded as if the ponies had caught a chill, but as they were discharging mucus they should be over the worst of it and with three days complete rest should recover. It was reassuring, but what the vet was not aware of, in making his diagnosis, was that the wind had increased to near gale force and rain was sweeping horizontally in from the sea. Trying their best to shelter from it were two shivering ponies.

Back at the farm I explained the situation to Malcolm and asked if I could stay for a few more days. He readily agreed, but somehow there was a strange atmosphere about the place.

An old proverb says that bad weather is always worse through a window, but when I looked through the tent door there were no optical illusions and the following day there was no doubt about it, it was getting worse. Pulling on my waterproofs, I went to look at Thor and Lucy and found them standing, backs to the storm, with rain streaming off their faces. They snatched at a bar of chocolate containing a cough tablet, but they had lost their usual perkiness. The prospect of hanging round the tent for two days was not very thrilling and I hit on the idea of crossing over to Mull the next day and visiting Tobermory. I walked to Achosnish and phoned Kilchoan post office to find out the times of the ferries. Gillespie's wife, Catriona, answered and said that I would have to be at Mingarry Pier, a mile out of Kilchoan, for eleven o'clock sharp. Returning to the tent I prepared a gastronomic extravaganza by opening a packet of yellow powder which the instructions promised could be easily transformed into a delicious omelette. I am sure I obeyed the instructions to the letter but the revolting mixture would not solidify and a thick spongy mass glued itself to the pan. It was my only pan and before I could make my usual chicken supreme I had to pull my waterproofs on again and go down to the loch to scrape the plastic omelette into the water. A flock of gulls descended on the pieces like vultures, but they soon dropped them again.

In the evening when I gave the ponies their medicine the mucus seemed to have cleared away and I just hoped my vet's prophecy about recovering after three days proved to be right. The weather looked anything but cheerful and on the hills above the farm tiny rivulets that for most of the year trickled down unnoticed had swollen to foaming torrents, scattering stones and chunks of peat across the road. Strong wind and rain battered the tent and it was one hell of a night. About midnight the lighthouse fog siren started up and between that and the noise of flogging canvas and rain I hardly slept a wink.

When dawn broke the prospect of walking to Mingarry Pier in the gale rather took the edge off my enthusiasm for a day in Tobermory and I must have dozed off while I was thinking about it. I woke with a start and, glancing at my watch, found I had under two hours to walk the seven miles. There was no time to look at the ponies. Stuffing cameras and lenses into a rucksack, I struggled into my waterproofs and ran towards Achosnich. I felt confident that someone would give me a lift so, hearing a car coming along from the farm, I waved and jerked my thumb in the direction of Kilchoan. It was a car I had seen parked alongside one of the caravans, but although the driver was alone he glared and accelerated past me. As he looked at me through his driving mirror I hoped he could understand what I was calling him. It hardly seemed possible that the rain could increase, but it did and I tramped along, kicking up clouds of spray where water poured across the road from overburdened culverts. Near the Sonachan Hotel faces looked miserably out of caravan windows as they watched me trudge up the steep hill, but no one waved. It was not that sort of day. Across the bleak moorland the fog siren continued to bellow its mournful call, reflecting the mood of all of us.

The minutes ticked by as I strode along at a cracking pace, soaked with rain on the outside and lathered with sweat within; but even so, time seemed to go faster than I did. At Kilchoan post office I had twenty minutes in which to cover the mile to the ferry and I was heading full into the strong wind and rain. As the pier came into sight I saw the ferry nosing in to tie up and I broke into a run, scattering pools of water and a flock of sheep a farmer was driving along the road. Fortunately for me, a car driven by an elderly chap was very firmly wedged between the walls of the narrow approach to the pier and I arrived breathless at the end of a small queue of passengers. With the none-too-gentle assistance of a couple of brawny crew members, the car was dragged off the walls and the queue surged forward. A woman was heaving a fish box full of salmon towards the gangway and as no one offered to help her I grasped one of the rope handles on the box.

'It's quite all right, thank you. I can manage,' she said, icily, in one of those expensive voices that told you right away she was no fishwife, but actually owned the salmon river. Letting go the handle, I followed the valuable cargo as she dragged it on board and then I retreated into the passenger saloon to drip water over the seats. There were about ten other passengers on board. Two middle-aged Americans, having closely inspected the rather bare interior of the saloon, went out on deck and clung to the rail as the ferry rolled slightly in the swell.

'Doggone it Mamie, I ain't never seen anything so bootiful,' exclaimed the man.

Thinking a shaft of sunlight had broken through to illuminate the crumbling ruins of Mingarry Castle, I rushed on deck to get a photograph, but the man and his wife were staring, starry-eyed, at a mile or two of heaving grey sea, merging with a sombre black rain cloud.

An elderly member of the crew came round for the fare and he had a quaint Highland way of collecting it. He took the money from each passenger, wrote the details on a battered piece of cardboard, then clambered up a ladder into the wheelhouse. A few minutes later he came back brandishing a fistful of tickets, but meantime he had forgotten whom the tickets belonged to.

'You will be the chentilman with the three bicycles who is going on the *Columba* to Oban,' he said to me in a beautiful lilt. I replied it was more likely to be the trio in shorts in the corner.

'Aye maybe it is. Well, are you a single or a coming-back?' he enquired, shuffling a bunch of tickets like a riverboat gambler with a pack of cards.

'Coming-back,' I said, leaping on the lovely description, and his gnarled hand thrust a long brown ticket into mine.

As we approached Tobermory, the usual bunch of old sages to be found on every pier in Scotland were watching us intently. They have a grand life, seemingly with nothing to do and all day to do it in. The arrival and departure of every vessel is discussed at length and they talk about the vagaries of weather and tides with a knowing nod and a wink, as though they are in direct contact with Neptune himself. As the ferry nudged into the wall they scrambled to take our mooring ropes and slip them over bollards, then stood back to scrutinise the passengers. Not having had time for breakfast before my mad dash to the ferry, I was ravenous, but first I had to find a bank. When I found one it was bursting with people and a long queue spilled out onto the pavement. I hate waiting in queues, but without money I could not eat, so I had no option. The clerks worked like fury and soon I was inside out of the rain, wedged in between a group of yachting types in dazzling oilskins and an old lady who struggled to control a dog almost as big as herself. The manager came out of his office and, finding the bank full, he came along the queue to each local person and led them into an anteroom to be attended to without having to wait with us tourists. It was a very nice gesture and one that locals in other tourist honeypots might appreciate.

Outside the bank, my nose led me towards the aroma of fish and chips and the entrance to the Brae Restaurant. It looked a bit dingy from outside, but it was clean enough and the attractive waitress actually smiled. I peeled off my waterproofs to find that not only was I wet with sweat, I was also soaked with water where the rain had seeped through my supposedly waterproof coat and trousers. As the sweat cooled and I began to feel cold the waitress obligingly moved an electric fire closer to my table. She took my order and handed the menu to a family of man, wife and two whining children on the next table. The wife read every item out loud then said she could not decide and handed the menu to her husband. He also read it out loud, but slowly and deliberately, as if there was a world of difference between 'Fish and Chips', 'Pie and Chips', 'Beefburgers and Chips' and so on. The poor waitress was trying very hard to keep her temper and was not helped by the brats shaking salt into the sugar bowl and whining 'I dinna like that' each time Dad read something from the menu.

'The prices are a lot higher than they are in Paisley,' complained the woman, in a voice that could be heard throughout the building. 'Nearly a pound for fish and chips, it's robbery.'

'Be reasonable, Effie,' argued her husband. 'It costs a lot of money to bring food to the island you know.'

She was not convinced, 'Och it cannae cost much to live in these country places.'

The long-suffering waitress had heard enough. 'Would you like to order now Madam,' she said. 'There are other people waiting.'

'We'll have a pot of tea for two and two glasses of orange for the bairns,' said the woman.

I caught the waitress's eye as she went past and I could almost hear what she was thinking.

It was a real luxury to pour hot tea out of a pot instead of slopping water onto a tea bag in a mug and I drank three large cups full before my meal arrived. Finishing off with a large piece of apple pie and cream, I paid up, pulled my soggy clothes on and went out into the rain. The leading boats in a yacht race were beating into the harbour and as each one crossed a line between the pier and a large yacht dressed overall with signal flags, anchored in the bay, a shot was fired from a gun. Despite the rain and poor visibility, I wanted to try and photograph the harbour and I found a path that led to a good viewpoint. Dozens of inflatable dinghies headed for the shore from the newly arrived yachts and when I returned to the harbour road it was crammed with the crews shouting excitedly to each other and arguing about who had won the race. The rain was coming down like stair-rods and, looking for somewhere to shelter, I came across the local folk museum in the Masonic Hall. For twenty pence I was able to look around a wonderful assortment of old tools, books and photographs of by-gone Mull. The enthusiast in charge was a Mr Yule, an absolute mine of information. The story of the sunken galleon in Tobermory Harbour has always intrigued me. Although it is often reported as being the *Florida*, Mr Yule said that recent evidence strengthened a theory that it was not the *Florida*, but a ship with the imposing name of *St Juan du Bastista de Ragusa*. The story really started with Francis Drake who, on 19th July, 1588, had his game of bowls interrupted by the news that the Spanish Armada had been sighted in the English Channel. To avoid panic, he calmly finished his game and, on 25th July, he gave the Spaniards a hiding off the Isle of Wight and scattered the Armada in all directions. Several ships fled North and three, the *Florencia*, the *Florida* and *St Juan du Bastista de Ragusa* found their way to Tobermory and put in for provisions. McLean of Duart agreed to provide food but kept two Spanish officers hostage to prevent the ship sailing away without paying. Word seems to have got round that the *St Juan* was bulging with treasure and one day in November 1588 she mysteriously blew up and sank in the harbour with, according to a Mull legend,

'The fruit of Aladdin's gardens
 Clustering thick in her hold,
 With rubies awash in her scuppers
 And her bilge ablaze with gold.'

It is generally believed that the ruthless McLean was responsible for the explosion, but whether or not he managed to get his hands on any of the treasure is not recorded. The story of the treasure attracted others to look for the wreck and, according to some records, a cannon, preserved at Inverary, was lifted from the wreck in 1670. In 1883 a diver nearly lost his life when his airpipe burst while he was working on the wreck for the Duke of Argyll. No further exploration was carried out until a ship's anchor brought up a few Spanish coins in 1903 and sparked off another gold rush. The Glasgow

Salvage Association obtained a lease in July 1903 and although they worked for less than a month they found a number of Spanish coins and a breach-loading cannon. Another cannon, supposedly from the galleon, sold in London in 1904, was described as a bronze breach-loading cannon, four feet six inches long. The buyer had the added bonus of finding the breach still loaded with powder and shot.

There have been other attempts in recent years to discover the bulk of the Spanish treasure, but the thick silt lying in Tobermory Harbour has so far defeated even the most modern diving technology. Mr Yule said that someone in Yugoslavia claimed to have evidence that the *St Juan du Bastista de Ragusa* was in fact a Yugoslavian ship commandeered by the Spanish, and so the mystery deepens.

There is another, less publicised, version of the story of the Spanish galleon in Tobermory which involves a Spanish princess, one Viola Bheola. She was haunted in her dreams by a handsome man and she could not rest until she had found him. During her long search for Mr Right, she sailed in the galleon *Florida* into Tobermory and met the debonair McLean of Duart and fell in love with him. But there was one black cloud which threatened this otherwise perfect romance; McLean already had a wife. Mrs McLean was not amused when the señorita started flashing her castinets at her husband and, since gunpowder was quicker than litigation, arranged for one of her servants to drop his fag end into the ship's magazine while the princess was enjoying her evening *paella*. It must have been an almighty explosion, because she is buried in Morvern.

I spent an enjoyable hour in the folk museum which housed one of the most interesting collections of local artefacts I have seen for some time. Out in the street it was still sluicing down, but somehow the throng of holidaymakers managed to look cheerful as they drifted from shop to shop or, in the case of the yachtsmen, from pub to pub. I bought a few groceries, half a bottle of whisky and half a dozen films for my cameras and walked back to the waiting-room of the pier to shelter from the rain and enjoy a meat pie and a can of beer. The room was crowded with waiting passengers, including a fair sprinkling of clergymen. Not wishing to sit in front of them slurping beer and biting off chunks of pie, I found a little side room which was empty except for a bench. I was happily chewing my pie when I heard the sound of a toilet being flushed and a door at the end of the room opened to reveal an elderly lady hauling up her bloomers. To my horror I realised I was in the ladies' rest room, but it was too late. She screamed and, abandoning beer and pie, I fled into the waiting-room, expecting to be arrested at any moment. An old chap sitting by the door almost choked with laughing.

'My gawd, laddie,' he said, wiping tears from his eyes, 'Ah know ma missus isnae much tae look at, but I didnae think she was that frightenin'. Ah been married tae her for forty years and maybe you've seen somethin' ah havenae.'

The rest of the room collapsed with laughter and it dawned on me that instead of pointing out to me that I was walking into the ladies' room, they had said nothing and sat back waiting for the fireworks. The enraged lady stalked in and I hurried out to the safety of the crowded pier.

Sitting on the bollards, the old sages were discussing the imminent arrival of the Outer Isles ferry *Columba*.

'She is half an hour late,' said one, examining the cracked face of a battered pocket watch.

'Well yes, I am thinking it will be the heavy swell running off Ardnamurchan. The wind against tide will be throwing up a nasty sea and the captain, he will be taking it easy.'

'Och yes,' chipped in a third, 'he will not be wanting the tourists to be emptying their stomachs all over the saloon.'

They were distracted by an old trawler chugging in from the sea. Given a coat of paint and renamed the *Isle of Tiree*, she had a new role as a cargo boat and was calling to collect stores for the island. She turned to come alongside the pier, but the sages waved her away.

'Stand off. Stand off. The *Columba* is coming,' they chorused excitedly as if she was making the only visit of the year.

Swearing angrily, the skipper hauled the engine control to astern and, spinning the wheel, went backwards in an arc round the edge of the yachts. The Kilchoan ferry was also moved from its berth to make more room and it had just departed when the black hull of the *Columba* appeared round a headland. From the wing of the bridge, the captain manoeuvred the ship gently alongside the pier; heaving lines were flung ashore to be pounced on by the sages, who pulled thick mooring ropes off the ship and looped them round the bollards. Capstans whirred, fore and aft, pulling the ship tighter against the pier; bells jangled on the bridge and were answered in the engine room and the *Columba* had arrived. A hydraulic lift on the foredeck whined upwards until it was level with the pier and a ramp was lowered to allow cars to drive straight off the ship. After all the excited anticipation, I expected to see the ship alive with activity, cars being driven off, cattle loaded into the hold, lorries backed up and unloaded. It was a dreadful anticlimax to see about ten passengers leave the ship. Only five, including the three cyclists, walked up the ramp on to it. A crewman shouted, 'Anymore?' There was no response and the ramp was raised, the lift sank into the hold and the ropes were cast off. Having taken little over five minutes, the *Columba* was on its way to Oban. A motor boat came racing across the harbour with a woman standing in the bow, shouting, 'Wait please, I have to get to Oban tonight.'

'I'm sorry, but you are too late,' a crewman shouted back from the departing ship. He looked up at the bridge, but the captain shook his head, the propellors churned up the water and the gap between the *Columba* and the motorboat widened rapidly. The woman burst into tears and the man driving the boat did his best to console her. Years ago, I remember the *Loch Seaforth* putting back at Stornoway for someone seen running along the pier. She nudged alongside while two crewmen grabbed the late arrival and hauled him aboard by the seat of his trousers. Perhaps in these days of rules and regulations, it would be more than a captain's job was worth to allow a passenger to join a ship unless it was by the approved gangway.

The Kilchoan ferry returned to the pier and I went on board. The *Isle of Tiree* came alongside, quickly loaded a cargo of calor gas bottles and miscellaneous boxes and put out to sea again. I was the only passenger on the ferry and at ten past six it cast off and backed out towards the yachts.

Rain lashed the deck as the ferry ploughed across the Sound and I sat in the warmth of the saloon, tired and wet after my day in Tobermory, and not looking forward to squelching the seven miles back to the tent. The rain never eased off for a minute as I trudged along the road from Kilchoan and I reached the tent utterly weary and soaked to the skin. I staggered across the field to look at Thor and Lucy, but it was difficult to tell how they were feeling. Falling into the tent, I pulled off my wet clothes and stacked them in a heap by the tent door. The warmth of the stove stopped my teeth chattering, but I was too tired to eat. Wriggling into my sleeping bag, I sipped a mug of coffee well laced with whisky. The fog horn on the lighthouse was still groaning but a good dram was more effective than ear plugs and I slept undisturbed.

The following day, Tuesday, 17th July, was my birthday and perhaps the best way of describing it would be to quote verbatim from my diary.

'Today I am 45 years old. "What does it feel like to be forty-five?" would be the standard question from a reporter. My answer would have to be "Warm and Dry". Yesterday when I was forty-four, I was cold and wet, but now I am forty-five and enveloped in a down sleeping bag. If the reporter had not experienced such bliss he would go away muttering that I was round the bend.

'I have just opened a sealed envelope marked 'To be opened on 17th July" which Sue gave me on the day I started my journey. Miraculously, it has survived the damp and on a birthday card inside is the following:

While riding through the Highland glens
With Lucy and with Thor,
I hope that you're not soaking wet
And your backside's not too sore.

I hope it's not too long before I see your smiling face
And Lucy with her itchy skin
And Thor, who sets the pace.
I hope you're feeling fit and well,
Zestful and alive!
Because, it's true, I'm sad to say,
Today you're forty-five!

'For some, birthdays are a time for reflection and the older a person is the more he is expected to reflect. Normally I prefer to look forward rather than back, but since on this occasion I have nothing better to do than lie in my tent, listening to the rain lashing against the canvas, it is an opportunity to look back on my disordered life.

'There are those who go through life without any apparent effort. Successful school career, well-filled, memorable holidays. Do well at college or university, land a good job and marry well. Produce happy children and enjoy the satisfaction of watching them grow up and go through the same process. Fate touched me with a different brush and left me with an affliction called wanderlust. Had it been any other kind of lust it may have been satisfied by now, but for wanderlust there is no cure, merely a temporary relief. Instead of lying in a gale-lashed tent on a Scottish hillside, any sane forty-five-year-old family man would be at home relaxing in the garden. So why do I do it? Bravado? Hardly. There is no one around when I think I am being brave and anyway most people have the impression that wandering around the countryside with two ponies is one long holiday. It is all to do with wanderlust, that constant urge to do something different, not with any financial motive, but simply because people like me are made that way. Robert Service, the Yukon poet, wrote a poem about us wanderers which is so true it is uncanny.

> There's a race of men that don't fit in,
> A race that can't stay still;
> So they break the hearts of kith and kin,
> And they roam the world at will.
> They range the field and they rove the flood,
> And they climb the mountains crest;
> Theirs is the curse of the gipsy blood,
> And they don't know how to rest.
>
> If they just went straight they might go far;
> They are strong and brave and true;
> But they're always tired of the things that are,
> And they want the strange and new.
> They say "Could I find my proper groove
> What a deep mark I could make!"
> So they chop and change and each fresh move
> Is only a fresh mistake.

'In forty-five years I have done a lot but achieved very little. One of the exciting things about life is wondering what the next day will bring. Sometimes it is disappointment or grief, but occasionally a memorable day turns up which makes up for the bad ones. I do not believe in life after death, nor am I in any way religious. At the same time, when I am in the mountains or at sea in a small boat, I am aware of something immensely powerful watching over me. Whether it is called God, Buddha, Mohammed or any other name is not really important. The insistence of individuals and nations that only their interpretation of the wishes of our creator is the right one is causing untold suffering and misery throughout the world. Surely, instead of asking their followers to prepare for a life after death, church leaders ought to be helping to make the one they have a bit happier.

'Having reflected and offered my brand of philosophy, I have now to come to grips with my immediate problems, not least the condition of the ponies. Despite the long rest, both Thor and Lucy still have coughs and streaming noses. Even above the lighthouse fog siren I can hear the barking cough and I am faced with an awful dilemma. I cannot keep them out in this weather much longer; nor can I continue my journey in the hope of finding shelter for them. To bring a vet from Fort William will cost at least thirty pounds, but unless the ponies have shelter, whatever medicine they are given would be wasted. The only option left to me is to take them home and start the journey again when they have recovered. Altogether it is one hell of a worry. Rain continues to batter against the tent, Thor and Lucy continue to cough and the tent is stacked with sodden clothing, with no hope of getting it dry. I have racked my brains for an alternative to abandoning my journey, but I cannot find one. The condition of the ponies is urgent. I shall have to take them home.'

Strangely, that extract from my diary makes no mention of the rain being driven under the flysheet and dripping into the tent. Within a very short time a pool had gathered on the groundsheet and, though I mopped it up frequently, with wads of toilet paper, I was fighting a losing battle. To add to the fun, I was invaded with earwigs. They arrived in the tent on the first day and, as the weather deteriorated, they told their friends and families of earwigs swarmed everywhere. From time to time I swept a heap into a plastic bag and emptied it outside, but having tasted the good life, and my food, they were soon back again. There was always a line of flattened corpses under my sleeping bag where several earwigs unwisely happened to be taking a stroll at a time when I turned over during the night. The more adventurous ones had discovered the luxury of a down sleeping bag and refused to come out. It was only when I felt one scampering over my unmentionables that I managed to grab the squirming little horror and bash its brains out on the groundsheet with a tin of meths.

In those conditions, life in the tent was very tedious and the one bright spot each day was the postman, who always stopped his van for a chat and produced a tin of humbugs 'to drive away the damp'. He had a croft in Kilchoan and was worried that, the weather being so bad, his oats would be ready for harvesting before he was able to get his hay in.

16

Glenfinnan

With the help of two weeks' warm, dry weather at home in Cumberland and liberal doses of antibiotic magic, Thor and Lucy recovered completely and romped around the field like a pair of foals. Kind friends offered us their horse-box wagon and early on Sunday 5th August my wife, Sue, and our neighbour, Brian Burscough, and I thundered back over the border, heading for Glenfinnan at the head of Loch Sheil. I had hoped to start again at Swordle, in Ardnamurchan, and follow the coast as far as Loch Shiel then on to Glenfinnan, but it would have used up a lot of time and the stalking season was approaching rapidly. Cutting out Ardnamurchan, the most obvious place to start was Glenfinnan.

The weather was fine and clear when we left home, but by the time we reached Strathyre the windscreen wipers were hard at work coping with a downpour. In Glencoe it was raining so hard the wheels threw up clouds of spray on either side like a snowplough clearing a drift. On we went, over Ballachulish Bridge and along the edge of Loch Linnhe, to rest for a while in a car park by Fort William railway station. There cannot be a less inspiring town in the whole of Scotland than Fort William on a cold, wet, blustery Sunday morning. Tired and bleary-eyed, we shuffled along the main street in the rain, ankle-deep in discarded chip cartons, beer cans, bottles and cigarette packets, searching optimistically for a café, tea bar or anywhere we could get breakfast.

When I lived in the area in the 1960s there was as much chance of finding a café open on a Sunday in Fort William as there was of seeing nude bathing off the town's pier. To be standing now in front of a restaurant door that was not only open, but open at eight o'clock in the morning, was nothing short of a miracle. The three of us trooped in and joined a small queue of lorry drivers, one or two locals striving to recover from the effects of a dram too many and hikers thawing out after spending the night stretched on benches in the bus terminal. We moved slowly forward as the girl behind the counter handed over what has become the standard breakfast in every café from John o'Groats to Land's End: beans on toast, egg on toast and a number of permutations which sometimes included bacon, or, if you are really discerning, a few shrivelled mushrooms. Two American lads reached the counter in front of us.

'Ham and eggs, please,' said the first one.

'Sorry, we only serve bacon and eggs,' replied the girl.

The American looked puzzled. 'Do you call ham bacon in your country?' he asked politely.

The girl sounded irritable, 'Don't know. We only serve bacon and egg.'

'Well how about a couple of poached eggs on a piece of your bacon,' the American persisted.

Breaking off a conversation with someone in the kitchen, the girl looked over her shoulder, 'Sorry,' she said, 'it's too early.'

'Too early for what, goddamit,' exploded the American. 'Don't Scots hens prodoose eggs in the mornin'.'

'We only serve a set breakfast,' replied the girl huffily, 'You can have bacon and eggs or you can have a roll.'

Turning to his friend, the American laughed. 'How about that Hank. We can get a roll!'

'Say,' said Hank, looking at the girl with a mischievous gleam in his eye, 'd'you know what an American breakfast is?'

'No, what is it?' said the girl sullenly.

'It's a roll in bed with honey,' laughed Hank.

'We don't serve honey,' said the girl. 'You can have beans on toast, eggs on toast, egg and ...'

'Next please,' shouted an assistant at the end of the counter and we moved up without hearing whether Hank and his friend eventually got something to eat.

Rain was bouncing off the pavements as we drove out of Fort William for Corpach and followed the Mallaig road along the edge of Loch Eil. Apart from the café where we had breakfasted, every shop in the town and every garage, hotel and tea bar along the road were firmly locked and barred. There was no sign of the great Highland awakening to cash in on the needs of summer tourists whose restricted annual holiday often compelled them to travel on the Sabbath. Years ago two distraught American women called at my cottage in Glen Moriston one Sunday and begged me to make them a pot of coffee and a meal. Unaware of the power of the Scottish Sabbath, they had driven all the way from Prestwick Airport to Kyle of Lochalsh on a Saturday night, hoping to cross to Skye on the Sunday. When they found the ferry was not operating they tried in vain to find accommodation for the night. In the end they were forced to sleep in their car. Early the following morning they drove to Sheil Bridge and knocked on the door of a house displaying a 'Teas' sign, only to be greeted by the lady of the house with a tirade of abuse and told that their misfortune was God's punishment for travelling on the Sabbath and they would get no refreshment from her that day.

'Are these people crazy, or sump'n?' asked one of the American women as they thawed out in front of my fire and drank coffee. I explained as best I could that in the West Highlands the ten commandments were taken very seriously and they had broken the fourth.

'Gee, is that a fact?' said the second lady, a smile flickering across her face. 'Say Sybil,' she continued, turning to her friend, 'I guess that when we were at college we must have broken every cotton pickin' one of 'em, so what the hell.' They drove away, vowing to dump their hire car in Inverness and catch the next plane to London.

I can sympathise with the people who want to retain the Scottish Sabbath as part of a way of life, but there are those who take it to ridiculous extremes. Spiritual salvation may be important to the ministers and elders of the churches, but in these changing times it is economic salvation the Highland region is desperately in need of. In the long term that salvation lies in tourism and, however abhorrent it is to the Church, the Scottish Sabbath will have to move forward into the twentieth century.

Throughout history the churches have been puritanical in the extreme. Professor Smout, in his *History of the Scottish People*, wrote that kirk discipline led to an increase in infanticide and homosexuality. Homosexuals, men and boys, if detected were burned alive, 'sometimes two together'. In 1694 the General Assembly of the Church of Scotland, in an attempt to bring the country back to what they considered was the path of morality, recited the sins of the nation:

'God is dishonoured by the impiety and profaneness that aboundeth ... in profane and idle swearing, cursing and Sabbath breaking, neglect and contempt of Gospel ordinances, mocking of piety and religious exercises, fornication, adultery, drunkenness, blasphemy and other gross and abominable sins and vices.'

There were many rumblings of discontent about the way the established church was run. Some wanted a different form of service, others wanted to break from the constitution and there were heated disputes over what form the church service should take. The disruption of 1834 split the established church apart and the Free Church of Scotland was formed. But even then they could not agree among themselves and, on 27th July, 1893, the Reverend D. Macfarlane and the Reverend D. MacDonald, both of Sheldaig, met together with Alexander Macfarlane, a schoolmaster from Raasay, and 'resolved to meet next day, and, in the name of the Head of the Church, form themselves into a separate Presbytery, not owning jurisdiction of the courts of the presently subsisting church calling herself the Free Church of Scotland.' So the Free Presbyterian Church of Scotland was formed, but not without a good deal of criticism. An enraged reverend gentleman described the new church as 'the most mischievous movement of modern times and calculated to do the most serious harm to the cause of truth and godliness in our beloved Highlands.'

With the exception of parts of the Outer Hebrides, both the Free Church and the Free Presbyterian Church have maintained a strong grip over the Highlands and Islands and their puritanical 'hell fire and brimstone' brand of religion has probably done more to drive the young people away from church than anything else. When, as a young lighthouse keeper, I was sent to the Butt of Lewis lighthouse, I had hardly been on the island a week when I fell foul of the Wee Frees. Keen to explore the island, I borrowed the Principal

Keeper's bike and rode through Port of Ness, enjoying my day off and whistling a tune. As I pedalled slowly past a croft a man came out and started to shout in Gaelic and wave his arms. I jumped off the bike thinking he wanted to find out who I was, but his gestures were far from friendly. He started to hurl lumps of peat at my head and the Principal Keeper's bike was minus a few spokes before I managed to escape. I found out later that I had been 'called' from the pulpit for defaming the Sabbath by riding a bicycle and whistling. What the men of black cloth and grey faces did not know was how much the youngsters hated and despised them and used to chant:

'The Wee Kirk, the Free Kirk,
The Kirk without a steeple.
The old Kirk, the cold Kirk,
The Kirk without the people.'

Whatever the youngsters wanted to do, the minister or the elders invariably condemned and local people suffered very much from their killjoy 'everything you do is a sin' outlook on life. The damage inflicted on community life by the churches has caused a lot of concern over the years and, in his *West Highland Survey* Fraser Darling comments, 'our observations lead us to the opinion that a very small and remote community would have a greater chance of survival if it were Catholic than if it followed one of the stricter sects of Presbyterianism.' William MacKay, who wrote the *History of Urquart and Glenmoriston* made an even stronger indictment against the Church. 'It has to a great extent destroyed the songs and tales which were the wonderfully pure intellectual pastime of our fathers; it has suppressed innocent customs and recreations whose origin was to be found in remote antiquity; and it has with its iron hand crushed merriment and good fellowship out of the souls of the people, and in their place planted an unhealthy gloominess and dread of the future entirely foreign to the nature of the Celt.'

It is because of this stranglehold the ministers have over the population that the dreary Scottish Sabbath has continued to exist, but how long can it last? When the old people have passed on and the Highland churches stand empty maybe the

General Assemblies will ask themselves why, but then it will be too late. It would take more than a church to suppress the Highlanders' sense of humour altogether though. There used to be a story circulating round the Island of Lewis about the ferry, *Loch Seaforth*, leaving Stornoway one night, bound for Mallaig. As she steamed down the Minch one of the crew shouted, 'Man overboard!'

'Who is it?' shouted the captain.

'It's the minister,' replied the deckhand.

'What church?' shouted the captain.

'Free Church,' came the reply.

'Full steam ahead,' roared the captain.

Clouds hung low over Loch Shiel when we reached the Scottish National Trust's Visitor Centre at Glenfinnan and drove into the car park. It was raining so hard we could barely see Prince Charlie's monument two hundred yards away and I sat for a long time, putting off the evil moment when, rain or not, I would have to saddle the ponies and start my journey again. Dashing across to the Visitor Centre, I asked them if there was a building nearby where I could shelter for the night. A very helpful man behind the counter scratched his head in thought for a moment, then said, 'Hold on a minute, I'll ring Sandy Walker, the stalker in Glenfinnan and let you speak to him.' Sandy said there was a bothy three miles up the glen and a fenced enclosure where I could keep the ponies. It was the one bright spot in a miserable day and, saying goodbye to Sue and Brian, I spurred Thor forward up the glen, with the ever-faithful Lucy following his tail.

Water cascaded down from the high viaduct carrying the Fort William to Mallaig railway and dollops of icy-cold water gave my newly waterproofed suit quite a severe test as we rode under the arch. In its brochure the Scottish firm who manufacture the range of 'thornproof' coats and trousers I was wearing claimed that they were waterproof and timeproof. I'm not sure what they meant by timeproof but, in driving rain, one hundred per cent waterproof they most certainly were not. While I was at home waiting for the ponies to recover, I had carefully washed the suit and given it a thorough coating of waterproof dressing. It withstood the cascade from the railway

Ardnamurchan Lighthouse

A chance to dry out — Glenfinnan bothy

A rotten bridge which almost cost Lucy her life — Loch Hourn

The Prince's bed — Prince Charlie's Cave, Glen Moriston

arch, but there was a long way to go before my journey would be over.

The stalker's new bungalow loomed up through the murk and his two young children braved the weather to run out with a piece of bread for Thor and Lucy. Sandy came out with them and said that there were a few bits of wood at the bothy and I would be able to dry out over a fire. Higher up the glen, the white building of Glenfinnan Lodge looked down from a high knoll and below it, nestling by the edge of the tumbling River Finnan, was Corryhully bothy and a good field for the ponies. The owners of the estate had gone to a lot of trouble to think ahead and landscape the glen for the future. A large number of broad-leaved trees had been planted around the Lodge and alongside the track, each with its own fence to protect it from foraging deer and sheep.

The bothy was typical of most Scottish bothies, a one-room building with stone walls and a corrugated iron roof. Inside it was sparsely furnished with a roughly constructed wooden bench for cooking on and two benches piled high with scruffy mattresses. In one end there was a stone fireplace with a stack of firewood ready for use and in no time I was basking in the warmth of a good fire, watching the shadows flickering up the wall. As darkness fell the rain drummed on the tin roof of the bothy with renewed vigour, but snug in my sleeping bag I drifted into a much-needed sleep.

The next morning I lay in my sleeping bag until ten o'clock. It was still pouring with rain and the river was running high so that crossing it would have been extremely hazardous. In the afternoon the rain stopped and I was overjoyed to see the clouds break up and the sun come out. I rushed out to see how the ponies were and almost ran into a magnificent golden eagle sitting on a wall. While we stared at one another I wished I was holding a camera, but he did not give me time to get one. With a loud shriek he stood on the tips of his curved talons and launched himself into the air like a hang glider jumping off a cliff. The heavy body dropped for a second until the giant wings bit into the air. Then with a slow flap the eagle climbed higher into the sky and, holding his wings rigid, soared effortlessly down the glen.

Conditions were perfect for photography so, first checking that the ponies were quite happy in their field, I walked down the glen to the Visitor Centre to photograph the monument commemorating Bonnie Prince Charlie's Rising of 1745. Silhouetted against a pale sky, the monument would have made a fine picture, but the warm sun had brought out hundreds of tourists and each time I looked through the camera's viewfinder a group of people emerged onto the parapet and peered intently up the stone kilt of the Highland figure or made funny faces at their friends below.

Before walking back up the glen I browsed round the Information Centre and chatted to the man who had phoned Sandy Walker for me.

'There's a lot of people climbing the monument today,' I said laughingly, 'I hope it doesn't end up like the Tower of Pisa.'

'It's funny you should say that,' he replied. 'As a matter of fact the monument is reckoned to be nine inches out of plumb and its moving a rate of three eighths of an inch each year. But it's quite safe,' he added hurriedly, 'the engineers calculate it would have to be three feet out of vertical before it would fall over and that will be in the year 2030. But it won't get that far. The Trust are working on it.'

When I returned to the bothy it was a gorgeous evening and I hung the saddle blankets over a fence to dry and coated the saddle with a layer of leather preservative. For dinner I ate the last of my chicken supreme and looked forward to a change of diet during the rest of my journey.

During the night clouds drifted in from the West and the new day dawned overcast and with a light drizzle. A newly bulldozed road beyond the bothy provided easy riding for a short while, before ending abruptly at a ford crossing the river. The route ahead rose from one hundred feet above sea level to about fourteen hundred in just over a mile and was so rough and wet there was no possibility of riding up it. I was lashing one of Lucy's packs to Thor's saddle when Sandy Walker arrived with a stalking party and suggested I follow him. There was no proper path and soon the ponies and I were lathered in sweat with the exertion of clambering over rocks and floundering through bogs. Some way below the summit of the ridge the already difficult route deteriorated further into a maze of boulders washed down by centuries of floods and the going became exceedingly strenuous. We crossed and recrossed the stream a dozen times, clambered over boulders and picked a way across scree and sharp rocks. As we climbed higher the drizzle increased to a downpour and thick cloud came down off the high tops, reducing visibility to a few yards. The stalking party turned off to climb the steep face of Streap and with a wave they were swallowed up in the mist.

I pushed on with the slipping, slithering ponies behind me and it was only when the ground started to slope the other way I realised we had reached the summit of the ridge. Tying Thor and Lucy to an old fence post, I flopped against a rock, but two mugs of orange and a chocolate bar soon revived me and, before my sweat had time to cool, I was leading the way down into Glean a Chaorainn. The climb up was awkward enough, but when we dropped below the clouds I looked down on several hundred feet of very steep hillside followed by five miles of wet wilderness. Both ponies puffed and snorted with fear as I carefully picked my way down and on the floor of the glen I let them graze while I studied the way ahead through binoculars. There was no path, just mile after mile of bog and rock, flanked by high mountains on either side. I tried to keep to a straight line, but that soon proved impossible. We floundered through acres of bog then staggered for miles across expanses of tussock grass so exhausting I had to rest the ponies every few hundred yards. To add to the difficulty, the rain increased and thick cloud rolled into the glen. I was soaked to the skin and my boots were full of water, but I was past caring as I drove the ponies on, swearing at Lucy for not following Thor and getting herself in a position where I had to go back and rescue her. When the nightmare of the tussocks ended I thought we were through, but the worst was yet to come. Thor plunged into a bog up to his chest and I had to scoop the wet peat out with my hands and pull his legs forward. On the move once more, we had hardly gone fifty yards when he went in again. In all, he sank into the bog five times before we reached safe ground. With a final heavy shower the rain and clouds cleared away like magic and a warm sun beamed down out of a blue sky. It was like having crossed the forbidden mountain range and reached Shangri-la.

The tip of Loch Arkaig sparkled in the sun far below and

through the binoculars I could see a range of buildings and a large sheep pen. Near the edge of the loch were one or two cottages and a few caravans, but no sign of life anywhere. A long, steep ridge led down to a river flowing from the loch into Glen Pean and with some hesitation the ponies plucked up courage to cross a rickety bridge. A newly erected forest fence forced us to follow a wet route along the river bank and in a place where a long section of the bank had been washed away I had to wade down the river, towing Thor behind me like a barge. Trying to coax him back onto the bank was no easy matter. Each time he tried, more of the bank collapsed under his weight and he soon worked himself into a terrible state. Finally with a mighty grunt he hurled his great body at the bank and, in a flurry of hooves and flying mud, he landed gasping on the grass. While all this was going on, Lucy had stood and watched from the other side of the gap. With a superior expression on her face she jumped into the river, waded upstream and, without any assistance, climbed easily up the bank and started to graze.

'OK, clever pants,' I called to her as I helped Thor to his feet, 'don't forget Thor is a lot older than you. Wait till you get middle-age spread.' Thor snorted his agreement and, to show that there was still plenty of life in him yet, he bucked a couple of times, raising his back feet all of twelve inches off the ground.

The sheep pens and clipping sheds I had seen from the hill had a good, fenced-in paddock alongside them, but they were choked with rushes and grass was almost non-existent. As I let the ponies through the gate I gave them a chocolate bar each to make the rushes taste better. The sheds were stacked high with fleeces and the whole place reeked of marking fluid, but with two wooden benches pulled together to make a table, I soon had the stove going and the dominant aroma was ground coffee bubbling in the pan. Stripping off my wet clothes, I squeezed as much water out of them as I could and hung them over a fence. I was reluctant to put my warm dry feet back into wet boots so, spying a couple of polythene bags lying under some wool, I cut them to size, pulled them over each sock and put my boots on.

17

Inaccessible Knoydart

I enjoyed a very restful sleep and woke the next morning to find the sun trying to burn a hole in the tent. At first I could not believe it, but when I looked out it was real enough. All the hills were bathed in a red glow and even the glen I had fought my way down the previous day looked inviting. The midges came out in force to enjoy the morning sun and exercised their wings by chasing poor Lucy round and round the paddock. To save time and temper, I brought the ponies into the shed and was able to load up without having to cope with Lucy practising the Highland fling. A vicious rain squall appeared from nowhere as I was about to leave and I sheltered for an hour while it bounced off the shed roof and gurgled into the drains. It eventually drifted away and the sun beamed down again as though nothing had happened.

Behind the sheep pens was Glendessary and the path to Loch Nevis and the ponies strode along happily in the warm sun. Several people were sitting on a bench outside Glendessary House and a woman ran across to ask if I had seen a pony roaming the hills. She explained that a girl who had been travelling on horseback had gone out one morning to find that her pony had strayed. Even after searching for nearly a week, she had discovered no trace of it. I promised to look for it and continued on my way.

A thin path contoured round the hill, keeping close to a forest fence, but it was very wet and I constantly had to jump off Thor and lead him through nasty patches of bog. By the fast-flowing stream of Allt Coire nan Uth the path disappeared over the edge of a rocky gorge and I looked down to find it traversing diagonally across fifty feet of slippery rock to the stream bed. To make matters worse, on the other side of the stream was a fence but no sign of a gate. I hunted for an alternative route but the original line of the path had been lost and could possibly have crossed a bridge at some time. Leaving Thor at the top, I unloaded Lucy and coaxed her down the rock, keeping well away from her in case she slipped and crashed down on me. Very gently she inched her way down while I kept a light pressure on her lead rope and talked to her all the time. My heart almost stopped when her shoes lost their grip on the rock and she started to slide, but she dug in harder and managed to stop herself going over the edge. What a relief it was when she clattered down the last few feet and splashed through the boulder-strewn water to safety. I went back to collect Thor, but the silly fool had decided to find his own route and when I climbed out of the gorge he was heading rapidly down the glen. I shouted to him and he rushed back, whinnying that he had lost Lucy.

'Just follow me, you great mutton-head,' I growled at him, heaving him to the edge of the rock, but although he could see Lucy on the other side, he flatly refused to move. Lucy whinnied at him as though shouting, 'Come on you coward, I'm getting cold standing here.' The taunt strung him into action and he cautiously stepped over the edge and, moving very slowly, worked his way down the rock to the stream and across to the other side. I followed with the packs and spotted a gate in the fence a few hundred yards downstream. It seemed a good opportunity to rest for lunch before loading up again. A pan of coffee was nicely bubbling on the stove when I felt a spot of water on my neck and looked round to find the sky as black as coal and thick clouds pouring down the crags. I jumped up and just managed to scramble into my waterproofs when a tremendous deluge lashed down and poured off the ponies' backs as if someone had emptied a bath of water over them. Crouching against the fence, I tried to shelter from it, but the weight of water forced its way through the seams of my jacket and under the hood and within seconds rivulets of cold water were trickling down my back. A gust of wind knocked the Primus stove over and sent the pan of coffee spinning into a cluster of boulders, but I had to leave it to its fate. Easing only for a moment, the squall returned with renewed ferocity and the ponies huddled together for protection as the wire fence bowed under the pressure of the wind. It seemed an eternity before the wind eased off and I was able to stand up and load the equipment onto Lucy. Except for a large dent, the billycan was all right and the Primus was none the worse for its roll in the heather.

The path up the glen was awash with water so that the ponies' hooves kicked up clouds of penetrating spray as we pushed on through the rain. Huge patches of bog barred the way, but there was no alternative route round them. Dark, menacing crags glistening with water towered on either side. It was a case of keep going and hope for the best. Bogs gave way to boulder fields with their own particular hazard of concealed holes waiting for the unwary leg and at times I had to walk in front of the ponies, testing the ground with my boot. Having negotiated one rather nasty expanse of rock, the ponies halted on the edge of a stretch of spongy grass. There was no way round it and I urged Thor forward. He sniffed the bog, made a slight detour or two and splashed confidently across, with Lucy close behind. The rain was beating on my jacket hood like a drum and, hunched in the saddle, I let him find his own way. I half turned to see how Lucy was, when Thor broke through the surface and rolled on his side, trapping me underneath him. The more he fought to get out the further I was pushed into the wet peat, but my left foot was still in the stirrup and I could not pull it free. Thor continued to struggle, but only sank further, dragging me with him, and I was soon up to my waist.

'Steady Thor old lad, steady,' I hissed in his ear, trying to calm him down while I fumbled in the slime for the buckle of my stirrup leather. With a heave I managed to pull the leather off the saddle and I was free. Gasping for breath and spitting out lumps of moss, I crawled away from Thor onto firm ground and turned to help him, but there was nothing to do. Free of my weight he had clambered to his feet and pushed forward to climb out beside me. Lucy sniffed the large hole left by Thor and found her own way across. In the shelter of an overhanging rock I examined Thor for any sign of damage, but the way he snatched a handful of mints was a sure sign there was nothing wrong with his innards. Apart from being plastered with sticky peat, he was no worse for his ordeal. For a dreadful moment I thought my cameras had been ruined, but although they had been submerged in the bog inside the cases they were bone dry. Kicking off my waterproof suit and boots to empty the water out of them, I scooped lumps of moss and peat out of my hair and trousers. I was soaked to the skin, but there was no point in changing into dry clothes: it was still raining and I would have been as wet as ever within an hour.

Away from the bog, the path improved as it climbed upwards. Soon, however, it broke away again and I led the ponies through a nightmare maze of bog and rock to a large cairn marking the top of the pass. Thick cloud swirled off the crags and I could hardly see more than a few yards as we tripped and stumbled through the most harrowing stretch of country I have ever experienced with ponies. The path, where it existed at all, followed an erratic course over very difficult shattered rock, disappearing every few yards into the most desperately dangerous holes full of slimy moss. It took a long time to coax and cajole Thor and Lucy up rocky ledges and down the other side, to jump across bogs with scarcely a place to land on the other side because a vertical rock face barred the way, and to descend narrow gullies choked with loose boulders and scree where more than once the packs became jammed between the walls and Lucy had to be unloaded. A long glacial hollow had filled with water to form Lochan Mhaim and I rested the ponies and tightened the clenches on two of Lucy's shoes. The path below the lochan was easier for a while, then it turned and climbed across the face of a steep cliff. The situation was impressive, but it was no place for nervous ponies and I hoped that Thor would not notice that there was a lot of air below his feet.

At the top of the climb I rested for a few minutes and looked down on the welcome sight of Loch Nevis. It had been a tough journey through Glendessary but the guardians of the glen had a final test for us. The path zigzagged down the steep hill to a deep ford at the foot of a waterfall on Allt Coire na Ciche and at the water's edge I halted the ponies and weighed up the situation. Swollen with rainwater, the waterfall foamed over the rocks in a fearsome torrent as if a dam had burst high in the hills. The force of water pouring directly into the normally shallow pool that served as a ford churned up the surface into a boiling maelstrom and it was impossible to see how deep it was. Two ropes had been stretched across the ford to assist walkers to cross safely, but for ponies the only way was through the water. There was absolutely no alternative. On the right was the waterfall and on the left a deep gorge down which the overflow from the pool cascaded on its way to Loch Nevis. Breaking a thin branch off a nearby birch tree, I sounded the depth of the pool. It was little under six feet deep and it meant swimming the ponies across. That was all very well, but if there is one thing in this world Thor dislikes more than anything, it is water rising above his knees, and even then he prefers it to be warm. Persuading him to plunge straight into a deep, ice-cold pool and pull Lucy in at the same time was not going to be easy. There was also the cheerful prospect of being swept over the edge into the gorge. It had to be done in one go and as quickly as possible. Walking the ponies back a few yards from the ford, I tightened the saddle girth, checked the lashings on the packs, climbed on Thor's broad back and fastened Lucy's lead rope behind my saddle. Standing up in the stirrups, I let out a piercing yell and cracked the end of the birch branch down on Thor's rump. He shot off like a scalded cat, straight into the pool. I felt Lucy's lead rope tighten behind me, then slacken as she was pulled forward. Thor never hesitated and plunged into the water, sending a bow wave right over us. The cold water took my breath away as Thor sank under the surface and I yelled at him to keep going. The roar of the waterfall was deafening and I dared not look round to see if Lucy was still with us. Thor's short legs thrashed the water as he swam madly for the opposite side. As the swiftly flowing stream pushed us ever nearer to the edge, I looked straight down the gorge to the rocks below.

'Keep going Thor, keep going,' I screamed above the noise. His feet found rock on the other bank and he surfaced, still running. On he went full tilt up the path until, spying a patch of grass, he lurched to a halt and started to graze calmly, as if swimming across torrents was something he did every day. Looking quickly behind me, I half expected to see Lucy still floundering in the pool, but to my amazement she was right behind Thor with her nose well into the grass. Sliding out of the saddle, I put my arms round Thor's neck. 'Thor you old devil,' I said, giving him a hug, 'I'm sure you'd travel to the moon if someone gave you a big enough whack on the bottom.' They both stopped grazing long enough to chew a chocolate bar.

We had passed all the tests set by the guardians of Glendessary and they rewarded us by turning off the water and sending the sun to warm our backs and drive away the damp. I stripped off and rubbed my frozen lower half with a towel to get the blood circulating. Bashing my wet clothes against a rock got rid of a lot of water, but it did not put any warmth into them and pulling on trousers caused a chill in some very uncomfortable places.

We descended slowly to the deserted meadow land on the shore of Loch Nevis and pitched camp close to Sourlies bothy, a very attractive one-roomed building renovated and maintained by the Mountain Bothies Association. Having given Thor and Lucy a thorough check over, I put the hobbles on their forelegs and turned them loose. There were very few places they could stray to and I was sure even Lucy would not tackle the ford wearing hobbles. I carried my food and stove inside the empty bothy and made a large beef curry from my stock of powdered delights. It tasted exactly the same as chicken supreme and I began to wonder if my taste buds had been permanently affected. A well-filled visitors book showed that the bothy was very popular with walkers on treks through Knoydart and Morar. In their search for firewood they had hacked chunks off a rowan tree close by the bothy and this act of vandalism had prompted the custodian to hang a message on the wall which read, 'Please leave the tree alone – Thanks. After all as that Gaelic phrase "Cha neil i beag boidheach no mor granda" goes, "She is neither tiny and pretty nor big and beautiful".'

While I was washing up after a dinner a cheerful young couple on a walking holiday arrived and pitched their tent near mine. They introduced themselves as Marilyn and Doug Graham from Durham and we sat in the sun and talked until the midges came out for their evening's sport. The ponies had wandered along the shore to inspect the grass around the ruins of an old house called Finishaig and I walked over to see if the hobbles were secure. In its day it must have been a thriving little holding with neat, walled-off fields reaching down to the loch, but it looked as if it had been abandoned in a hurry. Rusty bedsteads lay scattered in the neglected grass and half hidden in a clump of nettles was a large cast-iron cooking pot of the type that used to hang from a tripod over a peat fire. There was an atmosphere of tragedy about the place and I had a feeling that the last tenants might have been victims of the Highland Clearances, when hundreds of people were evicted from their homes and left to starve to death by the lairds.

As the sun dipped behind the hills and the long shadows of evening advanced across the calm surface of the loch, I walked slowly back along the shore listening to the call of the sea birds and the soft hiss of the tide rolling pebbles up the beach. Snug in my sleeping bag, it was the same sounds that lulled me to sleep.

I woke to an absolutely gorgeous morning with burnished gold hills reflected in the perfectly calm surface of the blue loch. There was not a sound in the still air and I sat for a long time at the tent door, transfixed by the breath-takingly beautiful scene before me. It was almost sacrilege to break the silence with the roar of the Primus stove, but in a way the aroma of my breakfast coffee added to the flavour of the morning. Although I was up very early, there was no chance of leaving until the tide ebbed at about ten o'clock and uncovered a path along the beach that would take us from Morar to Knoydart and the mountain pass to Inverie. I was quite happy to be forced to stay a little longer in such a lovely place and when Marilyn and Doug left to climb Sgurr na Ciche I spread my wet clothes and boots out in the sun. By the time the tide had uncovered the beach the clothes and boots were dry. At eleven o'clock, with everything stowed in the bags and fastened to the pack saddle, we were on our way. Normally, I would check the ponies' feet before setting off each morning. On that morning I forgot and it proved to be a very stupid mistake.

At the end of the beach a headland jutting into the loch

forced us to leave the shingle and climb through high bracken swarming with flies to a high knoll with a view over the salt flats at the estuary of the River Carnoch. According to the map there was a bridge, but a glance through the binoculars revealed posts on either side of the river with nothing in the middle. I could now understand why there was a note in the Sourlies bothy warning travellers that several people had been lost trying to cross the Carnoch when it was in spate. A thin path dropped off the knoll onto the salt flats and I steered Thor in and out of an expanse of pools and ditches until we reached the river. It was about two feet deep but surprisingly Thor and Lucy walked straight in and waded across without hesitating. I suppose that after the ford at the end of Glendessary they felt they could tackle anything. On the opposite bank I searched for a path leading to the ruin of Carnoch, but the path that existed when the man from the Ordnance Survey first came along with his theodolite had long since fallen into the river and I had a few hair-raising moments when it looked as if the ponies might do the same. At the gaunt ruins of Carnoch Farm, with its remaining gable end pointing defiantly at the sky, I halted to relieve Lucy of some of her load and tie it to Thor's saddle. The path climbed from Carnoch to the summit of Mam Meadail, rising from sea level to over a thousand feet very quickly and it would be a long pull for the ponies.

Thick cloud drifted across the hills and hid the sun as I led the way up the hill through springy bog myrtle and broken rock, but the air was very warm and within minutes the ponies were soaked in sweat. At first I could not find the path in the thick heather and I blundered about for ages before I eventually discovered it much higher up the hill that I had anticipated. Lucy kept stopping and it took a good heave on the lead rope to get her moving again. The path snaked up the hill at a fairly reasonable gradient and soon Carnoch shrank to the size of a toy house. I had a fine view across to the sharp peak of Sgurr na Ciche. Through the binoculars I could see two minute figures toiling up the final ridge: I wondered if it might be Doug and Marilyn.

Lucy kept stopping every few yards but though I checked and rechecked her back for signs of chafing or sores I could find nothing wrong. At times I became very cross with her; she just stared glumly at the ground and moved forward when I pulled her lead rope.

'Lucy, what the hell is wrong with you?' I said angrily when she stopped for the umpteenth time in half an hour. Her large brown eyes were trying to tell me something, but what? 'Look,' I said coaxingly, 'I'll put another of your packs on Thor and it will give you a rest.' She seemed relieved to have the load reduced but she still kept stopping. At last, in thick mist, we reached the top of the pass and I called a halt for half an hour and unloaded the ponies and let them graze. I watched Lucy carefully but she seemed fine. There was rain in the mist and I sat against a rock drinking a mug of orange and letting the drizzle cool my steaming face. A shaft of sunlight pierced the mist like a laser beam, then another and another. Almost in an instant the rain cloud dissolved, revealing a superb view down Glen Meadail to the glistening waters of Inverie Bay and beyond to the Isle of Skye.

Reaching for my camera, I spotted several blobs of red on the path where Lucy had been standing. 'It looks like blood,' I said to myself as I lifted the camera to take a photograph. Then I froze. Blood! Lucy must be bleeding. I jumped to my feet and went over to her. There was no obvious sign of bleeding but when I walked her along the track she limped slightly on her right foreleg. Lifting the leg up, I found a swelling and a small cut that had dried up, but had opened again with the effort of walking up the pass. I put my arm round her. 'Lucy,' I said, 'I really am sorry for calling you all those nasty names. I'm a stupid idiot for not checking your feet before we set out.' I knew exactly what had caused it. The previous evening at Sourlies the midges had plagued the life out of her and as she dashed madly round wearing hobbles, the leather had cut into her leg. The swelling was more serious than the cut and it looked as if it would take several days rest before she would be sound again. I cursed loudly; I had been going less than a week after their recovery from coughing and now it seemed the journey was going to grind to a halt again. Soaking a rag in water, I cleaned and dried the cut and covered it with antibiotic powder. I loaded all the packs onto Thor and let him follow while I led Lucy slowly down the glen, wincing for her every time she slipped on a rock or plunged her leg into a wet patch. In contrast to the winding route from Carnoch, the path in Glen Meadail contoured gently down. Near the foot of the glen it crossed the Allt Gleann Meadail by a bridge and I was faced with an awkward problem. The bridge had been built on stones high above the water to prevent it being washed away and a steep ramp led up to it. On the far side, however, the ramp was missing, leaving a drop of about three feet onto a heap of boulders. It took a long time to coax Lucy down and prevent her landing heavily on her sore leg, but I managed it by building a ramp of pieces of wood and stones. A good path led to a rickety-looking bridge crossing the Inverie river, but both ponies walked over without hesitating. The sun was very hot and swarms of flies bombarded us as Lucy limped slowly along with Thor close behind. A wide track wound through a plantation of tall trees and joined a tarmac road near Inverie House. A young lad on a motorcycle stopped to ask where I was heading. I explained that I had a lame pony and was looking for the estate factor to ask if he would let me rest her in a field for a few days. He said the factor's office was a mile away and he would go and ask him for me. An hour went by and I thought he had forgotten about me. Then he came roaring back with a message that I could camp and put the ponies in a field near the factor's house. Leaning his bike against a wall, he led Thor through a little collection of houses at Inverie and past the pier to a field with two ponies in it. I was a bit apprehensive about the usual display of kicking and squealing that happens when strange horses are put together but I had little option.

'What's your name?' I asked the lad as he helped to unload the ponies.

'I'm Angus MacRae, my dad works on the estate.'

'Do you like living here?' I said.

'Och well, it's all right,' he replied guardedly, 'but it's a wee bit quiet. I think I'd rather live in Mallaig.'

Before turning Lucy into the field I wrapped a large poultice soaked in seawater round her leg to reduce the swelling. Bad leg or not, she immediately lashed out at a nice chestnut gelding who came to say hullo. I pitched the tent in a corner of the field and walked back to the pier with Angus. Pointing to a new building he said, 'You can get a drink in there if you join the club. I'm away home for tea now,' and with that he went to collect his bike.

Having signed the visitors book and handed over ten pence, I became a fully paid-up member of the Inverie Social Club and ordered a pint of beer and a packet of crisps. I was so dry the beer never touched the sides as I poured it down my throat and within seconds of ordering the first one, I was back at the bar asking for another. The bar lady gave me a knowing look that said she knew I was a twenty pints a night man the moment I walked in. Little did she know that I am not all that fond of beer and after as little as two and a half pints I am ready to go to sleep.

While I sipped and looked across the bay at the darkening hills on the Morar peninsula, a group of men came in and crowded round the bar. One of them came over to me and asked how the lame pony was. I laughed and said she would be all right, but how did he know about it.

'Och man,' he said, 'ye canny even go for a pee in this place without someone seeing you! aye and better than that, they can tell you how big it is!' The crowd round the bar roared with laughter, then launched into a heated discussion about football. The door opened again and this time a brisk, military-looking chap in plus fours came in with two girls in their teens.

'It's Nigel Macdonald, the owner,' hissed my friend. 'That man is a real gentleman.'

I watched with interest as he sat at the bar and chatted with the estate workers. I expected to hear polite, patronising conversation, the set piece of his one visit to the club during his annual holiday. But I was wrong. He was natural and relaxed and talked enthusiastically about a particular stretch of river he intended to fish that night. No one in the room seemed at all overawed by his presence, yet it was obvious he was well respected. As he left amid a chorus of 'Goodnights' from the men, I felt it was a pity that more employers did not have his gift for communication.

The interest the crowd round the bar showed in my journey kept me in the club longer than I intended and as a result of having too many glasses of liquid hospitality, I woke next day with a fearsome headache. I could not face breakfast when I eventually crawled out of my sleeping bag at midday and strolled down to the pier to take a few photographs.

A ship's siren out in the bay announced the approach of the ferry from Mallaig. As it was low tide the ferry, a large fishing vessel, could not come alongside the pier and passengers and stores had to be rowed ashore in a dinghy. I helped to carry crates of milk, an assortment of boxes and a mail sack up to the village shop. Loaded with bodies and rucksacks, the tiny dinghy was almost awash but the crewman rowed gently and soon everyone was aboard the ferry. With a farewell blast on its siren, the fishing vessel steamed in a wide arc and set course for Mallaig. The newly arrived passengers were enthusiastically greeted by friends. Among them was John Laming, the stalker from Morvern. He had come over with his wife, Jeanette, to compete in an annual clay pigeon shoot, due to take place the next day. Friends whisked John and his wife away and I walked across to the factor's office to thank him for the use of the field. He greeted me very warmly and insisted I went home with him to meet his wife and have a meal. They refused to let me sleep in the tent and went to a great deal of trouble to give me a room in the house and said that I was welcome to stay until Lucy was fit again. I shall never be able to repay Sandy Macdonald and his wife, Patricia, for their kindness. Had providence not led me to them, my journey may well have been abandoned. When I looked at Lucy's leg that evening, the lump had burst and Patricia helped me to clean out the pus and treat it with antiseptic.

Early the next morning the ferry from Mallaig, crammed with men carrying shotguns and large plastic bags full of beer cans. They had come to take part in Inverie's biggest event of the calendar, the annual Open Clay Pigeon Shoot. I recognised a number of faces from my youthful days in Glen Moriston and several figures in full Highland dress provided a splash of colour among the tweed suits. Almost as soon as the first boat had emptied its passengers, another one arrived and I joined the throng as they made their way up to a field on the east side of Inverie House. While the estate

Renewing worn shoes — Glen
Garry

Merchard's Font, Glen
Moriston

Culachy House, Fort Augustus

Start of the Lairig Ghru Pass in the Cairngorms

Almost 3,000 feet above sea level. The summit of the Lairig Ghru Pass

workers tested the clay pigeon traps, the competitors queued excitedly at a small hut to fill in entry forms. Old friends shook hands and greeted each other in Gaelic. Hip flasks were being passed from hand to hand and already the red flush betraying a large intake of Scotland's national beverage was spreading across the faces of many of the spectators. Casual jeans and the vivid colours of nylon anoraks clashed horribly with the traditional plus-four suits of the stalkers and shepherds, each tweed identifying a particular estate. A small group of intense-looking types, lovingly caressing expensive automatic shotguns, were dressed even more garishly than the anorak brigade: in multi-coloured jockey caps with long peaks and windproof jackets covered in large American-style badges. These were the clay pigeon fanatics, whose whole life was devoted to the sport and who followed shoots all over Britain. The locals, some of them with very antiquated guns, might well have felt rather inferior to these grizzly professionals, but no one seemed to care.

The weather was fine although the sky was overcast and it was very humid. It was a perfect day for midges and they made the best of it. Every midge in Knoydart descended on the field and everyone was scratching furiously and rubbing midge repellent onto faces, necks and arms. An announcement was made that the shoot was about to start and the crowd hushed while someone made an opening speech. I was standing on the back of the crowd. In front of me, listening intently and looking very important, complete with feathered bonnets and leaning on ornate shepherd's crooks, were a number of clan patriarchs in Highland dress. The midges, spying bare flesh, zoomed around the kilts and the old gentlemen were obviously suffering considerable pain, but being men of standing and importance they could hardly resort to anything as common as having a good scratch. Finally, the most ancient of the ancients, a bent figure with white hair who could have been St Columba himself, could stand it no longer. Looking round furtively, he hung his crook over his arm and pulling a large aerosol tin of flyspray out of his pocket of his tweed jacket, squirted a long blast up his kilt then, as if nothing had happened, returned to leaning on his shepherd's crook. To my astonishment, the next old gentleman did the same and then the next, each returning to listen intently and look important, leaning on his crook. Watching a line of serious, elderly Highlanders calmly squirting flyspray up their kilts was the funniest sight I have seen in a long time and I laughed so much I forgot to take a photograph.

When the shoot got under way the smell of cordite hung in the air and the hills reverberated with the volley of shots as the competitors at the butts shouted 'Pull' and the clay discs whizzed into the air. A group of young bloods arrived sporting cowboy hats, one or two with the regulation Clint Eastwood cigarillo dangling, unlit, from the corner of their mouths. They fired shot after shot without as much as knocking a sliver off a 'bird'. One red-faced youth departed with the scorn of his attractive girlfriend ringing in his ears:

'I say, you'll really have to learn to shoot a lot better than that if you want to meet my parents. Daddy is frightfully keen on shooting.'

The next group were the badge and jockey cap boys who were so accurate in their shooting I could not see how the judge was able to decide who was the winner.

My ears were beginning to feel the affect of the barrage so I walked across to the refreshment tent where the wives of the estate workers were doing a roaring trade in cups of tea and venison sandwiches. John Laming was drinking tea and talking to an oldish chap and he shouted me to join them.

'I've got to go and shoot now,' he said to me, 'but let me introduce you to Donald MacDonald. He and his wife live at the loneliest post office in Britain, it's just down the loch at Tarbet, on Morar. There can't be many post offices without a telephone.' And with that he dashed off into the crowd.

Donald said he had heard about my journey with the ponies and asked what it was like coming through Glendessary. He shook his head when I told him about the rough time we had had.

'It's a terrible shame the way that old route has been left to get into the state it is,' he said, 'I can remember sheep and cattle being driven through there to Loch Arkaig and on to Fort William in the 1930s and it was a good path.'

I asked if he knew anything about the ruin at Finishaig.

'No, it has always been a ruin as far as I can remember,' he replied, 'but did you see the buildings at Carnoch?'

I said I had gone past on my way over Mam Meadaill.

'Well,' he continued, 'that was once a farm, but Crosthwaite-Eyre, who was the laird then, had it destroyed because poachers were living in it and helping themselves to the salmon in the river.'

Several of Donald's friends came to talk to him. Glad to leave the noise of the clay pigeon shoot behind, I strolled back to the pier. Across the far side of the bay I could see a white object sticking up on the headland.

'Is that a lighthouse?' I asked a man who was working on the pier.

'Hell no,' he replied, laughing, 'it's a statue of the Madonna with her arms outstretched, but I don't know whether she's blessing the loch or telling us about the one that got away!' He dragged a few boxes to the end of the pier then came back again.

'You've set me thinking now,' he said, staring across the bay. 'I'm a Catholic myself and yet in all the time I've lived here I've never actually been up to that statue. I do know it's built of fibreglass and it was put there by Sir Oliver Crosthwaite-Eyre, who owned the estate some years ago.'

Later that evening, I was relaxing in the depths of an armchair in Sandy Macdonald's lounge. We listened to records and helped the music along with well-filled glasses of whisky.

To the Highlander, drinking whisky comes as naturally as drinking tea. It has been the drink of the country for so long there was a time when the clergy were undecided whether the drinking of tea or the drinking of whisky was the most depraved. One minister is said to have salved his conscience and that of his parishioners by pouring a little whisky into the cup 'to correct all the bad effects of the tea'.

It was often said that drinking whisky in a cold, damp climate like that of Scotland was good for the health. It is probably as a result of this belief that the name whisky evolved, first from the Latin *aqua vitae* (water of life) and then the Gaelic equivalent, *uisge beatha*, which became the anglicised 'whisky'. The claim that it was good for the health was probably, as it still is today, only an excuse for drinking large quantities of it. The outlandish claim for the power of *uisge beatha* in Holinshed's *Chronicles of England, Scotland and Ireland*, published in 1579, sounds like a quote from an early whisky advertisement: 'Beying moderatlie taken, it sloweth age, it strengtheneth youth, it helpeth digestion, it cutteth flume, it abandoneth melancholie, it reliseth the harte, it lighteneth the mynde, it quickeneth the spirites, it cureth the hydropsie, it healeth the stranguary, it pounceth the stone, it repelleth gravel, it puffeth awaie ventosotie, it kepyth and preserveth the head from whyrling – the eyes from dezelyng – the tongue from lyspyng – the mouth from snafflyng – the teeth from chatteryng – the throte from rattlyng, the weasan from stieflyng – the stomach from wamblyng the harte from swellyng – the bellie from wirtchyng – the guts from rumblyng the hands from shiveryng – the sinowes from shrynkyng – the veynes from crumplyng – the bones from soakyng ... trulie it is a soveraigne liquor.'

If whisky could achieve all that, then, at 1s 10d a Scots pint in 1770, it is hardly surprising the Highlanders consumed it in large quantities. A French traveller, Louis Simond, observed that a Highlander drank a quart a day. In the early eighteenth century one William Larkin noted that, 'Whisky is to the full as much a staple commodity as black cattle, sheep and wool ... and the smuggling of whisky is the only resource for the regular payment of rents.' The landlords may well have taken whisky as a payment of rent, but it was not a drink favoured by the gentry and they probably sold it elsewhere. The upper class palate preferred French brandy or claret and even humble ale and beer were considered superior to locally distilled whisky. What the gentry disliked about it was its raw taste. According to Fynnes Moryson, a sixteenth-century traveller, there was whisky available in the isles that had been distilled four times and was so strong that as little as two spoonsful could endanger a man's life. That vitriolic observer, Dr Johnson, during his travels with Boswell in the Western Isles, tasted the native *uisge beatha*, but was not impressed and commented, 'It was strong, but not pungent, and was free

from the emypreumatick taste or smell. What was the
process I had no opportunity of inquiring, nor do I wish to
improve the art of making poison pleasant.'

As the distillation process improved, so the demand for the
Highlander's 'water of life' increased and inevitably
Government, in the shape of excisemen, saw it as a new source
of revenue. Stills were raided and destroyed, but it only made
the distillers more determined not to lose a good source of
income. Illicit stills sprang up in remote glens and in caves in
the hills. Smuggling became big business and strings of pack
ponies carried whisky all over Scotland. Joseph Mitchell, who
was engineer to the Commissioners for Highland roads in the
early nineteenth century, was inspecting the road through
Glenmoriston when he met a band of smugglers with a string
of twenty-five ponies, each loaded with two kegs of whisky.
Luckily, he was able to convince the smugglers that he was not
an exciseman or he might have ended up as part of the
foundations of his road.

The Honourable Mrs Murray, the author of *Murray's
Beauties of Scotland*, wrote 'the Highlanders were stout men but
will do anything for whisky.' Could it have been this same
lady who started the first Ben Nevis race? According to a local
tale, a fashionable lady, having climbed Ben Nevis,
deliberately left a bottle of whisky on the summit. When she
returned to Fort William she laughingly mentioned it to a few
locals and they immediately rushed off, competing with each
other to be the first to reach the bottle.

The present-day highly inflated price of whisky does little to
deter the Highlander from drinking lots of it, often with tragic
social consequences. If Scottish policemen were promoted
according to the number of successful convictions for 'driving
under the influence', then a new recruit standing outside
Inverness sheep sale could rise to be Chief Constable within
the year. But to ask a Highlander to give up his dram is like
asking the French to declare Vichy water their national drink
or telling Rasputin he could satisfy his sexual drive by reading
Playboy.

Lucy's leg had almost fully recovered when I inspected it

the following day and I decided to leave immediately for Loch Hourn. Although I could have lived at Inverie quite happily for ever more, I had set out to make a journey through the Highlands and I intended to complete it. With luck I might even manage to cross to the Isle of Skye and explore the Cuillins. Rain had been threatening all morning and a tremendous deluge swept across Inverie Bay as I packed the tent so that I wished I had done it the previous day in the sunshine. Clouds of midges drove me frantic as I splashed about in the rain, thumping wet canvas into a manageable roll and trying to keep my sleeping bag dry. Even though I plastered my skin with midge cream, the little brutes burrowed through it and by the time I had dumped the packs in a shed at the edge of the field my face was covered with lumps and looked like a relief model of the Himalayas. Even inside the shed there was no escape from the midges and they gathered in a thick cloud on the window. Finding a tin of aerosol fly spray on a shelf, I squirted prolonged bursts at them like a half-crazed soldier whose nerve snaps under the strain of combat so that he leaps from the trenches wildly firing his machine gun at the enemy. With sadistic glee I watched them plunge, writhing to the floor, as I fired burst after burst of deadly pyretheum into the fiendish hordes. Drunk with power, I pressed the button again and again, annihilating the battalions on the window ledge and repaying some of the misery they had caused me. The ground troops dealt with, I turned on the airborne division, but my trusty aerosol gave a gasp and dribbled at the nozzle. I had run out of ammunition. Flinging the can to the ground, I ran through the rain to the estate office.

In the office, Sandy and I stared miserably through the window at the grey rain sweeping across the bay.

'You can't leave in this,' he said. 'Stay another night and I'll run your packs and saddles up to the Black Lochan tomorrow. It will take the strain off Lucy for at least five miles.'

Listening to the wind howling around the roof, I did not need a lot of persuading.

'It's a good opportunity to go and see John MacKay,' Sandy continued. 'I told him you might call.'

John MacKay was a retired shepherd who lived with his

brother, James, in the village. He had lived all his life on the estate and I wanted to ask him about his early days as a shepherd.

The MacKays lived in a row of estate cottages and, with typical Highland courtesy, they invited me to sit by the fire and handed me a glass of whisky. James was more at home with Gaelic than English and though I tried out my rusty Gaelic, learnt in Lewis many years ago, I soon exhausted my vocabulary and John did most of the talking. I always enjoy hearing about life in the remote communities before the arrival of television and radio and John told me about the ceilidhs they had in each other's houses. Anyone who could sing, play an instrument or tell a good story was in great demand. The shepherds and crofters would travel miles to a ceilidh and they were always held on the night of a full moon so people could find their way home. The invention of the electric torch with dry batteries increased the scope for winter visiting during the long nights.

'I remember buying my first torch in Mallaig,' said John, smiling as the memory of the big day came flooding back. 'But you needed a pocket full of batteries. You couldn't rely on them, they sometimes went flat after a minute or two.'

I said I could not understand why there was a post office in such a remote and inaccessible place as Tarbet on Loch Nevis. John thought for a moment.

'Ah well now, that was to do with the fishing,' he said and went on to describe how in the 1920s and 30s there was a fleet of herring drifters based at Tarbet and the post office was opened for the benefit of the fishermen. There was also a shop and an inn, and a schoolhouse at Camusrory on the Knoydart side of the loch, but they had long since closed. The fickle herring deserted Loch Nevis and the boats moved away. 'It was a sight to remember, I can tell you,' sighed John. 'We used to watch the fleet sailing into the loch, dozens of boats with black hulls and tanned sails racing back to Tarbet. Those days are finished, they'll never come back.'

He stopped to rattle the coal in the grate with a poker and for a few minutes no one spoke. Outside the cottage the wind had reached gale force and it howled through the trees.

'*Tha an la fuar* [it's a cold day],' said James. John nodded and stared through the window at the loch, white with spume.

'It's a good job there are no boats crossing from Mallaig today,' he said quietly.

James sipped his whisky and said, 'I remember when I was a boy in Mallaig. They were just building the railway line to Fort William. Hundreds of navvies came over from Ireland and when they got their pay there would be a terrible *sabaid* [fight].'

John replied that he was working away as a shepherd at the time and he missed all the excitement.

'While I've been here I haven't seen a single sheep,' I said. 'Why did the estate sell them off?'

John drew in a sharp breath and I knew I had touched a sore spot.

'They got rid of them because there are times when the owners take too much notice of the accountants instead of listening to good sense. When I was a shepherd there were eight thousand sheep on Knoydart and the laird sold the lot. They brought in a good return and buyers came from all over when there were Knoydart sheep in the sale. The subsidy alone was worth more than they get these days chasing after deer. There are times when you wonder how some of these lairds came by their fortunes, they don't seem to understand that if they want estates like this one to make money, the only chance they've got is with sheep and maybe a few head of cattle.'

John stooped to poke the fire again and I took the opportunity to change the subject and ask him about a period in the history of Knoydart about which there was been a great deal written, often with wildly differing versions.

'Were you working on the estate at the time when some of the workers tried to take over estate land?' I asked.

He looked at me quizzically for a moment, then snorted. 'Yes, I was and I wouldn't mind a pound for all the different stories I've heard about it. It was called the land raid and it happened in 1948, when Lord Brocket owned the estate. A lot of people condemn Lord Brocket and though I'm not going to say he was that good at all, I think in some ways he was made out to be worse than he was.' John eased himself more comfortably into his chair then went on, 'Well now, it's a long story, I think it all started because there was a lot of trouble about low wages and when Brocket wanted to go stalking he would take the men out of the gardens or the joiners shop or from anywhere on the estate to act as ghillies, but he would never pay them any overtime. Then about that time, a young priest came to live at Inverie and tried to get better conditions for the men. He said that a lot more could be done for Knoydart and agitated to get a road in and get more land cultivated. Well, one thing led to another and a few of them got together and decided they would take over some of Brocket's land and divide it amongst themselves as crofts. The newspapers called them the Seven Men of Knoydart, but in fact, there were eight of them and they had it well organised weeks in advance. They had arranged for reporters and photographers to come on this day and the men marched through Inverie carrying spades and scythes and hammered stakes with their name on into the ground in the fields they were taking over.' John paused for a moment and laughed as a memory of the event came back to him.

'One of the men always chewed black twist tobacco and there was a story that when Brocket was passing after the men had staked their claim he saw that one of them had picked a terrible wet piece of land for his croft. Looking at the name on the stake, Brocket remarked, "I don't think Henry will chew much black twist tobacco on what he will make out of that land." '

'What happened about the land?' I said. 'Were the men allowed to keep it?'

'Och no,' replied John, 'There was an interdict served on them. They weren't to walk on any of Brocket's land from that day. They took their case to the land court and a man by the name of John Cameron from the Department of Agriculture was sent to see if Knoydart was suitable for crofting. There was a lot of talk at the time that people would come out from the islands to work crofts in Knoydart. The priest was a Uist man and he had a scheme for the land to be divided into about forty crofts, but anyhow the decision of the land court went against them.'

'Well you've been a shepherd and crofter all your life,' I said. 'Do you think that forty crofts could have made a living?'

John stared into the fire for a while before answering. A silence fell on the room and outside the gale was increasing. The mechanism of an old clock on the wall whirred into life and struck one chime for the half hour.

'Well it's hard to say. There was a lot of bitterness over the land court's decision, but there wasn't much of a living in crofting at that time and for many a year after that.'

'So what happened to the men who tried to seize the land?' I enquired.

'Well they lost their jobs on the estate,' John replied, 'though Brocket did offer them what we call the peninsula, a piece of land between Scottas and Sandaig, for sheep grazing. But they wouldn't accept it. They wanted the whole crofts or nothing at all. Many people at the time thought they were very foolish. The ground was stocked with sheep and maybe they could have taken them over. It was very likely that Brocket would have employed them part-time on the estate again, but they refused and that was more or less the end of it.'

He looked at the clock on the wall and checked the time against his watch. 'I'll make a drop of tea,' he said, climbing stiffly to his feet and rummaging through a cupboard for cups and teapot. Scones and jam appeared from another cupboard and while he waited for the kettle to boil he sank back into his chair by the fire.

'It's interesting to hear a first-hand account of the land raid,' I said, 'but what about Lord Brocket himself, he seems to have had a very bad reputation. What was he really like?'

John did not hesitate with his answer this time. 'He was a shrewd man, I'll say that about him, but he was a hard man too. He had plenty of money, y'know, but he would fight for a sixpence sooner than fight for a hundred pounds. He wasn't bad to the workers, it was just that the wages were small and we were only paid every six months. The best I ever had was twenty-four pounds for the half year and two pounds came out of that for National Insurance. Brocket's wife was a queer sort of woman though, what you would call an eccentric. She stopped the children of the estate workers playing on the sandy beach in front of the big house. Then there was a time when she was clearing out a lot of furniture from the house to take in some new stuff, but rather than give it to anybody, and there were plenty that needed it about here, she dumped it in the sea. Och the woman was very queer right enough, she didn't like coming here and she didn't like crossing in the boat from Mallaig. In fact, once or twice, maybe more, rather than spend an hour on the boat, she rode a pony to Kinloch Hourn and had a car waiting for her.'

The wail of the whistling kettle in the kitchen cut the conversation short and John set about preparing tea and handing round plates of cake and scones.

Later that evening, I read the Department of Agriculture's report on Knoydart, compiled by John A. Cameron, the Board's official, who assessed the feasibility of crofting for the land court enquiry following the Knoydart land raid. I was surprised to discover that, in 1940, part of Lord Brocket's estate on Knoydart had been requisitioned by the Government because he had not responded to a request for his deer forest to make a contribution to the nation's food supply. A year later, the estate agreed to take part in the scheme and the land was returned to its owner. The results, however, were not a success and in the words of the report, 'tended to create in the mind of the estate a defeatist attitude towards food reproduction from these hills'. Read 'between the lines' the report gave me the impression that if the author had been able to come down on the side of the crofters, he would have done so, but the facts were inescapable. 'For so large an area there is a very small amount of land capable of cultivation or the provision of winter feed for cattle ... the absence of "mossing" to any extent limits its sheep-raising capabilities to a moderate type ewe and a moderate lambing percentage ... I do not recommend development as separate units indicated in the Department of Agriculture scheme, featuring nineteen holdings, nor under the Father Macpherson Scheme, featuring forty holdings ... cost would be out of proportion to production results, and the livelihood would be certainly insecure and with little comfort.' The report went on to recommend that Knoydart should be developed as a single farming and sporting unit by Lord Brocket, but the let off for the estate had a sting in its tail. If by the end of ten years the estate had not achieved and maintained a stocking target of sheep and cattle, then the property was to be compulsorily purchased and handed over to the Forestry Commission.

John Cameron ended his report with a touch of benevolence all too rare among officialdom. 'I regret the nature of my report, as I am well aware that the natural instinct of Highlanders is to have their own individual holdings, both for cultivation and the raising of stock, rather than for wage-earning employment, whether in agriculture or forestry, but I cannot see that it would be in their interests to recommend the development of such holdings in Knoydart.'

The weather forecast in the evening reported storm-force winds and devastation in the English Channel, but promised better things to come for Scotland. I went to bed early to make the most of a comfortable mattress and clean sheets. Soon it would be back to a sleeping bag and lying on the hard ground.

18

Loch Hourn and Near Disaster

The weather man's prophecy was right. When I sprang out of bed the following morning the sun was streaming through the windows and I lost no time in saddling the ponies and setting off for Loch Hourn. It was gorgeous to feel the warmth of the sun but it was short-lived. By the time the Black Lochan came into sight, the sky had turned to ink and rain was sweeping in from the sea. To ease the strain on Lucy on her first day out, I loaded one of the packs onto Thor's saddle. Keen to be on my way before the weather worsened, I led the ponies into the downpour and along a good path that climbed steadily to the summit of Mam Barrisdale. The thick cloud lifted briefly to allow me to look down on Loch Hourn, but it was only a tempting glimpse and the veil of rain soon closed round me again.

All the way up, the surface of the path and the bridges were in good condition, but on the Barrisdale side the path had been dreadfully neglected and years of floods had washed away the surface and reduced it to a quagmire. I had a few anxious moments negotiating yards of peat bog that had once been a path. Gaping holes where bridges had crossed the fast-flowing streams caused more problems and the only solution was to wade into the water and lead the ponies after me. The heavy rain found its way through my jacket and by the time I had coaxed the ponies through a quarter of a mile of bog and reached level ground I was thoroughly wet. There was a new bungalow close to a range of outbuildings at Barrisdale and when a young girl opened the door I asked if I could camp and graze the ponies. She consulted her mother who said I would not need to camp as they had a bothy and it would be fifty pence for the night. It was a relief not to have to pitch the tent in the rain and I carried the packs into the bothy kitchen. It boasted a calor gas cooker, a Rayburn and even a bath and toilet, but no firewood. Changing into dry clothing, I sat in the kitchen with a mug of hot tea. I felt quite homesick for Inverie and missed the company of Sandy and Patricia enormously.

'You've gone soft with all that good living,' I told myself and set about preparing the beef curry mix for dinner.

A young lad came to tell me that his father said I could turn the ponies into a field behind the bungalow. He helped me to take the saddles off and led Thor while I followed with Lucy.

It was fairly late in the evening and I hoped I would have the bothy to myself to catch up on my notes. However, as it was going dark there was a crash at the door and three walkers burst in, laden with packs. Two of them were quite pleasant but the third was a loud-mouthed 'know-all' for whom nothing was right. He had an answer for everything and expounded his views on subjects ranging from compulsory euthanasia (he considered that people over sixty were a burden to society) to the repopulation of the Highlands.

'And how would you set about achieving that?' I asked.

'Dead easy mate. All the land in places like this should be taken off the owners and divided into small-holdings and given to people who want to be self-sufficient.'

'But if nothing will grow because the ground is sour and it's all peat and rock, what then?' I said.

'All it needs is patience,' he replied in his 'know-all' way.

'And some knowledge of agriculture, surely?' I persisted.

'The trouble with people like you, mate,' he sneered, 'is that you're defeatist and when the revolution comes you'll be the first up against the wall. You must be a bloody capitalist anyway to have time to wander round on a horse.' He rounded on his companions, 'I came with you two to camp, only pouffs stay in bothies. Let's pitch the tents.'

Seizing his pack he marched out into the dark and the pouring rain.

'I'm fed up with him and his mouth,' said one of his friends.

'Well you asked him to come,' retorted the other.

'I know,' was the reply, 'but he's been out on strike for weeks and he was hanging round with nothing to do. Come on let's go and pitch the tents.'

Out they went into the night and left me to finish my dinner in peace.

A bedroom contained two bunks with very dubious-looking mattresses and I spread my sleeping bag on the less evil of the pair. An eerie wind sprang up and moaned round the building, rattling the doors, and it took me ages to drop off to sleep. I was jolted awake by a loud crunching noise. When I switched my torch on the crunching stopped. I looked at my watch, it was 3 am. As soon as I switched the torch off the crunching started again. I shone the torch under the bed and found a lump of polythene sheet wedged in a hole in the wall and something on the other side was doing its best to pull it through. I banged on the wall and the crunching stopped. I was nicely dozing off when it started again. I banged the wall again and the crunching stopped but started up again a few minutes later. Looking under the bed, I could see whatever it was had now dragged most of the polythene into the wall. Climbing out of my sleeping bag, I crawled under the bed and pushed the rest of the polythene into the hole. The crunching stopped. I shone my torch into the hole and waited. A large mouse stuck its head out and looked at me.

'Perhaps now we can both get some sleep,' I said. The mouse gave a loud squeak and shot back inside the hole. I was not disturbed again.

After a night of continuous rain, the whole glen glistened with running water and Thor and Lucy stood huddled behind a wall. 'Know-all's' tent had leaked and a stream of four-letter expletives let the world know his feelings about camping and Scottish weather. An uncomfortable night had drastically changed the views he expressed the previous evening and now, 'no one in their right effing mind would want to live in such an effing awful country. No wonder the effing Scots drink a lot, this place would drive anyone to drink.' This new outburst was obviously the last straw for his companions and half an hour later when 'know-all' staggered up the path heading for Inverie, they departed in the opposite direction.

Discovering that the gas stove had a grill, I toasted a few slices of the bread Patricia had given to me. I longed for some cheese to put on it but a piece I had been carrying with me for weeks was coated with a green hairy substance. It seemed a shame to throw it away, so I pushed it into the hole for the mouse. I stood at the bothy door drinking my mug of tea, wondering whether I should brave the weather or stay another night, when a dazzling sun pierced the cloud, creating a gigantic brilliant rainbow that arched across the glen like the entrance to a mythical kingdom. Slowly the rainbow faded into the hills and the clouds rolled back revealing a Mediterranean blue sky and a hot sun that raised clouds of steam from the waterlogged grass. Swiftly loading the ponies, I paid my fifty pence overnight charge to the shepherd's wife and hurried Thor along a wide track past Barrisdale House and along the edge of the bay to a headland. Here the path turned right to climb a short steep hill with a fine view down the loch to the Sound of Sleat. Loch Hourn is an odd-shaped loch resembling a bent funnel, the wide mouth being the Sound of Sleat. The bent spout, at the end of which is Barrisdale Bay, is about six miles long. On the right-hand edge of the spout, the headland where I was standing, the loch narrowed to less than half its width and continued for a further six miles, to Kinloch Hourn.

A glance at the map will reveal that Loch Nevis and Loch Hourn are surprisingly similar in shape and, like Loch Nevis, Loch Hourn once had a thriving herring fishing industry. During his travels in the Highlands in 1786, John Knox saw 'from eighty to one hundred herring busses, packing and curing the gleanings of their late captures. Towards the upper part, the loch is divided into reaches or sections, and in the very uppermost of these, the herrings are usually caught in sixteen fathoms water ... They fish in the daytime and some persons have been driving the herrings into the nets with their oars. They frequently intermingle their nets and are obliged to cut them with knives before they are separated ... Though Loch Urn is a capital herring fishery, it has no other recommendation as a proper station for a town. The hills rise to a great height on both sides and all intercourse with the inland country is nearly cut off, consequently there are few inhabitants on this water.'

When herring fishing came to an end and the boats left,

never to return, the agricultural life at Barrisdale carried on much the same as it had done for generations. Estate owners have come and gone, but today, as in John Knox's time, there are still very few inhabitants. The weather does not seem to have changed much either. Knox reported that 'In order to preserve the trifling crops of grain that are raised here, the corn is carried in wet weather and as soon as it is cut down, into barns built with wicker, where it is dried by means of sifting the air.'

Loch Hourn is fortunate that it is considerably less accessible than Loch Ness, otherwise it might have been subjected to a similar amount of commercialised razzmatazz, attracted by the story of a strange creature seen swimming across the loch on a bright sunny day in 1872. A party of six people cruising on Loch Hourn on board the cutter *Leda* saw, on 20th and 21st August, what appeared to be a line of black humps, sometimes three or four, long and fat, or at other times, seven or eight, smaller and more rounded. The cruising party observed the creature with the naked eye and through a telescope at a distance of between one hundred and two hundred yards, and at other times moving rapidly some distance away. They estimated that it was forty-five feet long when eight humps were visible and sixty feet when four humps were visible. As far as I am aware, it has not been seen in Loch Hourn since, so perhaps it was Nessy herself, enjoying a breath of sea air and a meal or two of fat west coast herring. When I looked down on the loch from my resting-place on the headland, the only thing disturbing the otherwise mirror surface were two cormorants arriving in the bay on a fishing expedition.

Heaving the protesting Thor and Lucy off a patch of succulent grass, I picked my way cautiously along an extremely wet and boggy path. I was so intent on preventing the ponies from stepping into holes, I did not have much chance to admire the view. While crossing a bridge Thor put a hind leg through the rotting timbers and I had a terrible time calming him down while I cut away the spongy wood and lifted his foot out. The path descended to the edge of the loch and followed a most delightful route beneath Scots pine and birch, close to the water's edge or high above it where a slip would have been disastrous. For most of this section the path was safe, but there were many signs of erosion. If something is not done it will become impassable to horses and one of the most beautiful and exciting bridleways in the Highlands will be lost.

Curving away from the loch, the path had been cut into the hillside above the old building of Runival, once a schoolhouse. It was almost a ruin when I last visited it in the late 1950s, but it had been restored to a dwelling and smoke curled from a chimney. The path climbed steeply again and the ponies had difficulty finding a foothold in a jumble of soft peat and rounded pebbles gouged out by the rain. A group of women and children were making their way down towards us and Thor and Lucy were soon the centre of attention, gobbling sweets and pieces of chocolate as though they had not eaten for a week. I was surprised to discover that one of the ladies was the wife of Christopher Hanson-Smith, the National Trust's Public Relations Officer in the English Lake District, and she invited me to join their party for supper that evening at Kinloch Hourn Lodge. It was only when the last sweet and piece of chocolate had vanished that the ponies could be persuaded to continue to climb and in a welter of sweat and flying stones we reached the top and rested. I could hardly believe my eyes when I looked round to see a chap with a pick and shovel busily digging drains.

'I think you'll reach retirement age long before you reach Barrisdale,' I said, laughing.

He smiled and replied, 'I'm only attempting the worst bits on this section of the path. It's becoming quite difficult to reach Runival. I've had the lease of the house for several years and each summer when I come to stay for a few weeks I find that the path has got worse.'

We sat and talked about Runival and in the course of the conversation he told me his name was Mark Stevenson and he was a history master at Winchester School. He was upset that someone had stolen all his oil lamps out of the house while he had been away. To prevent walkers breaking the door in to find shelter for the night, he left the house unlocked with a note inside informing people they were welcome to stay but asking them to treat the house with care.

'That's the sort of thanks you get these days,' said Mark sorrowfully.

Leaving him to carry on with his draining, I led the ponies down a very steep hill to the edge of the loch, only to climb again, up a wet, boulder-strewn path, to a tremendous viewpoint. Both Thor and Lucy were tired and, as there was plenty of grass it was a good place to turn them loose to graze while I assembled the stove and made coffee. Sitting with my back to a rock, I was able to enjoy a rare view of the lower end of the loch. The bright sun illuminated every tree and rock as far as the eye could see. Along the shore I could make out the ruins of the many crofts that eked out a living in days gone by. The amazing thing was that people living among the mountains endured incredible hardships, yet often lived to a very old age. They had no elixir of life, the secret was contentment.

'The mountayne men live longer manie a yeere,
Than those in vale, in playne, or moorish style;
A lustie hart a clean complexion cleere,
They have an hill that for hard living toyle,
With ewe and lamb, with goats and kids they play,
In greatest toyles to rub out wearie day;
And when to house and home good fellows drawe,
The lads can laugh at turning of a straw.'

The warmth of the sun and the peace lulled me to sleep. Two hours later I woke with a jerk and remembered that the ponies were not tethered. I jumped quickly to my feet, but the grass was good and they were still where I had left them. Loading the ponies, I followed a rough, wet path slanting down to the loch and a fence surrounding Skiary House. At one time Skiary was an inn and it shows how important the Barrisdale to Kinloch Hourn path must have been in the days of the drovers. I am not sure when Skiary ceased to be an inn, but it was certainly open in April 1897 when a party of Scottish Mountaineering Club members anchored off Barrisdale in the steam yacht *Erne*. The report of the Yachting Meet for Easter 1897 records, 'The mountaineers ascended Ladhar Bheinn and Luinne Bheinn, while those who had not recovered from the voyage made boating excursions to the head of the loch and tested the resources (very limited except as regards whisky) of the hotel at Skiary.'

Climbing up again, through bracken and large boulders, the path crossed a fast-flowing stream and waterfall by an ancient wooden bridge. I went ahead to test it by jumping up and down in the middle: though it looked rather moth-eaten, it seemed sound enough. I led Lucy forward and we had reached the centre of the bridge of creaking planks when there was a loud crack and Lucy plunged through with both hind legs. She struggled furiously to pull her legs out and as she did so more planks snapped under her weight and she was in imminent danger of falling through the hole to certain death on the rocks below. Blood spurted from cuts in her legs and stained the water, but I dared not let go of the lead rope to see how badly injured she was. The packs jammed against the planks and saved her from falling and gave me the chance to pull her forelegs forward and, with her stomach resting on a sound plank, I heaved like blazes on the lead rope. Inch by inch she moved forward, her hind legs flailing as she fought to get a grip and the bridge splintering ominously. With a loud crack the plank supporting her stomach snapped like a match and she fell, dragging me along with her. Again the packs wedged in between the planks and saved her life and I lay full-length, hanging on to her head collar, looking straight down the waterfall. Lucy's whole weight hung on the girth strap of the saddle and it was only a matter of time until it snapped. Crawling back along the bridge to the bank with the lead rope, I braced my feet behind a rock and heaved with all my strength. Lucy moved forward and I prayed that the head collar or rope would not part with the strain. One of her flailing legs somehow managed to catch on one of the girders supporting the planks and she heaved herself forward, but she went too far, rolled to the very brink of the bridge and almost went over. I pulled with every ounce of strength left in me and with a lurch she dived forward and we rolled down the bank into the bracken. Blood dripped from cuts on her hind legs but happily they were not too deep and I washed and dressed them with Terramycin. She was badly shaken and I spent half an hour talking to her and feeding her with mints.

At the first hint of trouble Thor had rebounded from the

bridge and stood whinnying nervously on the far bank. Jumping across the blood-stained, splintered planking, I grabbed him and followed the edge of the stream, searching for a place to cross. Swollen by the heavy rain of the past few days, the water roared over the rocks in a tumbling mass of foam and debris and it took me ages to coax the trembling Thor through a deep pool.

When the ponies were reunited I had to wait while they snickered, rubbed noses and exchanged a few pleasantries.

'Thank goodness you're all right,' snickered Thor. 'The man's an idiot, taking you across that heap of matchwood.'

'Oh I'm all right,' snickered Lucy, 'just a fright and a graze or two. Saw you floundering about a bit in that pool. Was it deep?'

Thor always reacts to sympathy. 'Deep! I'll say it was deep. The water was splashing round my ...!'' He realised he was speaking to a lady, 'Hm, well it was deep anyway. He ought to remember I'm a land horse, not a sea horse.'

I was reluctant to break up the conversation but there was still a fair distance to go to Kinloch Hourn. Lashing one of Lucy's packs onto Thor, I led the way along a narrow path that had been hewn out of solid rock a few feet above the surface of the loch. It wound in and out of bays and inlets for perhaps a mile and, except for one awkward rock step that took a few minutes to negotiate, we reached the safety of a tarmac road leading to a range of farm buildings. I knocked on a house door and it was opened by a man I recognised as Peter MacRae, who had lived there in the 1950s when I used to ride over from Glen Moriston on my old motorcycle. He was very helpful and said I could camp for the night and put the ponies in a walled sheep pen that had plenty of grass.

I was uneasy about accepting the Hanson-Smiths' invitation to join them for supper. After being subjected to regular soakings and rapid drying-out over Primus stoves and in hospitable houses, my clothes were looking very much the worse for wear. Stitches in the seams of my trousers had rotted and I had repaired them, not very prettily, with thick sailmakers twine. The zip fastener on my flies had long given up working and was held together with the aid of a large safety pin. The dye in what had once been a plaid shirt had been bleached out and blacks, red, greens, yellows and whites had merged into a sort of seasick brown. My only pair of boots were caked in mud, as were my once grey socks. This party-going ensemble, with matching accessories of grubby sweater, weather-beaten anorak and scorched woollen balaclava helmet, were more than adequately complemented by the unmistakable lingering aroma of Parfum des Chevaux.

At eight o'clock I knocked on the imposing front door of Kinloch Hourn Lodge and was greeted very warmly by Christopher Hanson-Smith and his family. I was introduced to a seemingly endless number of relatives and friends and altogether twenty-one people sat round an enormous table to eat. It was a lively, informal affair, with food and conversation passing up and down the table, helped along by plenty of wine. The chatter had a distinct international flavour, with the polite hesitant accent of France and the precision of Germany mingling with varying shades of English, in discussions ranging from World politics to the fishing prospects of the loch. The meal over, we crowded into the library, a marvellous room lined with leather-bound books and furnished with well-used settees and chairs. It had all the atmosphere I imagined a Highland shooting lodge might have had in the days when it was the done thing for the well-heeled to move lock, stock, barrel and retinue of servants from their London homes to Scotland for the summer 'season'. Among the paintings on the walls there was one of a steam yacht and one of the guests told me that Robert Birkbeck, the first owner, had cruised into Loch Hourn some time during the last century and dropped anchor off Kinloch Hourn. He was so captivated by the beauty of the area he persuaded the laird to rent him the forests of Armadale and Kinloch Hourn. Some years later he bought the land and built his dream home, Kinloch Hourn Lodge, overlooking the loch and planted the garden with eucalyptus trees.

It was certainly going from one social extreme to the other when later that night I left the pleasant company in the Lodge and crawled into my travel-worn tent, but I was quite happy with my lot.

19

Glen Quoich to Glen Moriston

I was up early the next morning and sat outside the tent with a mug of coffee in my hand. It was an unusually warm morning but overcast, with tiny cotton-wool clouds hanging motionless above the peaks like blobs on a child's painting. There was no sunlight yet the colours of the hillsides, trees and crags were separate and distinct, forming that tonal pattern that makes the Highland landscape so unique. I was drinking in this superb canvas when an unmistakably Scottish sound floated across the glen, adding an extra dimension that not even the finest painting can achieve. The thin wail of the bagpipes broke the still air, scattering the crows in the tall trees surrounding the Lodge and disturbing the spell of early morning. The cotton-wool clouds became alive and marched, almost in time with the music, across the hills in the direction of the Isle of Skye. A curious sun opened a window in the grey sky and beamed down on the lone piper, parading up and down across the grass by the Lodge. Thor and Lucy, who had been stretched full-length in the sheep pen, clambered stiffly to their feet and stood, ears pricked, listening to the strange sound. The piper finally squeezed the last pocket of air out of the bag and, with a parting squeal, the pipes were silent. Thousands of midges left their beds to dance an unaccompanied jig and I withdrew to the shelter of the tent to have breakfast and study the maps, trying to decide whether to press on over the hills to Glenelg and Skye or to give Lucy an easier time and turn inland for Glen Quoich. After the ordeal on the bridge it was a miracle she was able to walk without a limp. Even so she was not her usual perky self and I decided against making for Skye.

While I was loading up Christopher, his daughter,

Gabrielle and her friend, Catherine, walked over from the Lodge to say hello to the ponies and take photographs of us as we set off up the steep, winding hill leading out of Kinloch Hourn towards Loch Quoich. The gradient gradually eased and Thor and Lucy plodded steadily along the road, keeping roughly parallel with an ugly scar across the hillside gouged out by the movement of machinery during the building of miles of electricity pylons. By the tiny loch, Corrie Shubh, the ring of the ponies' hooves on the surfaced road disturbed a flock of mallard ducks and they rose in a black cloud, quacking angrily. The road followed a twisting course through a tumbled mass of wet hillocks for over three miles, until the long expanse of Loch Quoich appeared, grey and silent beneath the conical peak of Gairich. Some years ago a hydro-electricity dam built at the east end of the loch stemmed the flow of water into the River Garry, increasing the surface area of the loch and submerging the original road and many old footpaths beneath its cold waters. A new road has been built and when I looked down on the sterile tidemark at the water's edge, the hallmark of every man-made reservoir, I could see the bleached remains of the old road and its little arched bridges following a winding route to nowhere in a wilderness of washed-out peat hags.

The road curved round a headland to a concrete bridge spanning a fiord the flood water had pushed into Glen Quoich. I stopped to rest the ponies and study the map to see if there was an alternative to the miles of boring tarmacadam ahead. I knew of a track up Glen Quoich to Glen Loyne, then by a hill route to Cluanie Inn in Glen Shiel. I had walked it many times in my youth and, although it was wet, it was quite passable for a pony. While I pondered I left the ponies and walked up the Glen Quoich track. I had only gone a few hundred yards when the decision was made for me. A wire fence and a padlocked gate blocked access to the glen. It made me very angry to see yet another right of way obstructed and I was tempted to remove the chains and go through. The thoughts of Lucy's cuts and bruises and the possibility that the hill path may have eroded changed my mind and reluctantly I rode Thor across the bridge in the direction of Glen Garry. Low cloud slid down off the hills, hiding what would have been a fine view and the plod along the road was deadly dull. A stunted forest of old pine, birch and beech at the side of the loch relieved the stark scenery a little, but a cold wind made me retreat into my anorak and leave Thor to follow the endless ribbon of road at his own lumbering pace. The grey clouds turned inky black and threatened to demonstrate that Loch Quoich's reputation as the wettest place in Britain was not a myth. Mercifully, there was only a slight shower and the wind chased the clouds away.

After following the edge of the loch for several miles, the road relieved the monotony by climbing sharply to the top of a headland with a superb view. It is a shame that the panorama has done little to inspire the Ordnance Survey to give the headland a name. The viewpoint was a popular stopping-place for motorists and to show how much they had enjoyed their stay they had left the usual tokens of appreciation in the form of waste paper, cigarette packets, a well-used baby's nappy, beer cans, bottles and orange peel. I was busy burying the worst of it when a Land Rover pulled up and an estate stalker jumped out to look at Thor and Lucy. He told me the estate had locked the gate into Glen Quoich because coach-loads of anglers came from all over Scotland and left such a mess and caused so much damage that the owners had no alternative but to stop coaches driving up the glen. The stalker said that he had very often seen coach drivers sweeping out their vehicles and leaving dozens of beer cans, whisky bottles and other rubbish by the side of the road. If he said anything to them the usual reply was a tirade of abuse and sometimes even threats of violence. He cursed and looked down at the heap of rubbish.

'Who would believe that visitors who come to enjoy the glen would leave the likes of that?' he said, pushing a heap of cans with his boot. Climbing into the Land Rover he sighed, 'There are times when I hate people.'

As I covered the mess with a heap of stones I shared his feelings.

At the great concrete rampart of the Quoich dam, the road descended towards Glen Garry. Sheltered from the wind, the air warmed rapidly and I was able to remove my anorak. The road rolled on and on, by Coille Mhorgil where electricity generated by the dam sprouted out of the ground in a space-age cluster of insulators and climbed to the top of a pylon on its way to the power-hungry industrial towns of the East. Curving above Loch Poulary, the narrow road dipped to Tomdoun, a tiny cluster of houses and a hotel that faded into obscurity when the hydro-engineers dammed Loch Loyne and severed the main highway from Tomdoun to Kintail as if it were a disused artery.

Both ponies were very tired and a metallic clinking signalled that Thor had a loose shoe. Tying the ponies to a fence by a phone box, I spied a little church, well fenced-in and surrounded by good grass. It was an ideal place to camp and put the ponies in for the night and I went across to see if there was anyone about. A lady arranging flowers in the porch was rather taken aback when I enquired if she thought the minister would mind if the ponies cut his grass for him. She hastily explained that the minister lived in Spean Bridge and she did not think he would take kindly to the ponies wandering round the churchyard or to me pitching a tent. She was very helpful though and said that the hotel owner had a field next to the house that she and her husband were building, opposite the church, and he would probably let me use it. I trudged up to the hotel and sniffed the mouth-watering odour of food while one of the staff went to find the owner. He was very French and very courteous.

'M'sieur, you can use my field with pleasure,' he said, emerging from the kitchen and disappearing into it almost before the sentence was finished.

'He's very busy just now,' said the receptionist apologetically.

I unloaded the ponies by the newly built house and they bounded away to have a long roll and rub the sweat off their backs.

Evening was advancing rapidly and already the setting sun was casting long shadows across the glen. It was the signal for the midges' playtime and out they swarmed in their thousands to clog my nose, bite my hands and face and buzz furiously in my ears as I hurried to pitch the tent. I dived inside to light the stove and make a mug of coffee and was about to rummage through my food bag when the lady from the house arrived and asked if I would join the family for a meal. I accepted gladly and was soon seated at the table being introduced to Alistair and Mary Biggart, who were on holiday with their family from London. They had spent their holidays in Glen Garry for many years and had eventually got around to building their own house. It had taken longer than they had anticipated because of delays in the delivery of materials. At times this had exasperated Alistair who was an engineer and accustomed to working to a tight schedule. We talked about the easy-going ways of the Highlanders and I told a story about a man in Lewis who never got round to painting his boat because he always argued that 'tomorrow it will be a better day for painting'.

'Oh I can tell you a story about that,' said Alistair. 'A Highlander and a Spaniard met one day and they got to discussing the customs of each other's country. "This word *manyana* that you Spanish have," said the Highlander, "what does it mean?" "Ah *si*," replied the Spaniard, "it means never be in a hurry, take things easy, never do anything that can be put off till tomorrow or the next day, or maybe even the day after that." The Highlander looked puzzled for a minute or two, "Well now," he said, thoughtfully, "I do not think we have a word in the Gaelic for anything as urgent as that!"'

It was late when I left the house for the tent and the midges were driving the ponies berserk; all night they raced up and down and kept me awake.

Lucy and Thor were still careering about at seven o'clock the next morning but at nine when I packed the bags and went to collect them they were not in the field. I searched for an hour before I spotted them about half a mile away on the bank of the River Garry. Somehow they had managed to get over the fence and were on a narrow strip of land between the river and a fence enclosing a newly ploughed forestry plantation. They were grazing quite happily when I reached them and to show there were no hard feelings I gave them half a chocolate bar each and searched for a way round the fence back to the road. At one side of the forestry fence a narrow strip of land separated it from the adjacent field, providing an obvious route. I led the ponies up to a gate and was busy removing

yards of wire when a car stopped and a lady demanded to
know what I was doing. Her manner softened quickly when I
told her about the straying ponies and she insisted on taking
me to meet her husband, who, she said, knew all the pony
routes in the area and might be able to advise on a way to
Glen Moriston. Leaving Thor and Lucy tied securely to a fence
I climbed into the car and was whisked away to a house to
meet Ian Gilmore, who was involved in long-distance pony
trekking. It was pleasant to chat over coffee and biscuits but I
was anxious to replace Thor's loose shoe before I left. Ian ran
me back to the ponies and on the way he told me about a girl
whose horse had lost a shoe in Glen Garry and who had to pay
£30 to bring a blacksmith out. It turned out to be the same
pony the people at Glendessary Lodge had asked me to look
out for. Ian said it was missing for over two weeks before a
stalker found it in a high corrie. The poor girl who owned it
must have had a harrowing time; I hope it has not killed her
enthusiasm for exploring on horseback. Ian also said that
there was no route from Tomdoun to Glen Moriston, but three
miles down the glen there was a sheep park between two
forestry plantations which was a short cut to the new
Invergarry to Glen Moriston road and would save about six
miles. He gave me the owner's name so I could ask his
permission to go through.

Thanking Ian for his help, I led the ponies back to the
Biggarts' house. All the way Thor's loose shoe rang out across
the glen like a curfew bell. When I looked at his feet, all the
shoes needed replacing. To save time later I also fitted Lucy
with three new shoes to match the one I had put on at Inverie.
Over two hours went by before the last nail was banged home
and I was able to straighten my aching back. Waving goodbye
to the Biggarts, I rode over to the hotel and thanked the owner
for the use of his field. The sky was still overcast with grey
cloud but it was pleasantly warm and we jogged along the
road to a scattered group of houses at Inchlaggan. About a
dozen Icelandic ponies grazing at the side of the road
obviously thought I would lead them to a happier world and
fell in behind Lucy in a long line. I tried all ways of chasing
them off, but they stared at me with innocent faces and
refused to budge. A chap on the staff of the pony trekking

centre arrived in a car and tried to chase them back down the road but they just galloped past him and followed Lucy again. In the end he said he would follow me to the sheep park and drive them back from there. In the rush to get away from the Icelandics I forgot about asking the owner's permission to go through the sheep park and I was half way up the steep hill, riding alternately between bracken and bog myrtle, before it dawned on me. The climb was quite strenuous and at a gate in a fence I stopped to rest and look down on Loch Garry and its glen.

The sun burst through the clouds as I gathered the ponies to continue the climb, but it was soon engulfed again. Higher up the hill I could see a stream of cars pouring along the road. It took almost an hour of hard slog before we reached a gate and joined the noisy throng. The main road was agonisingly long and tedious as it first climbed, then descended, towards Loch Loyne dam. Sombre clouds hanging menacingly above the long spiky ridges of Kintail and Cluny and a wide expanse of peat bogs surrounding the almost empty loch combined to give the scene the appearance of a sepia tone photograph. As we reached the dam and the edge of Beineum Forest, the temperature plummeted and the bitterly cold wind returned. A final hill to descend to Bun Loyne House and we reached level ground at the junction of the Invermoriston to Kintail road. For the first time since I had left there in the early 1960s, I was back in Glen Moriston and I wondered what changes I would find. Tying the ponies to an AA telephone box, I was dialling my home number to report all well when an AA patrolman drove by in a Land Rover. Seeing the ponies tied to his telephone, he stamped on his brakes, then realised that giving advice on how to repair a bandaged pony was outside his province, accelerated again and was gone before I even had time to wave. Tired and hungry, I pushed on down the glen to Ceannocroc Lodge and asked if I could camp. The Girvans, who owned the estate, remembered me and Tom Girvan led Thor to a field while I followed with Lucy. A large meal, several cups of coffee and a generous dram soon drove the aches out of my muscles and I slept like a top.

It rained hard all night but faired up by morning to become cloudy and warm. Both ponies were stretched out fast asleep in the soft grass, making the most of a well-earned rest. I enjoyed a leisurely wash and shave by the side of the river, then crept past the sleeping ponies on my way to Balintombuie to visit Clachan Mhercheird, a tiny churchyard hidden on the banks of the river. Although it has been in existence for centuries it has escaped the notice of the Ordnance Survey and there is no reference to it on their maps. Glen Moriston abounds with stories of saints and mysterious happenings and a very old man named Ewen Dubh, who lived near Dalchreichart, told me a great many of them. Ewen's English was not good and my Gaelic was worse, but he told me that the founder of the church was Erchard, a travelling preacher who came to Glen Moriston from Strathglass. There, according to legend, while working with two other preachers he noticed a white cow stood by a certain tree each day. Though it never ate anything, it was always well-filled. Erchard dug under the tree and found three bells, bright and new as if they had just been made. He kept one of the bells himself and gave the others to his friends. He told them to go out into the country and the bell would ring three times. When the bell rang for the third time they were to build a church. Erchard journeyed to Glen Moriston and when he reached the top of a hill, now called Suidhe Mhercheird (Merchard's Seat) his bell rang for the first time. He continued up the glen to Balintombuie, where the bell rang again at Fuaran Mhercheird (Merchard's Well). Below Balintombuie, on the bank of the River Moriston, the bell rang for the third time and there Erchard, or Merchard as he became known, built his church, Clachan Mhercheird. The name Merchard comes from Mo Erchard, meaning my Erchard, a term of affection. Merchard's church has long since crumbled to dust, but his bell was kept in the churchyard until sometime in the late 1880s, when it went missing.

I opened the gate of the little churchyard and wandered round looking for another wonder of the glen old Ewen Dubh had shown me. Hidden in the grass and not easy to find was a small stone, hollowed out on one side and filled with water. It is reputed to be a font where Merchard baptised his converts and its magical power will never allow it to become empty of water. If the water is removed it will have returned, mysteriously, by the next morning and many an eminent scientist has offered his theories as to the reason for the phenomenon.

On my way back to the gate, two names on a gravestone caught my eye and I was saddened to find that they were the two brothers Dunc and Willack, who owned a smithy in Invermoriston. They were hilarious characters who spent the day arguing furiously with each other while shoeing a horse or repairing an implement. Both of them were rather short in the leg and I have a vivid memory of one tiny man hanging on to the foot of a huge Clydesdale horse, hurling abuse in Gaelic at his brother, who was hammering with all his strength on a glowing shoe and covering himself and everyone else in a shower of sparks. If a customer had travelled any distance to reach the smithy, he would always be given a mug of tea and a cake. Their only water supply for the house was the River Moriston, running past the back doors of the smithy. When work started on the hydro-electric schemes higher up the glen, the brothers were warned that they must not drink water out of the river as it could be contaminated with sewage. A short time after the warning, I called to collect an implement and was handed my usual cup of tea.

'I hope this isn't made with water out of the river,' I said jokingly to Willack.

He exploded with indignation. 'Indeed it is not,' he replied gruffly, 'I'll never a drink a drop of that filthy water again. We just use it for washing the dishes.'

The sun was doing its best to push through the cloud as I walked back towards Ceannacroc. At Balnacarn House, I sat on a rock and watched a bee humming its way from flower to flower in a mass of hedge bindweed trailing across the garden wall. It was a gorgeous summer sound and it mingled with the hoarse cry of a crow and the occasional bleating of sheep, the only sounds in the quiet glen. Across the other side of the river by the steadings of Achlain Farm, I could see a man working sheep near the foot of the old military road that crossed the hills from Fort Augustus. As I watched, the sheep were scattering in every direction, clambering over a heap of stones by the road that once gave shelter to Dr Johnson and his friend, James Boswell, on their way to visit the Isle of Skye and the legendary Flora MacDonald. 'Between twelve and one, we set out,' wrote Boswell, 'and travelled eleven miles through a wild country, until we came to a house in Glenmoriston, called Anoch, kept by a M'Queen. Near to this place we had passed a party of soldiers under a serjeant's command, at work upon the road. We gave them two shillings to drink. They came to our inn and made merry in the barn. We went out and paid them a visit, Dr Johnson saying, "Come let's go and give them another shilling apiece." The poor soldiers got too much liquor. Some of them fought and left blood upon the spot and cursed whisky next morning. The house was built of thick turfs, thatched with thinner turfs and heath. It had three rooms in length and a little room which projected. Where we sat the walls were wainscotted as Dr Johnson said, with wicker neatly plaited. Our landlord had made the whole with his hands.'

The humming of the bee faded into the distance as it carried its cargo of pollen across the fields towards Clachan Mheircheird. Looking at my watch, I was amazed to find that I had been staring across the glen for over two hours. As I walked back to Ceannacroc through Tomcrasky Farm and by the old settlement a towering black cloud, advancing from the West, engulfed the sun and the sky turned very threatening.

When I prepared my dinner that evening I was disturbed to find that I was running very short of food. Apart from a bag of beef curry mix, all I had was a handful of muesli, a few oatcakes, margarine, two bars of chocolate, a packet of peppermints and a few raisins. The nearest shop was a long way off and what food I had would have to last until I reached Fort Augustus.

The roar of torrential rain battering the tent woke me the next morning and put paid to my plans for the day. I had hoped to visit a cave about nine miles away in the hills, where Bonnie Prince Charlie had hidden while the Redcoats hunted for him in the glens.

Old Ewen Dubh had told me where to look for it way back in the 1950s and it was a great thrill when I actually stumbled on it after a lot of searching. If books about Scotland mention the cave, they often state that it is in Coire Doe. It is not in Coire Doe but in Corrie Mheadhoin. It was one of the hideouts of a band of Glen Moriston men who had taken refuge in the hills after the disaster of Culloden and revenged the loss of their homes and families by ambushing parties of soldiers, killing as many as they could before vanishing into the hills laden with food and arms. While the Glen Moriston men were leading the lives of outlaws, the Prince, having been pursued the length and breadth of the Hebrides, landed in Morar and made his way with three of his followers to Loch Hourn and on to Glen Shiel.

The whole glen swarmed with soldiers and a man from Glengarry guided the party to the safety of Sgurr nan Conbhairean, a mountain dividing Glen Moriston and Glen Affric, 'where the only shelter his Royal Highness had being an open cave where he could neither lean nor sleep, being wet to the skin with the rain that had fallen all day; and having no fuel to make a fire with, his only way to make himself warm by smoking a pipe.' The Glen Garry man made contact with the Glen Moriston outlaws and the Prince and his party were given shelter and food in a cave in what one historian describes as Coire Sgrainge, at the head of Corrie Doe. (Nowadays it is marked on the map as Coire Sgreumh and when I questioned Ewen Dubh, who had stalked all his life in the area, he had no knowledge of a cave in that particular corrie.) While he rested, the Prince was uneasy about the comings and goings of the band of men and worried that a careless word might lead the soldiers to his hiding-place. He asked them to swear an oath 'That their backs should be to God and their faces to the Devil, and that all the curses the Scriptures did pronounce might come upon them and all their posterity if they did not stand firm by the Prince in the greatest dangers.' The seven men of Glen Moriston, as they came to be known, moved the Prince and his followers to another cave in Corrie Mheadhoin and he stayed there for four days before crossing the hills to Poolewe in search of a French ship.

It was the cave in Corrie Mheadhoin that I wanted to visit, but the heavy rain showed no sign of slacking off and I stayed in the tent, repairing large holes in my disintegrating socks. Towards evening the weather improved so, pulling on my waterproofs, I climbed a small hill behind Ceannacroc Lodge and looked down on a dark, forbidding, rain-soaked glen, glistening under a fan-shaped ray of pale sunlight that moved slowly across the landscape. It paused for a brief moment, illuminating the stark crosses in the graveyard of Clachan Mheircheird, as if to remind the World of the horrors and atrocities committed against the innocent and defenceless people of the glen by the Duke of Cumberland. Not content with routing the Jacobite army at Culloden, he turned his mob loose and they slaughtered the wounded and the prisoners with savage and uncontrolled butchery. The eighteenth-century writer, the Honourable Mrs Murray, attempts to exonerate Cumberland by claiming that his orders were to succour the Highland wounded, not to kill them, and it was a certain Colonel Hobby who was responsible for the carnage and afterwards actually boasted about it. It might be possible to believe this story had the Duke put a stop to the unbelievable barbarity of his men against the people of Glen Moriston. The well-populated glen was only a few miles from Cumberland's headquarters at Fort Augustus and his officers and men roamed, unchecked, revelling in murder, plundering, setting fire to houses and stripping and violating women and children. Thousands of cattle, sheep, horses and goats were driven away and sold to dealers from England the proceeds divided between the soldiers. Men, young and old, working in their fields, were shot down like deer for the fun of it. The terror-stricken people fled into the mountains where, without food and clothing or shelter, they died like flies when the winter snow covered the glen. Desperate with hunger, some of the poor creatures even begged for food at Cumberland's fort, but they were turned away. The Duke had ordered 'There is no meal to be sold to any persons but soldiers, their wives are not allowed to buy it. If any soldier, soldier's wife or any other persons belonging to the army, is known to sell or give any meal to any Highlander, or any person of the country, they shall first be whipped severely for disobeying his order, and then put upon meal and water in the Provost for a fourthnight.'

While the starving Highlanders and their families were dying of hunger and cold, Cumberland and his men lived in luxury in the Fort. The City of London sent £4,000 to be divided among the non-commissioned officers and soldiers and many of them grew rich with the money received from the sale of stolen animals. To keep his men entertained, the Duke organised horse races and an observer at the time reckoned, 'The Duke gave two prizes to the soldiers to run heats for, on bare backed galloways taken from the rebels ... These galloways are little larger than a good tup, and there was excellent sport. Yesterday his Royal Highness gave a fine holland smock to the soldiers wives, to be run for on these galloways, also bare backed, and riding with their limbs on each side the horse like men.' It was strongly rumoured that as the ale flowed and excitement ran high, the soldier's wives rode naked in the races. The Reverend James Hay complained in a letter to Bishop Forbes, 'The women running races at Fort Augustus, having no clothes but their shirts, and women upon horses, some with short coats, others with soldiers coats, who, by turning of the stoup fell from the horses, which was a fine diversion to Cumberland and his hellish followers.'

It is said that more Highlanders died from starvation in the two years after Culloden than had been killed on the battlefield. Broken in spirit and barely clinging to life, the survivors were subjected to a final outrage. They were prohibited from using arms or wearing Highland dress and worse of all were forced to swear an oath, 'that I have not, nor shall have, in my possession, any gun, sword, pistol, or arm worst of all were forced to swear an oath, 'that I have not, nor the Highland garb; and if I do so may I be cursed in my undertakings family and property; may I never see my wife and children, father, mother, or relations; may I be killed in battle as a coward, and lie without a Christian burial in a strange land, far from the graves of my forefathers and kindred; may all this come across me if I break my oath.' What a bitter pill for the proud Highlanders to swallow.

But the greatest insult to the Highlanders must surely have come from the Church of Scotland. At the time when innocent people were being massacred, the General Assembly wrote to the Duke of Cumberland: 'The Church of Scotland is under peculiar obligations to offer their most thankful acknowledgement to Almighty God, who has raised you up to be our brave defender ... and guardian of all our sacred and civil interests ... since this part of Great Britain has been blessed with your presence.'

The light faded quickly as more cloud scudded across the sky from the West. Guided by the lights of Ceannacroc Lodge, I clambered down the hill and returned to the shelter of the tent. Heavy rain lashed down throughout the night and it was bitterly cold. At first light I made a mug of coffee, ate the last of my breakfast muesli and set off for Prince Charlie's cave. The morning sun was fighting to break through the clouds, but it lost the battle when reinforcements arrived and sat stubbornly on the hill tops, amusing themselves by emptying buckets of water over my head as I strode up Corrie Doe. I was surprised to see the figure of a man walking slowly ahead of me. When I caught up with him we stopped to pass the time of day and he told me he was a farmer on holiday from Australia and staying at one of the cottages by the Lodge. He complained bitterly about the loss of Australia's traditional markets since the setting up of the European Common Market and said cattle prices were so depressed that some farmers in the outback were shooting their beasts where they stood because it was not worth transporting them to the sale ring.

'It's a bloody crazy world, mate,' he said, thrusting his hands deep into his pockets. 'I spent four years in a Jap prisoner of war camp, being beaten up and bloody near starving to death and when I fly home next week I'm joining a group of farmers going out to Japan to try and get the buggers to buy our meat.'

A heavy shower poured out of the clouds and the Australian dashed back to the cottage for his breakfast while I pulled my anorak hood up and tramped through the downpour. A wide Land Rover track wound through a small wood of Scots pine then emerged into the open glen, keeping close to the bank of the swollen River Doe. Streaks of light played around the head of the corrie, but a sombre backdrop of black sky scarred with red warned of nasty weather on the horizon. On the opposite side of the river the line of a path that crossed to Glen Affric stood out clearly as it traversed the side of Meall Damh. Locals used to tell a gruesome tale about a barn that once stood by the river somewhere here. The barn was kept filled with hay to feed the deer in a bad winter, but several winters had been mild and the hay remained undisturbed. One day an estate worker happened to be caught in a storm in Corrie Doe and hurried to the barn for shelter. Unable to open the door, he climbed through a skylight in the roof and dropped onto the old hay. Unknown to anyone, the warm hay had attracted hundreds of adders, who made their homes in the barn. The unfortunate man landed among them and was bitten to death.

Ewen Dubh, the stalker from Dalchreichart, once told me an interesting story about taking the late Sir Winston Churchill stalking in Corrie Doe. Churchill had recently escaped from the Boers in South Africa and was nervous that an attempt might be made on his life. He made Ewen walk in front of him carrying the stalking rifle and insisted on keeping the ammunition in his own pockets.

'The laddie was terrible full of himself,' mused Ewen. 'He used to boast that one day he would lead the country, but he would not get my support, he was awful mean with his tips.'

The head of Corrie Doe forms a trident with Gleann Fada the right-hand prong. Corrie Mheadhoin the middle and Corrie Sgreumh on the left. There was a shepherd's bothy at the head of Corrie Sgreumh and I sheltered in an outbuilding for an hour while the rain drummed on the corrugated-iron roof and poured like a river along the track. When it eased off I climbed above the bothy looking for a particular boulder in Corrie Mheadhoin which was a marker to point me in the right direction. Local folk had no use for maps and for centuries boundary lines between crofts or estates had been decided on by the use of prominent landmarks such as streams, large boulders, ridges and mountain tops. One ancient deed I was once shown for a property in Glen Moriston described the boundary as '300 paces West of Allt Tarsuinn to a square rock. At noon on Midsummers day follow the direction of the shadow of the rock for 200 paces.' It was in a similar way that Ewen Dubh had told me how to find Prince Charlie's cave.

The corrie was rough and wet and I stumbled over a confusion of peat hags for three very tedious miles. Every hill was alive with deer and I sat on a rock and counted over a hundred in one herd. They were as curious about the stranger in their midst as I was of them and stopped to stare long enough for me to look at them closely through binoculars and pick out three magnificent stags with full antlers. As the black crags at the head of the corrie came into view, a vicious rain and hail shower swept down off the hills, leaving behind a brilliant rainbow arching over the cave like coloured lights above a shrine. A large rock guided me to the entrance and I ducked inside in time to avoid another downpour. I was relieved to find that the interior had changed little since my last visit in the 1950s. The absence of beer cans and the other rubbish the modern backpacker feels obliged to leave behind showed that visits to the cave were rare. The cave is formed by a large glacial boulder lying with its flat side across another large boulder. The south end has been blocked off, perhaps by the Seven Men of Glen Moriston, and a narrow cleft at the north end provides an entrance. Inside, it is roughly twenty feet long by six feet wide, rising to about ten feet at its highest point. A narrow stream flows through the cave and, just inside the entrance, a stone bed built with infinite care is spread with bracken.

The Battle of Culloden and the Prince's flight through the hills has faded into history, but over two hundred years after the event the cave is still charged with atmosphere. I could almost see the exhausted and travel-weary Prince, fast asleep on the stone bed, his plaid wrapped round him to keep out the damp, cold air of the cave. It would be too dangerous to light a fire lest the patrolling soldiers should spot the smoke. What food the party had would have been eaten raw and washed down with whisky. Even though the cave sheltered the Prince from his enemies, he would have found it difficult to escape from the weather. With each rain squall a cold gust of wind whistled through the entrance and water dripped incessantly off the roof to run in rivulets across the rocky floor. After four days in the cave, the Prince must have been very relieved when the time came to leave for Poolewe.

I spent some time taking photographs inside the cave and

was puzzled by a peculiar musty smell that hung in the air. Crouching down to photograph the Prince's bed, I discovered a dead fox lying at the head. It was only a youngster and had not been there very long. There were no signs of gunshot wounds or that it had been poisoned, but the fox had come into the cave and laid on the bed to die.

Rather than flounder back down the Corrie, through the peat hags, I thought it might be easier to follow the Allt Corrie Mheadhoin. As it turned out the only difference was that the rain now thumped the back of my head instead of driving into my face. The terrain was just as rough and I fell, cursing, into peat holes and sank over my boots in slimy moss. Every muscle in my body cried out for a rest and, reaching the River Doe, I lay against a rock and drank several mugs of orange juice. Trudging wearily back along the edge of the river, I followed the peat-stained torrent as it thundered its way down towards Ceannacroc, tearing great chunks out of the river banks as it flexed its watery muscles. Near the bridge the North of Scotland Hydro Electric Board had built a dam and diverted the river down a tunnel to feed the turbines. The trickle that escaped over the dam threaded a silent and rather bewildered passage through a desert of bleached boulders that was once the river bed. It was rather like watching a young stallion bursting round a field, then seeing the difference after a visit from the vet.

The sun broke through and warmed my back as I reached the Lodge, but dark clouds poured across the towering face of Sgurr nan Conbhairean and the cowardly orb dived for cover. I beat the rain to the tent and the heat from the Primus stove was melting the goose pimples off my legs before the first drops rattled onto the canvas. During a break in the showers, I took my wet clothes across to Mrs Girvan to ask if I could dry them. She said the hot water system in the Lodge was bubbling its head off and would I like to run some of it off and have a bath. Within minutes I was up to my neck in soap suds, feeling the hot water reach deep into the frozen marrow of my water-logged limbs and I almost fell asleep. A refreshing shave and a vigorous teeth-brushing completed the beauty treatment and I emerged warm and glowing into the kitchen to find that Mrs Girvan had set a place for me at the table.

Her daughter, June, was an enthusiastic dog breeder and kept several German pointers. It was a change from talking about horses although there is only one dog that really excites my interest, the working border collie.

Waves of rain lashed the tent when I crawled into my sleeping bag later that evening but, still glowing with warmth, I slept undisturbed.

20

Whirlwinds and Monsters

During the night a strong wind sprang up and when I woke at six o'clock and looked out it was playing a merry game, driving rain clouds down from the hills to empty their water tanks over the glen. I could hear the wind screeching down the glen even above the rear of the Primus stove, but whatever the weather I had to leave: I was almost out of food. Breakfasting on a handful of raisins and two oatcakes, I began the drudgery of packing the bags inside the confined space of the tent. I eased myself out through the tent door into the full force of the wind-driven rain and what a miserable morning it was. Sheep huddled behind clumps of rock and trees, fences and buildings were shrouded in thick grey cloud, swirling in a confused mass before the wind. Cold water seeped through every seam in my waterproof jacket and trousers as I knelt in the grass thumping the sodden canvas of the flysheet and tent into a roll small enough to fit into the bag. Mud-caked tent pegs were thrust on top and the whole lot laboriously lashed onto the pack saddle while Lucy stood dejectedly in the lea of a gate-post. I rode across to the Lodge to thank the Girvans and was promptly invited in for coffee. The ponies were nicely sheltered under a verandah and I was glad to escape from the storm and sit, once more, in the warm kitchen. Tom Girvan talked about the many problems affecting Scotland and, in particular, the way the lairds had been forced to change their methods of management.

'The foreigners who buy estates in Scotland,' said Tom, 'often get their fingers burnt because they've neither an understanding nor knowledge of the limitations of the Highlands. Many estates are bought purely for sporting purposes, by people who've got as much idea about deer management as I have of rearing cuckoos.'

He paused for a moment as though reluctant to give away any secrets, then went on, 'To be successful, every deer forest has to have a glen or corrie that's kept as a sanctuary where the deer are never interfered with, no matter how many good stags are lying there or how many clients are paying a thousand quid a week for their sport. If the deer haven't a place where they know they're safe, they'll look for one on someone else's property and you can say goodbye to any income you hope to get from deer.'

While we talked the rain and wind died away and a gorgeous sun came out and lit up the trees. Collecting Thor and Lucy, I climbed into the saddle and set off for Fort Augustus. I had intended to ride along the main road to the ruin of the inn at Anoch, then join the old military road crossing the hills to Fort Augustus, but Tom said that with the flood of holiday traffic the road would be dangerous. I took his advice and followed the back road through Tomcrasky Farm and by Baltintombuie and Dalchreichart to join the main road at Torgoyle Bridge.

I led the ponies across the bridge and along the very busy road for a short distance to a gate in the forest. Tom Girvan was right about the amount of traffic on the road and motorists were tearing along at a crazy speed. A shiny Ford saloon with a brand new registration number overtook several cars on an incredibly dangerous bend. I was not surprised when the squeal of tortured rubber echoed across the glen, followed by the crunch of tearing metal and the tinkle of shattered glass. Looking up the road, I could see the Ford and a large lorry embracing each other, but the way the driver of the lorry was waving his fists as he jumped from the shattered cab conveyed anything but love and affection. There were plenty of other car drivers milling around to pull the vehicles and the drivers off each other, so I opened the gate and took Thor and Lucy into the peace of the forest.

High up in the wood the track merged with several paths radiating out in different directions and I wasted an hour riding up and down trying to find the right one. The task was not made any easier by short but nasty rain squalls, gusting down off the hills and driving stinging hailstones into my face. A path churned to black mud by tractor wheels seemed to head up the hill and trusting to luck, I turned Thor onto it. Both ponies floundered heavily as the soft surface gave under their weight but for once our luck was in. The tree line ended and a few hundred yards above it was the forest fence and a gate.

A bitterly cold wind brought the rain with renewed vigour and the weather deteriorated rapidly as I unwound yards of wire and heaved the gate open to let the ponies through. The sky darkened and the view faded as the wind screamed across the glen like a tornado, spiralling the saturated clouds hundreds of feet into the air and bending the tall pines as though they were made of bamboo.

Quickly tying the ponies to a post, I crouched against the fence. It was not a moment too soon. The wind howled through the wire like a thousand tormented souls and the rain struck Thor and Lucy with such force they reared and plunged in their efforts to escape. For ten minutes it was like lying under a waterfall; I have never experienced anything like it. As the whirlwind passed over it tried to pluck me off the ground and my hands ached with pain as I held tight to the wire fence. The reins I had left draped over Thor's saddle actually rose into the air and flopped down over his head.

When the roar of the wind ceased, the rain eased off and I was able to lead the frantic ponies away from the fence and join a barely discernible path through the heather to descend to the Allt Phocaichain, a fairly wide, fast-flowing river. Normally the ford would have been easy to cross but after the heavy rain of the past few days the river was far from normal. It was in spate and the surface was white with foam as the cataract boiled and thundered through the narrow canyon. The noise of the water was deafening as I rode along the bank looking for a possible place to cross. On a bend in the river I found a few yards that looked less lethal than the rest and not as wide. It took a lot of heel work to get Thor to plunge into the water and he staggered as the force of the water pressed against him. I shouted to Lucy to follow, but either she could not hear me above the din, or she chose not to. She stood with her feet firmly planted on the bank and all the time

Thor was moving further into the river. There was no turning back and I heaved desperately on Lucy's lead rope. She followed all right, but instead of stepping into the water she jumped in and sent a wave of water right over me. Thor gasped and snorted as the water rose over his knees and he fought to keep a footing on the rocky bed of the river. He struggled bravely for the opposite bank and we were almost there when he plunged into a deep hole and for one horrifying second I thought we were rolling over. Immediately the strength of the water swung him away from the bank and swept him like a piece of driftwood into the middle of the river. The cold took my breath away as I sank up to my waist in icy water, but Thor was not to be beaten. He thrashed out with his sturdy legs and miraculously managed to gain a footing. With a mighty heave, he scrambled out of the water onto the river bank. I slid out of the saddle and turned anxiously to see how Lucy was faring but she was already across and grazing happily on a patch of grass. Thor shook himself like a dog while I stripped off and squeezed gallons of water out of my trousers, shirt and socks. It was a waste of time: it started to pour with rain again and a horrible mist rolled across the hills, reducing visibility to a few yards. Teeth chattering like a woodpecker boring into a tree and my whole body shaking with cold, I pulled my wet clothes on and played leap-frog over boulders to restore my circulation. Half an hour of hard, physical exercise almost wore me out, but at least I was tolerably warm. Taking out my compass to plot a course through the mist, I was puzzled to find the needle revolving like the sweep hand of a clock. Thinking I had damaged it, I tried my spare compass, but it did exactly the same. The visibility was very poor and I could not go on without a compass nor was there any question of trying to cross the river again. I tried the compasses once more but again they spun out of control.

'Perhaps the rock around here is magnetic,' I told myself, then glancing at the map I found the answer. Close to the river and hidden in the mist was a long line of pylons carrying electricity cables from Glen Moriston to Fort Augustus and it was interference from these that was deflecting the compass needle. Riding Thor carefully forward into the mist, I heard the crackle of electricity on insulators and the grey steel work of a pylon loomed out of the murk, dripping with moisture like a watery skeleton. To my joy I came on the old military road. Despite having been in existence for well over two hundred years, it was in remarkably good condition and easy to follow. Wind and rain blasted us across a fairly level plateau to a gate leading into Inchnacardock Forest and here the air was very much warmer. Easing quickly, the rain finally stopped and the mist rolled away to reveal a magnificent bird's-eye-view of the village of Fort Augustus sitting comfortably at the foot of Loch Ness. A good track dropped gently down through the forest and, finding a sheltered glade among the trees, I halted to rest the ponies and boil a pan of coffee. My waterproof coat and trousers helped to retain my body heat so that though my clothes were wet I felt remarkably warm. A mug of hot coffee and a bar of chocolate tasted better than a three-course dinner and I rested contentedly against a tree. A brave sun was fighting a duel with the sinister cloud that had followed me from Glen Moriston: as each shaft of sunlight broke through a column of swirling black cloud suffocated it. In the end good triumphed over evil and, snarling and spitting, the ogre slunk away to the West. The sun shone down on Fort Augustus and every building, every boat lined up waiting to go through the locks of the Caledonian Canal and every stone in the abbey stood out sharply in the newly washed air.

It seems odd that after all the suffering inflicted upon the Highlanders by the Duke of Cumberland, his memory is perpetuated in the name Fort Augustus. The old name of the village was Cill Chumein, after the saint Cummein, who was an Abbot of Iona; in my youth this was the name the older, Gaelic-speaking inhabitants used. When the Highland Uprising started in the 1700s a barracks was built at Cill Chumein. It was not large enough, however, to accommodate all the military and in 1729 General Wade built a fort and named it after the infamous William Augustus, the youngest son of George II. Impressive though it may have looked, the Jacobites proved that it was by no means impregnable and in March 1746, after besieging it for three days, managed to land a shot in the magazine and blow it to bits. It was later rebuilt and in 1867 the Government sold it to Lord Lovat, whose son gave it to the Order of St Benedict. William Augustus would hardly recognise the original building of his day. Much of the old fort has been knocked down or incorporated into the beautiful twin-spired building of the Abbey. Where the noise of battle and the rolling of drums once echoed across the green fields, only the sound of the Abbey bells disturb the wood-pigeons and crows. Time may have healed the wounds, but the scars will always remain.

Gathering Thor and Lucy, I continued down through the quiet forest to Jenkins Park, a housing estate on the edge of the village. Scores of people came to the doors of their houses or stared curiously at us through windows, as if I had arrived from Mars instead of Glen Moriston. A number of excited children came to look at the ponies and word spread fast. Boys and girls appeared from every corner and I felt like the Pied Piper of Hamelin as dozens of children streamed behind me. A large ship moving through the canal drew their attention and when they raced away to watch it sail into Loch Ness I tied the ponies to a railing outside the village grocery shop and went inside.

At the sight of shelf upon shelf stacked with food of every description I could have gone berserk, but my slim budget kept me in check and half an hour later I emerged with a small box of groceries, a few rolls of film and one luxury, a half bottle of whisky. I was ravenously hungry so, having stowed the groceries in the packs, I sat on a bollard by the side of the canal and ate a meat pie. A series of five locks descended from the canal to Loch Ness and several fishing vessels and yachts were being moved down, towering above the canal bank one minute, the next, twenty feet below it, in the bottom of the lock. I have sailed through the Caledonian Canal several times in a variety of small boats and it is an unforgettable experience. Stretching sixty miles, from Fort William on Loch Linnhe to Inverness on the Moray Firth, it joins together Loch Lochy, Loch Oich and Loch Ness and enables ships to avoid the long and dangerous passage round Cape Wrath and through the Pentland Firth. It was built by the Scottish engineer, Thomas Telford, famous for his bridges, roads and canals all over Britain, this is one monument to his work he would probably want to forget about. Instead of taking the estimated seven years to build it took eighteen and by the time the first ships passed through in 1822 there was no need for it. Steam ships were rapidly replacing sailing craft and as they increased in size they became too large to pass through the canal. The long delay had got nothing to do with bad weather, lack of materials, or protracted negotiations with the lairds: it was simply that the Highlanders labouring on the canal were unused to a regular job and returned at frequent intervals to their crofts for peat-cutting, planting or harvest. For months at a time work on the canal was at a standstill. In November 1804, the exasperated engineer in charge of construction wrote to Telford complaining that very little work had been done that year because many of the men had gone home 'to get their little harvest and potato crops and are not yet returned. Indeed many of them do not intend to return before the spring never having been used to work in the winter in this country.'

Fortunately for history, work was in progress on the canal on Thursday, 16th September, 1819, during Robert Southey's tour of Scotland. In his journal he wrote a graphic description of the locks at Fort Augustus. 'Went before breakfast to look at the locks, five together, of which three are finished, the fourth about half built, the fifth not quite excavated. Such an extent of masonry upon such a scale, I had never beheld before, each of these locks being 180 feet in length. It was a most impressive and rememberable scene. Man, horses and machines at work, digging, walling and puddling going on, men wheeling barrows, horses drawing stones along the railways. The great steam engine was at rest having done its work. It threw out 160 hogsheads per minute; and two smaller engines were also needed while the excavation of the lower locks was going on, for they dug 24 feet below the surface of water in the river, and the water filtered thro' open gravel. The dredging machine was in action revolving round and round, bringing up at every turn matter which had never been brought to the air and light. Its chimney poured forth volumes of black smoke, which was no annoyance in beholding because there was room enough for it in this wide clear atmosphere.'

The canal was later enlarged and the work completed in

1847. Nowadays, instead of having to employ an army of men to operate the gates and sluices, it is all done by remote control and ships can pass through from the Atlantic to the North Sea with the minimum delay.

As I watched from my bollard, the fishing vessels and yachts reached the last loch basin and chugged into Loch Ness. With a hum of electric motors, the gate closed behind them, the road barriers swung up and the long line of waiting traffic poured across the bridge.

Tom Girvan had given me the telephone number of a Mr Biggs at Culachy House on the edge of Fort Augustus who, he said, might let me camp on his estate. Spying a telephone box, I rang him up. He was most helpful and said to make my way up to the house and meanwhile he would arrange with his farm manager for a field to put the ponies in. I steered Thor past the entrance to the Abbey and around the foot of Loch Ness and was almost at a junction where a minor road turned off for Culachy when a large foreign car with a German registration plate pulled in ahead of me. A man festooned with Leica cameras got out and held up his hand, indicating I should halt.

'Could you please tell me,' he said in a thick accent, 'vere I can photograph the Loch Ness monster. I haf been here for one week and seen nothing.'

At first I thought he was joking but when he produced a card bearing the name of a popular German magazine and explained that his editor said he must bring back a photo of the monster at all costs, I realised that he was serious. It is difficult enough trying to explain the legend of Nessy to those who understand English, but confronted with a man whose English was very limited and worse, expected the monster to pop up on demand, taxed me to the utmost. Each time I attempted to tell him what little I knew about the monster he smiled politely and said, 'Please, I do not understand.' He became quite agitated when I explained that people had sat for weeks waiting to film the monster and had gone away disappointed.

'Ok, ok,' he said, irritably, then a flash of inspiration lit up his face and he beamed with enthusiasm. 'My editor say I have to have photographs for zis weekend, so I photograph you and zer horses, yes?'

Before I could answer he leaped around us, clicking furiously with the Leicas. I wrote my name in his notebook for him and, with a cheery wave and a loud *Aufwiedersehen*, he drove away. If his editor had set his heart on having a photograph of the Loch Ness monster he must have been greatly puzzled by a photograph of me grinning at him from Thor's back and the large hump of Lucy's pack sticking up behind me. I have often wondered if I appeared in the magazine with the caption 'An exclusive picture of the Loch Ness Monster taken last week in Scotland by our staff reporter.'

The narrow road leading to Culachy climbed steeply for a short distance. At the top I let the ponies chew the grass in a lay-by while I photographed the view of Loch Ness. The surface of the loch was calm and I laughed to myself at the thought of Nessy suddenly appearing while I looked through the camera viewfinder. Every newspaper and magazine in the World would have clamoured for a print and the proceeds would have financed my horseback expeditions for many years. If Nessy had shown her face though, I would probably have missed the shot as I have never been able to fully accept the stories of the monster and would probably have dropped the camera in surprise.

It is well over a thousand years since Adamman, the Abbot of Iona, first reported the monster and told how Saint Columba came on a group of men on the bank of the River Ness, burying a man who had been killed by a water monster. Columba asked his companion to swim across the river and bring back a boat tied to the bank on the other side. He was halfway across when the monster appeared again and was about to have him for breakfast when Columba shouted, 'Thous shalt go no further nor touch the man; go back with all speed.' At the sound of the Saint's voice, the terrified monster fled 'more quickly than if it had been pulled back with ropes.' Ever since that day the monster, or Nessy as it has affectionately become known, has shown a head or waved a scaly fin in different parts of the loch to show there is still plenty of life in the old body but, as far as I am aware, has never eaten anyone. People have come from all over the World hoping to catch a glimpse of Nessy and elaborate schemes have been hatched to capture the beast and put it on public view. Bertram Mills, the circus owner, offered a prize of £20,000 to any person who could capture Nessy alive. Happily the wily creature has evaded the speculators and might endear itself to the World if it devoured a few of them. During their long vigils huddled behind batteries of ciné and television cameras, scores of film cameramen from different countries have provided endless sport and a change of diet for the Loch Ness midges, but to date Nessy had not obliged with a full frontal. One of the first, and perhaps the most famous, of the photographs taken of the monster was snapped in April 1934 by a London surgeon and shows the head and neck of a strange creature sticking up out of the water. Other photographs have been taken since, though scientists seem reluctant to stand up and declare them to be genuine. One of the reasons could be the number of hoaxes that have been played on the unsuspecting public and even the Press. It is amazing how many sightings of Nessy take place during the tourist season.

Little is really known about the monster, but even less information is available about the lower reaches of the loch itself. It plunges to over seven hundred and fifty-four feet at its deepest point, off Urquhart Castle, and many locals believe that there are caverns at the bottom of the loch. There is also a strong belief that there could be an opening into the sea bed, which might account for Nessy's long absences. This theory is given some credibility by a strange occurrence in 1775 when an earthquake destroyed a large part of Lisbon. The weather in Scotland was calm at the time of the earthquake, yet the surface of the loch was violently agitated and waves three feet high were driven up the rivers and continued to ebb and flow for over an hour. The agitation increased and the water level overflowed the river banks by more than thirty feet. No tremor of any kind was felt on land.

I have a feeling that one day Nessy will slither out of the water in full view of dozens of spectators, yet the momentous occasion will hardly receive a mention in the newspapers or on radio or television. Not even the most enthusiastic newshawk would dare file a story that the Loch Ness monster has been positively sighted in Fort Augustus main street on the evening of 31st December!

Turning my back on Loch Ness, I swung stiffly into the saddle and continued along the road by Ardachy Lodge and over the River Tarff to a drive leading to Culachy Estate. The drive wound· in and out of a wood, and reached a cottage where a lady answered my knock.

'You're not there yet,' she said with a laugh, 'they're expecting you at the house. Keep going, you can't miss it.'

The drive climbed above the wood with superb views across the glen to Fort Augustus and the military road crossing the hills to Glen Moriston. Thor and Lucy were tiring and I looked eagerly ahead for the house as they moved slowly along. When I saw it I stared in amazement. I was expecting a large farmhouse but there, filling the skyline, was an enormous turreted house as big as a castle. Pulling Lucy in on a short rope to keep her teeth away from a line of rosebushes, I led Thor in front of an imposing front porch and, praying that he would not disgrace me by leaving a load of droppings on the well-raked gravel, I rang the front door bell. The clanging echoed through the house but no one came. I turned to walk round to the back door and froze. Lucy had pulled away from the tree and was tramping across the neatly mown grass round the house, leaving great holes where her feet sank in. Racing across the gravel, I dragged her back and had just finished filling in the last hoofprint and smoothing the grass over, when a voice said, 'Hullo, you've made it then.' A cheery man advanced towards me. 'I'm Ian Biggs,' he said, extending his hand, 'you look jolly cold; come on, I'll show you where to put your ponies.' He led the way to a field close by the house. 'I hope you'll be all right here. Pitch your tent wherever you like and bring your wet clothes to the house when you're ready. We've got a splendid drying area.' He left me to get on with unloading the ponies and, having pitched the tent in the shelter of a tall hedge, I crawled inside to light the stove and peel off my wet clothing. Dumping the sodden heap outside the tent, I attacked yards of icy flesh with a rough towel to stir up my circulation. Warm and dry in my spare clothes, I dashed across to the house where Mr Biggs showed me a room to hang my leaky waterproofs and other clothes to dry. We chatted for a while over a glass of whisky, but I was so weary I could hardly keep my eyes open and I returned to the tent to make a meal. Later that evening the sky cleared and the stars came out in their millions. I had been looking forward so much to crossing the great Correyairack Pass from Fort Augustus to Laggan and the weather showed every sign of helping me to enjoy it by providing a nice day.

21

Over the Correyairack

For once the weather signs were right and the chatter of birds woke me early with the news that the morning was fine and bright. Thor and Lucy were fast asleep in the deep grass; the heavy dew on their bodies glistened in the sunlight as they rose and fell with their breathing. It was too early for the midges and I sat in the warmth of the sun, drawing in the aroma of bacon and coffee as I prepared breakfast.

Culachy House looked magnificent in the morning light. Taking my cameras, I walked round the garden to find the best angle for a photograph. Mr Biggs came out while I was busy clicking away and I commented on how attractive the house looked. He smiled and said, 'Yes, we are rather fond of the old place. I got the estate in 1963, but years ago it was owned by a rather remarkable person called Kennth Angelo; I believe he originated from Piedmont in Italy. He had some very progressive ideas on farming that were far ahead of his time and his buildings, roads and even a hydro-electric scheme were incredibly ingenious. Like most estate owners in those days, he employed a lot of men and was very well thought of. His great passion was stalking, but when his eyesight deteriorated he cross-bred deer hounds with wolf hounds and used them to course deer, though rumour has it that he ran into trouble with his neighbours when his hounds ran stags out of their ground. One of his neighbours was Lord Lovat and, because of some trouble between them Angelo began to construct a stone wall to separate the two estates, but it was a formidable project and never finished. You'll see some of it on the summit of Correyairack.' He paused to straighten a rose bush, then went on, 'Angelo married a lady from Ireland, far younger than himself and when he died she married an army man, General Beckett. She outlived him too and died, a very old lady, at Culachy in the early 1950s.' We had walked slowly along a terrace as Mr Biggs was talking and, reaching the end of it, looked down over the wooded estate. 'The interesting point of the story,' he continued, 'is that the old lady is buried in a small private graveyard in the wood down there, with Angelo on one side of her and General Beckett on the other.'

It was a rare pleasure to saddle the ponies and load up in warm sunshine and I took my time over it. Mr Biggs very kindly topped up my almost empty paraffin container and when I was ready to go he led the way to a gate opening onto the hill. Thor surged forward and, with Lucy following, we made our way up the most famous of all General Wade's military roads, the Correyairack Pass. Major Caulfield, the Governor of Fort George, is reputed to have exclaimed, 'Had you seen these roads before they were made, you would lift up your hands and bless General Wade.' The Governor said it jokingly, but at the same time it was a compliment to one of the most gifted road-builders of his time. He penetrated into areas of the Highlands that had been isolated for centuries. Along his roads, albeit constructed for military purposes, crofters were able to take their cattle and sheep to markets with considerably less effort and danger than crossing the bog-ridden hills. More of an engineer than a soldier, General George Wade was given the task of improving road communication throughout the Highlands to enable the army to move troops and horse-drawn equipment quickly and easily in the event of trouble. Between 1723 and 1740, he was responsible for building over two hundred and fifty miles of road and forty bridges. Ironically, many of the roads he built to move soldiers along were also used by the Jacobites and as Thor strode up the Pass I experienced a strange sense of excitement. Two hundred and thirty-four years before, almost to the day, Prince Charlie and his army had left Culachy and climbed Correyairack on their way to Edinburgh. The Prince and his aides on horseback, followed by two thousand five hundred clansmen, must have been an awesome sight, as they marched along the track, the hills resounding with the roar of

clan war-cries and the skirl of pipes. Drawn into the excitement
of the event, I spurred Thor on into battle and he puffed and
wheezed with the effort. I was busy leading a battalion of
sword-wielding, kilted Highlanders to victory when it dawned
on me I was English and had I been around on that day in 1745
I might have been scattered over the hill in little pieces for the
crows to fight over. Thor and Lucy were very relieved when I
retired from the chase and let them plod along in their own
good time.

The wide track zigzagged relentlessly up the steep hillside
and I marvelled at the way the soldiers had dug it out of the
earth and laid drains to prevent flood water from washing it
away. Five hundred soldiers were employed on the building of
the Correyairack. In the autumn of 1731 a traveller saw six
oxen being roasted as a treat for the men who had completed
'the great road for wheel carriages between Fort Augustus and
Ruthven, it being 30th October, His Majesty's birthday.'
Crossing the Correyairack by coach must have been a feat of
skill for the driver and a real test of nerves for the passengers.
Some of the hairpin bends were very tight and a slip would
have sent the coach and the horses crashing to destruction.
That much-travelled lady with a taste for adventure, the
Honourable Mrs Murray, stormed up the Pass in her coach in
1798, though I wonder if she did it more to show the Governor
of Fort Augustus what a wet he was than for her own
enjoyment. She had stayed at the Fort and at breakfast the
Governor gave her a horrifying account of a time when he had
crossed the pass on horseback, a journey 'of wild desolation
beyond anything he could describe and the whole of the road,
rough, dangerous and dreadful, even for a horse. The steep
and black mountains and the roaring torrents rendered every
step his horse took frightful; and when he attained the summit
of the zigzag up Correyairack he thought the horse, himself,
man and all, would be carried away, he knew not whither; so
strong was the blast, so hard the rain, and so very thick the
mist, and as for the cold, it stupified him.' The tough lady
probably smiled to herself over her breakfast toast, but before
leaving she had her coach checked carefully by a blacksmith
to make sure it would stand the journey. For extra power she
harnessed two plough horses to her own. At eight o'clock in

the morning she set off up the Pass and crossed safely to Laggan. I like to think she sent the Governor a postcard.

The track climbed up the hillside, keeping parallel with the deep, wooded cleft of Glen Tarff, then levelled out for a short distance before dipping and rising among the hills and crossing the picturesque hump-backed bridges on its way. High above, I could see the summit of the Pass marked by a stark line of electricity pylons and as I looked a film of grey cloud obliterated the green hills. It was an all-too-familiar sign of rain advancing down the Corrie. Resting the ponies for a while beside a stream, I pulled on my waterproofs and then set off up the final few hundred feet towards the summit. Years of storms had ploughed the track into a jumble of boulders and it was very tough going for Thor and Lucy. I kept to the edge of the track where I could, but they slipped and snorted and fell into holes and were soon lathered in sweat. The weather decided it was time to add a touch of spice to the journey and a ferocious wind thumped into us, sending Lucy reeling into the hillside. I hung onto Thor's mane, but the squall had not finished with us. Pausing for a moment, it returned with renewed force and this time it brought rain with it. A tremendous deluge of water swept horizontally across the face of the hill and for five minutes I clung to both ponies while the gale shrieked over us. The stony path streamed with water and I splashed through it, frozen to the marrow, towing the ponies behind me. What a contrast to the heat of the lower glen.

At the summit the rain stopped but the bitterly cold wind did not let up for a minute. The view was magnificent. I could see the whole length of Glen Garry to the mountains of Loch Arkaig, Knoydart and Skye, and across the Glen Moriston range to Glen Affric. It was too cold to linger more than a few minutes and I pulled Thor and Lucy behind a concrete building belonging to the Hydro Electricity Board. A plate on the door informed me that I was two thousand five hundred and seven feet above sea level, but it could not have been any colder if there had been another nought on the end of it. I gave up trying to chew a frozen chocolate bar and broke it into several pieces with a large stone. From where the building was situated I could not see the mountains in the West, but this was more than compensated for by a superb view down a long glen to Laggan and the Cairngorms. An ominous black cloud raced across the sky from the North-west and when it arrived I was thankful for the shelter of the building. A gale-force wind moaned through the steel lattice-work of the pylons and the world turned white as every rock and blade of grass was plastered with a thick layer of hailstones. The temperature was well below freezing point and I whacked my arms together and jumped up and down to keep the blood circulating.

There was nothing for the ponies to eat so once the squall had blown itself out they were more than happy to be on their way. I felt strangely reluctant to descend into Laggan. The Correyairack was the dividing line between the West Highlands I knew and loved and the East that had never really held much attraction for me. I had climbed and skiied many times in the Cairngorms and enjoyed their isolation, but had never felt at home.

A series of well-engineered zigzags descended to the floor of the glen where countless rainstorms had churned the track into a slippery morass. I let Thor pick his own way through it and progress was terribly slow as he stopped to sniff at each boulder before placing a nervous hoof on it. A family group, out for a walk cheered him up when they stopped to pat his nose and offer him pieces of chocolate. Lucy looked at the children with limpid brown eyes and put on her 'downtrodden pony' act. It did the trick and crunching a packet of sweets and an apple, she hurried on down the track. Both Thor and Lucy were tired and footsore when we reached a surfaced road at Melgarve and I looked round for a place to camp.

Later that evening I sat outside the tent and watched dark shadows sweeping up the glen as the setting sun turned the mountain tops pink before sinking finally behind the summit of the abandoned highway of Correyairack. The night sky was filled with stars and a sharp frost descended to slow the gurgling stream by my tent to a soft burble, as ice formed over the water. It was bitterly cold and even though I was wearing all my clothes inside my sleeping bag, I shivered. Every sound travelled far on the cold night air and the sharp bark of a roe deer far down the glen echoed among the hills.

At dawn the sun peeped over the eastern horizon but it was high in the sky before Jack Frost released his icy grip on the glen and winter became August again. By nine o'clock the ponies were loaded and I rode gently down the wide desolate glen to Garva Bridge, one of General Wade's more adventurous pieces of architecture, spanning the young River Spey. Not a thing stirred in the silent glen and it was as if the inhabitants had fled before the advancing Jacobite army. The old barracks that housed the soldiers guarding the approach to Correyairack stood empty and desolate by the side of the road. No soldier in red coat and black breeches challenged us as the ring of the ponies' shoes echoed across the empty courtyard.

The road wound on through a forest of Scots pine and crossed a new bridge over a man-made culvert connecting two small lochs. The culvert diverted the original watercourse and the new road had marooned one of General Wade's bridges like a monument in the middle of a meadow, leaving only time and the occasional sheep to pass under it.

The sound of the ponies' shoes on the road brought two men to the door of a hut at the edge of one of the lochs and they stared curiously as we approached. The elder one of the two asked if I had come over the Pass and when I said I had, but it was rather rough, shook his head.

'Och, they've let it get into terrible condition. I remember the time when you could drive a pony and cart over to Fort Augustus, no bother. I'll tell you what's done more harm than anything,' he continued, wagging a finger at his companion, 'it's they damned motorbikes. You'd think the County Council would have more sense than let them run competitions on a bonny path like that.'

The younger man was obviously a keen motorcyclist and a friendly argument broke out between the two of them. A Land Rover crammed with men clutching lunch boxes arrived and they joined in. The sides of the hut bulged as the argument became more and more heated. Gathering up the ponies, I quietly slipped away. There was a dam at the end of the loch with a complicated system of sluices to allow salmon up the river. A little way beyond it, the road crossed the river again, ran parallel with it for a mile, then swung left in a wide curve to join the A86 Fort William to Newtonmore road at Laggan.

The long glen had brought me to civilisation and before I could escape to the freedom of the hills again I was faced with at least ten miles of main road. The map showed a minor road leaving the main road at Cat Lodge, about three miles from Laggan and it seemed ideal. Pulling Lucy in on a short rope to keep her from wandering into the middle of the busy road, I turned Thor towards a narrow metal bridge crossing the Spey. It was only wide enough to take one lane of traffic at a time and was controlled by traffic lights. The lights were on red when we approached and I dutifully reined the ponies to a halt. A long column of cars built up behind us and as the lights changed to green I pushed Thor forward. As soon as his foot touched the metal surface of the bridge he jumped backwards as if it was red hot. Cursing, I pushed him forward again, but he reared up and flailed the air with his forelegs and very nearly threw me into the road. The impatient motorists sounded their horns and created such a racket it frightened Lucy, who tried to bolt. Jumping off Thor's back, I hung onto the reins and Lucy's lead rope and the pair of them dragged me along the road before I managed to hold them back. Nobody offered to help, the traffic lights had changed to red again and the motorists glared sullenly at me from the airless interiors of their metal boxes. The lights changed to green but this time the motorists did not give me a chance to lead them over the bridge. With a roar of engines they swept past, almost trapping us against the metal girders. I held tight to the ponies till the last car had gone by then pulled them onto the bridge. We were half way across when the lights changed again and the stupid motorists at the other side, instead of waiting, drove at us like unleashed hounds, only to jerk to a halt when they realised there was not room to pass. I was so angry I could have kicked the windscreen of the leading car to bits. When the fool at the wheel had the cheek to wind his window down and start to lecture me, my reply made the woman sitting next to him turn pale and he quickly wound the window up again. In the end a farmer in a Land Rover came to my rescue and made the motorists reverse off the bridge while I followed with the ponies.

'Thanks very much,' I shouted to him as I rode by.

'Och dinna bother yer heid laddie,' he replied with a wide grin, 'if some of they car drivers' brains were made of dynamite, they wouldnae have enough to blow their hats off.'

Turning onto the Dalwhinnie road, I kept Lucy on a tight rope, but fortunately there was very little traffic. Whether it was the heat or the fright on the bridge, I was not sure, but both ponies suddenly began to tire and the pace slowed to a crawl. I looked for a place to camp but although there were large fields on either side of the road I could not see a farmhouse. Painfully slowly, the ponies crawled up a long hill to Cat Lodge and the start of the minor road and I let them graze on a patch of grass alongside a telephone box, opposite the Lodge gates. While I was studying the map a young man in a camouflage jacket came out of the Lodge and asked if he could help. I said that I was looking for a place to camp and graze the ponies and wondered if he knew who owned the land hereabouts. He smiled and said, 'We do and I'm sure father will let you camp in the grounds of the Lodge.' Taking Thor's reins, he led him through the gate and showed me where I could pitch the tent.

'What about the ponies?' I ventured.

'Oh just turn 'em loose,' he laughed, 'the grass could do with being mowed. I'll tell everyone to keep the gates shut so they won't stray.'

I filled a bucket with water for the ponies and Thor drained it dry in two gulps. Lucy took longer but she too drank a full bucket before she joined Thor knee-deep in the juicy grass.

'By the way, I'm Richard Miller,' said the young man as he helped me to pitch my tent. 'We usually come up for a few weeks stalking each year. We've got a book of cuttings about our family somewhere in the house, I must let you see it.'

Richard's elder brother came out to chat and I talked about my journey until they left to bring down a stag they had shot that day.

In the evening I was hiding from the midges and writing my notes when a strikingly beautiful girl arrived at the tent door.

'Richard asked me to bring you this,' she said softly, handing me a book.

She turned and melted into the evening gloom as quickly as she had come and at first I thought it was a hallucination. The book was real enough, however, and I lit a candle and browsed through it.

22

Towards the Cairngorms

I was so weary I fell asleep reading the book and woke a couple of hours later, stiff and cold. The sky was ablaze with stars and around the tent the thick grass crackled and popped like breakfast cereal as a white frost spread over the ground. I kept my clothes on in the sleeping bag but even so I could not get warm and resolved that before setting off on another horseback expedition I would invest in a new sleeping bag. At four o'clock I could bear it no longer and lit the stove to warm the tent and make a mug of coffee. The heat from the stove had a remarkable effect on the weather outside. Within half an hour the winter scene, with its frosty air and clear sky, was gone. A white mist brought warm air and replaced the frost on the grass with a heavy dew.

About six o'clock I pulled on my boots and anorak and stumbled through the mist to a path leading up a hill behind the Lodge. The swirling white mist made rocks and trees look twice as large as they were and threatening shapes loomed out at me like figures in a weird nightmare. I must have climbed three or four hundred feet up the hillside when, as if I had sailed through time into another world, I walked out of the mist into brilliant sunshine and looked down on a most fabulously beautiful sight. Below me a carpet of cotton-wool mist, tinted pink with the morning sun, filled the whole valley floor of Glen Truim. Here and there purple hill tops protruded through the mist like islands in a frozen sea, each bursting into flame as rays of the sun flicked across it like a laser beam. Dark, claw-like hands, streaming with wisps of grey, reached up out of the hollows below sombre crags and were magically transformed into brightly coloured pine and birch trees. The world that had hung in suspended animation during the cold night burst into activity in the warmth of the sun. Swallows twittered happily to each other and the hoarse cry of a crow carried across the glen, echoing the mewing of buzzards soaring watchfully above their nest on a high crag. As the sun climbed higher the glacier of cotton-wool gradually melted and houses and fields took shape. Cows and sheep standing motionless like toys on a child's model farm came alive and called to each other. The staccato noise of a tractor engine drifted across the glen and signalled the start of a new day for the farmworkers. A faint roar of traffic rumbling along the main road on the opposite side of the glen did not distract the birds but it was sufficient to break the spell of the morning and I walked back down the hill to the Lodge.

The summer seemed to have arrived at last. It was gorgeously warm when I said goodbye to the Millers and rode down Glen Truim. Both ponies were refreshed and eager to go and it was a great joy to let Thor amble gently along and feel the warmth of the sun on my back. All the way the views were breathtaking, as the road climbed steadily above the glen and I could see the Correyairack hills very clearly. Richard Miller had said there was a path through Truim forest that eventually came out at the Falls of Truim. Looking at the map, I could see it would bring me nicely to the start of an old military road crossing a long plateau between Etteridge and Ruthven. The track through Truim Forest was a pleasant relief from the hard surface of the road and, though I had lost the view, the scent of the trees and the cool, winding track overhung with pine and birch more than made up for it. On the far side of the forest the track dipped to a gate and, leaving the trees, continued through a delightful carpet of heather in full bloom. Hundreds of bees droned back and forth among the delicate purple blossoms, carefully lifting out the pollen before flying off down the glen like a squadron of helicopters. A sign on the wall with the legend 'Right of Way to Perth road' pointed into a field. I squeezed Thor and Lucy through a rickety gate, but there were no more route markers and I was left to find my way through a series of fields. Luckily I discovered a track leading downhill and I steered Thor along it to a range of dilapidated farm buildings. It was saddening to find that what had once been a very attractive traditional farmhouse had been totally destroyed by fire. There was an air of neglect and abandonment about the whole place and I was glad to get away from it and follow a surfaced road to a bridge were the River Truim pours down a narrow gorge in a series of small but impressive waterfalls.

The forces of the water pouring over the rocks made a tremendous roar, but it was nothing like the din coming from the A9 trunkroad, a few yards above the river bank. A new road was under construction and it looked as if every piece of heavy machinery in existence had been assembled to work on the stretch of road I had to cross with the ponies in order to reach Etteridge. Enormous earthmovers and bulldozers rattled and squeaked, shoving great mounds of red earth to one side as they scraped the new highway level. Convoys of lorries with huge rotating mixers waited their turn to back up and add a few more yards to the slowly advancing ribbon of concrete. Contractors' cars, vans, diggers and lorries rushed about, carting, dumping, loading, surveying or just looking on. The roaring, squealing, yelling, jarring noise all but burst my eardrums and Thor and Lucy would have bolted if I had not kept a firm grip on them. A contractor's car pulled up and a man wearing a safety helmet shouted something and pointed to his watch. I could not hear what he said and waved to him to come over to me. He grinned and was opening the door of his car when a miracle happened. As though someone had pulled a motor switch, the noise was shut off and machinery stood motionless where only seconds before it had been tearing up the earth. The man was saying something, but my head still buzzed with the noise.

His voice broke through, shouting, 'I was trying to tell you we finish early on Saturdays and you would soon be able to cross.' Realising the noise around him had stopped, he lowered his voice, 'Sorry for bellowing,' he said, 'you get used to it in this job.' He walked round the ponies, then pushing his helmet to the back of his head, he rubbed his brow thoughtfully, 'By God, it sometimes makes me wonder what life's all about,' he said. 'Here am I, building a modern road to carry more traffic and you're travelling with a pack pony like they've been doing for centuries.'

Glancing at his watch, he cursed and ran to his car. It

started first touch and with a thumbs-up sign and a squeal of protesting tyres, he disappeared in a cloud of smoke and dust.

Threading my way through the lines of silent machines, I led Thor and Lucy the half mile to the farmstead of Etteridge and followed a wide track between the farm buildings into open country. It had been very hot all day but when a bank of cloud drifted in from the West and shut off the sun, a fresh breeze rapidly cooled my sweat-soaked shirt and I was glad to pull on a sweater. It was an easy track but Thor kept stumbling every few yards and, though I checked his feet and legs very carefully, I could find nothing wrong. General Wade had certainly planned his road very carefully and it wound gently through a vast expanse of heather, crossing streams by the now familiar bridges. It could not have been easier going for a pony yet Thor continued to stumble and he walked so painfully it was an effort for him to put one leg in front of the other.

Spreading out the map, I saw I was quite close to a farm called Milton of Nuide and only a few miles from the village of Newtonmore. I felt sure there would be a blacksmith somewhere in the area. The large bank of cloud covering the sun drifted away towards the Cairngorms and it was comfortably warm again as I led Thor and Lucy slowly down a wide, dusty track to the farmhouse. It took several hefty thumps on the door before a sleepy-eyed man appeared and informed me gruffly that he was only renting the cottage temporarily and I should continue for another half mile to Nuide Farm and see the manager there.

At Nuide Farm the manager was very helpful and said there was a blacksmith at Newtonmore but as it was the weekend it was unlikely he would turn out until Monday. He showed me a field where I could camp and graze the ponies then returned to his haymaking. Not wanting to waste the whole weekend hanging around, I quickly pitched the tent and walked the three miles to Newtonmore to see if I could coax the blacksmith to come out that evening. Blacksmiths are a fine race of men and life would be very dull without their banter and fund of tales, but they can often be as truculent and unco-operative as some of the horses they have to deal with.

'It's the heat and smoke that makes 'em bad tempered,' an

old farmer once told me. 'They can't kick the horses so they lash out at the owner instead.'

I knocked at the door of the blacksmith's cottage and it was instantly flung open. A hefty man with unruly hair and deep-set eyes looked me up and down.

'Whadyerwant?' he growled. I explained about Thor and asked if he would come and fit new shoes so that I could carry on to the Cairngorms before the weather broke again.

'I'm no coming out tonight, that's for sure, but I might manage it tomorrow. Where are you staying?'

I said, 'Nuide Farm.'

'Right,' was his reply, 'I'll come when I can,' and he shut the door. There was no point in trying to persuade him and with nothing better to do I wandered down the village main street.

A friend of mine, a Macpherson, once said that if I was ever in Newtonmore I should not fail to visit Clan Macpherson Museum, where I would be able to see the green banner of the clan, Cluny Macpherson's black chanter and the broken fiddle of James Macpherson, the Scottish equivalent of Robin Hood, who was hanged for stealing. Regrettably the museum curator either did not display the Macpherson memorabilia on Saturdays, or he had gone home for tea, and I rattled the door in vain.

The village was obviously a popular watering-hole for motorcoaches on tours of the Highlands. Hotel forecourts thronged with high-spirited visitors and, to the delight of a party of kilted pipers in varying degrees of intoxication, their arrival coincided with a continental coach full of lively French girls. It was soon plain that Scottish mythology had crossed the Channel.

'Hey, Jock,' shouted a swarthy Parisienne in tight-fitting jeans and a well-fitted blouse, 'What do a Scottish man wear under ze kilt?'

A huge sandy-haired piper looked at her through glazed eyes then, gently placing his bottle of 'Highland Mist' on the pavement, grasped the hem of his kilt with both hands and lifted it to his chest. The Parisienne turned white and screamed, '*Mon Dieu, c'est la Tour Eiffel!*' and all her friends crowded round to see the Scottish phenomenon. Full of whisky and hardly knowing what he was doing, the big Highlander swayed back and forth on his heels, still holding his kilt to his chest, until several of his friends ran out of the hotel shouting, 'Angus, you daft eedjot, are ye trying to land us all in jail,' and lifting him bodily they carried him into their coach, draped him over a seat and returned to follow the French girls into the bar.

What a Scotsman wears, or does not wear, under his kilt, has kept visitors of Scotland mystified for years. Like the sightings of the Loch Ness monster the day before they arrive on holiday, or the origin of the haggis, they are always held one step away from the truth. Only those with a genuine thirst for knowledge will have the secret revealed to them. Paul Steeman in his intriguing book, *Across the Highlands with Sweetheart*, tells the story of a kilted farmer who, when asked by an English lady if Scotsmen wore anything under their kilts, took her hand and said, 'Madam, I cannot tell you. I can only do as I did when I was young and a girl persisted in asking me this. I took her hand and put it under the kilt for herself to find out.'

It was in the Highlands that the prudish ladies of the Victorian era often had their first lesson in practical anatomy. Describing what Highlanders wore when he toured Scotland in the early part of the nineteenth century, Edward Burt wrote, 'This dress is called a quelt; and for the most part they wear this petticoat so very short, that in a windy day, going up a hill, or stooping, the indecency of it is plainly discovered. A Highland gentleman told me on a day merrily, as we were speaking of a dangerous precipice we had passed over together, that a lady of noble family had complained to him very seriously, that as she was going over the same place with a gilly, who was on an upper path, leading her horse with a long string, she was terrified with the sight of the abyss that to avoid it, she was forced to look up towards the bare Highlander all the way long.'

The smell of food wafting out of the hotels reminded me that I had not eaten since breakfast so on the way out of the village I treated myself to a meal of sausage, bacon and chips in a café. I was trudging back along the road to Nuide Farm when a van pulled up alongside me and a gruff voice said,

'Get in, I'm going to measure your pony's feet to make a set of shoes.'

It was the blacksmith and in a talkative mood.

'I've nae time for a lot of the pony owners these days,' he complained as the van bounced along the road. 'They buy a pony and they're all over me to come and shoe it, then when they think they've learnt the job they start telling me how it should be done. There's more money in mending farm implements and they're a hell of a lot less trouble.' He turned the van into the farmyard and waited while I went to collect Thor. 'Who put these on?' he demanded, lifting Thor's front leg.

'I did, about two weeks ago,' I admitted reluctantly.

He tapped Thor's foot with a hammer and said, 'There's nothing wrong with 'em it's just that you didn't trim his feet. The hoof's too long and that's why he's lame.'

I said I had thought of carrying a pair of hoof trimmers, but they were too heavy and I left them at home.

'Well, next time take 'em with you,' he grinned, 'they're cheaper than me.' He drove away and, absolutely worn out, I crawled into my sleeping bag and fell fast asleep.

I slept late the next morning and it was the familiar sound of wind-driven rain battering onto the flysheet that woke me. It was a lovely feeling not to have to strike camp and load the ponies with the rain dribbling down my neck and I made the most of it by snuggling deeper into my sleeping bag and going back to sleep. When I woke again and looked at my watch, it was almost midday. A faint breeze and light drizzle was all that was left of the heavy downpour and gale-force wind and a bright sun was doing its best to put some cheer into the damp scenery. On the edge of the field, a few yards from the tent door, four or five adult rabbits were hopping around, nibbling the grass while their tiny youngsters, with large floppy ears, played a game of 'chase me charlie' round a fence post. Suddenly there was a rustling in the thick grass by the tent and there was a stoat on his hind legs watching the rabbits like a tiger watching a herd of antelope. He was so close to me I could have touched him, but I held my breath and kept perfectly still. He sank out of sight in the grass, then a few seconds later popped up again even closer to me and I could see every hair on his handsome body, the light brown of his head contrasting with his smart white chest. The fine whiskers protruding on either side of his long face twitched with anticipation as the bright black eyes fixed hungrily on the rabbits. I could almost hear his mind ticking over as he worked out his strategy. Should he try and get closer to the older rabbits by creeping along the fence or would a surprise attack on the young be easier? Would it be best to go into the stack yard and hide behind the tractor parked near the gate? The young rabbits tired of chasing each other round the fence post and playing 'follow my leader' went first into the centre of the field and then turned and hopped straight towards the tent. Stoat sank silently into the grass and waited. Nature has built an early-warning system into all her animals and the adult rabbits, sensing something was wrong, drummed a warning on the ground with their back feet. The young rabbits turned and scattered, running like the wind for the safety of their burrows on the far side of the field. A brown thunderbolt exploded from the grass and the stoat streaked across the field, the black tip of his tail held up as he ran. A squeal of terror came from the rabbits when they saw him. They zigzagged across the field trying to shake him off, but he was too fast. He locked himself like a missile behind one of the young ones. Tiring rapidly, it weaved desperately from side to side, screaming for help. But nothing could save it. The stoat closed quickly and with a bound sank its teeth into the rabbit's neck. With a final piercing shriek, it lay still. The stoat stopped for a moment to watch a dozen white tails disappearing into a maze of burrows on the side of a hill then, heaving backwards with remarkable strength, dragged the carcase of the rabbit across the field and under the fence. When I went to look half an hour later there was no sign of the stoat or the rabbit.

Although the sun was shining, the sky to the West did not look at all promising and I spent the rest of the afternoon poring over the maps, searching for an alternative to the Lairig Ghru should the weather turn nasty. Bored with sitting around, I went for a walk in the evening, hoping to meet the blacksmith and hurry him along so I could get away early the next morning; but he did not appear. Before darkness fell a strong wind blew down off the hills and I was glad to return to the warmth of the tent and a mug of coffee laced with whisky.

The blacksmith's van rattled into the farmyard early the following morning and by ten o'clock Thor was striding along happily in his new shoes. It was a huge relief to know that his lameness was caused by nothing more than his shoes and I kept my fingers crossed that the weather would be kind for the final part of my journey through the Lairig Ghru. The new A9 road under construction passed close to the farm. Although it was not officially open, the farm manager said that no one would object to me taking the ponies along it. The ponies caused quite a flurry of interest as I rode along the long strip of concrete and the drivers of the contractors' vehicles twisted their heads in surprise as they drove along. A cheerful man in a Land Rover pulled up and got out to admire the ponies.

'Hell's bells,' he exclaimed, bursting into fits of laughter, 'I've seen everything now. Wait till I tell the boss that his fine new road has been officially opened by a horse.' He climbed into the Land Rover again and slid the side window back. 'I've got a job to do just now,' he called, 'but two miles up the road you'll see a caravan. Come and have a mug of tea with us. I'll have the kettle boiling by the time you get there.'

Sure enough, when I reached the caravan the tea was ready and he had even driven into nearby Kingussie to get me a pie.

'I'm Jim McBain and my pal here is Simon MacDonald, but never mind the formalities, get stuck into that,' he said, handing me a meat pie and a battered pint mug brimming with thick tea. Simon MacDonald had been a blacksmith and he looked critically at Thor's new shoes.

'Aye,' he said in a West Highland accent, 'he's no made a bad job of them at all, perhaps a wee bit long in the clenches, but no bad at all.'

The lunch break over, Jim had to leave with Simon on another errand. Unhitching the ponies from the caravan towbar, I thanked them for their hospitality and followed a deeply rutted access track down to the peace of a back road by the ruin of Ruthven Barracks.

The day became progressively warmer as I left Ruthven

behind me and rode steadily along the winding road. Normally I hate riding on roads designed for the motor car, but this one never lacked interest and there was always something new round each corner. Beads of sweat dripped off Thor and Lucy as they slogged along the shimmering tarmac and so, coming to a stream by a garden hedge, I let them drink. While they slurped, I glanced idly over the hedge into the garden and beads of sweat started to drip from me. It had nothing to do with the heat of the sun. Lying on her back on the lawn with her head on a cushion was a girl in her early twenties, wearing only a minute bikini. She was fast asleep and her well-formed breasts rose and fell rhythmically. Wisps of her long black hair had fallen across her lovely face and reached almost to the curve of her belly. All the manly urges rose inside me as I gazed at her and I envied the clan chiefs of old who, having spied such a beauty, would have whisked her off to their castle.

The chiefs certainly had this sort of power over their people, but one lecherous laird who lived in Ruthven Castle pushed his luck too far and came to a nasty end. Enticing away a local lass for a bit of slap and tickle was one thing, but when young Lord Walter Comyn decided to add spice to his sensual amusements by ordering the women on his estate to work naked in the fields, he was subjecting them to unbearable shame. Excited by the prospect of an unusual harvest time, young Walter rode through the hills to visit friends at Atholl, with the intention of returning within a few days to enjoy the fun. But he never did return. His horse arrived back, terrified and foaming at the mouth, with no rider on its back but with one of his legs hanging from a stirrup. A search was made for his body and it was found among some rocks with a pair of eagles feasting on it. It was said that Comyn's death was the work of witchcraft and the eagles were the mothers of two of the girls who were to be forced to work naked.

As I stared at the sun-tanned Cleopatra lying on the lawn, I experienced all of Lord Walter Comyn's weaknesses. But the thin face of the girl's mother glaring at me from an upstairs window looked so eagle-like I took fright and dug my heels into Thor's ribs for a quick getaway.

Reaching the edge of Inshriach Forest, I asked a man sitting in a Forestry Commission Land Rover if he knew of a place where I could camp.

'I dinna ken, laddie,' he said, hardly looking up from a newspaper he was reading. 'Ye'd best gang on doon the road tae the Forester's house and ask there.'

I found the house in a little clearing in a coppice of birch and I was warmly welcomed by Alec Herd, the Forester, and his wife, Mary. Alec arranged for me to stay at a nearby farm owned by the Russell family, who very kindly let me sleep in their comfortable caravan.

23

The Last Lap – the Lairig Ghru

I woke the next morning excited at the prospect of tackling the notorious Lairig Ghru Pass, but when I rode away from the Russell's farm the weather looked extremely threatening. Great banks of cloud were scudding across the sky at a tremendous speed and it looked as if I was in for a battering. Alec Herd guided me through the forest for a mile or two until we reached the boundary fence.

'I'll leave you here,' he said, 'just carry on through the gate and follow the reiver's road to Loch an Eilein.'

Away from the shelter of the trees I felt the full force of the wind and the gusts very nearly knocked me out of the saddle. The path through the heather looked like any other path crisscrossing the hills and woods, but in its day the reiver's, or robber's, road was one of the favourite routes of Rob Roy MacGregor for his raids into the cattle-rich country of Speyside. Cattle-raiding expeditions to the East were a favourite pastime with the warring clans from the other side of the Correyairack. One of the Rothiemurchus lairds, when he heard that raiders were in the area, used to tie a bullock to a tree close to the Robber's road. The bullock was always driven away, but the laird's herds were not touched. The path followed the base of a hill, past little Loch Gamha to the welcome shelter of trees surrounding Loch an Eilein. After the gorgeous warmth of the day before, the weather seemed to have gone mad. There would be a lull for a few minutes when all was quiet, then, with a noise like an approaching express train, the wind roared across the hills from the West, throwing up loose heather and grass in its path and turning the surface of the loch white with spume as it howled through the trees. It lasted perhaps five minutes then all would be quiet again until the next squall arrived. It was extremely cold and I halted in the shelter of a large tree to pull on a thick sweater under my anorak. Between the loch and the edge of Rothiemurchus Forest I had to cross open country and poor Lucy was almost bowled over as the force of the wind grabbed at the packs and spun her round.

Pummelled first one way then another as the wind bounced off the mountains and came at us from different directions, it was a great relief to reach the protection of the trees once more. I rested for a while by the side of a river to eat a bar of chocolate and decide whether to carry on through the Lairig Ghru or wait for the weather to improve. A plaque fastened to an iron footbridge spanning the river informed me that it was five and a half miles to the summit of the Lairig Ghru and fourteen miles to Derry Lodge on the Braemar side of the Pass. Providing the weather did not get worse I estimated it would take me three and a half hours to reach the summit and another four and a half to five to drop down the other side to Derry Lodge. I sat back against a tree and surveyed the weather. The wind was westerly gusting a good force eight in the squalls, but the black rain clouds had been replaced by a grey harmless variety. Although the clouds streamed in long banners from the lofty summit of Braeriach, there seemed little possibility of them sliding below the three thousand foot level, so visibility would be no problem. The Lairig Ghru ran roughly North to South, through a deep cleft between the long mountain barriers of Braeriach (3,888 feet), Eirich Carn (3,695 feet) and Cairn Toul (3,774 feet) on the West side and Lurchers Crag (3,459 feet), Ben Macdhui (3,927 feet) and Carn a' Mhaim (3,411 feet) in the East. Since the wind was from the West the pass should be fairly sheltered for most of the way. It was this final point that convinced me it was safe to carry on.

But first I had to overcome an obstacle that worried me far more than the prospect of being caught in the Lairig Ghru in bad weather. To reach the Pass I had to take the ponies through the river and it was in spate. There was no possibility of taking them across the footbridge. To prevent it from being swept away during the floods it had been built high above the river and was reached on either side by a flight of steps.

Taking a firm grip of Lucy's lead rope, I pushed Thor to the water's edge, expecting to have to fight with him before he placed a cautious hoof in the water. He amazed me by plunging straight in and Lucy followed without hesitating. I felt Thor brace himself as the water rose over his knees and splashed against his chest, but he kept going and never put a foot wrong. To keep my feet dry, I sat cross-legged in the saddle like a mahout riding an elephant and reached the safety of the opposite bank with hardly a spot of water on me. Scrambling out of the river, the ponies chewed happily on a few peppermints while I checked the pack lashings and girths. Then on we went, deep into the ancient forest of Rothiemurchus with its graceful pine trees rising out of a thick carpet of heather and blaeberry. There are few trees to equal the Scots pine for beauty yet it is only in recent years that anything has been done to preserve them. In only a very few areas of the Highlands can you see remnants of the original Caledonian Forest and had it not been for a wise man of Badenoch there might not have been a Scots pine left in the whole of Strathspey. According to legend, the King of Lochlan was jealous of the fine forests in the Highlands and sent a witch to destroy them with fire. She started with the great forests of Sutherland and soon hardly a tree was left standing. Everyone was in a dreadful panic as she moved South with her evil work, but because she remained hidden in the clouds no one could catch her. Her fire had reached the edge of Badenoch when a wise man hit upon an idea to make the witch show herself. He gathered a large number of sheep, cattle and horses together, then separated the sheep from the lambs, the cows from the calves and the horses from the foals. The cries of the young parted from their mothers and the mothers searching for their young set up such a tremendous noise that the witch stuck her head through a hole in the cloud to see what the commotion was about. It was just what the wise man hoped she would do. Having loaded his gun with a silver sixpence, he killed the witch and saved the forests.

I sent the wise man of Badenoch my own thanks as Thor and Lucy made their way along the forest path. If the trees had not been there to take some of the sting out of the wind, progress would have been very slow and uncomfortable. As we climbed higher and the trees thinned out the protection was less effective and in the teeth of the gale I led the ponies up the east side of the Pass to join the path from Loch Morlich. For a while the ponies floundered through rocks and bog until the Sinclair Refuge Hut came into sight and the path turned towards it, dropping steeply to a narrow gorge and the tumbling waters of the Allt Druidh. On the opposite side of the stream a narrow, slimy path slanted upwards out of the gorge towards the Sinclair Hut, then swung away from it to follow a very rough but well-defined route towards the summit ridge. Lashed by the gale, cloud streaked across the sky at a tremendous speed, but deep inside the Pass there was hardly a breath of wind and it was surprisingly warm. As we climbed higher I could see what looked like a thick layer of snow barring the way, but when I focused the binoculars on it I had to look twice to make sure my eyes were not deceiving me. A vast boulder field filled the Pass, reaching right to the summit and the path went right through it. I scanned the hillside for an alternative way round, but there was none. To a walker a boulder field is a minor inconvenience and he can hop from one lump of rock to another. For a pony it is a major hazard, where a slip or an unseen hole can result in a broken leg.

At the edge of the boulder field I left the ponies browsing on the sparse grass while I walked ahead to survey the route. It was not a cheering sight. In every direction it gave the appearance of the aftermath of an earthquake. Millions of tons of boulders and rubble were spread all around as if the summit of the Pass was a mountain peak that had been annihilated by the devastating force of nature. Returning to the ponies, I tethered Lucy to a boulder and led Thor slowly through the maze. He slipped and skidded and at one point worked himself into a frenzy when he jammed a hoof between two boulders, but I managed to prize it out and he reached the other side shaking, but otherwise unscathed. Lucy made it look easy by picking her way daintily across with hardly a slip and whinnied at Thor as if she was asking him why he had made such a fuss. I have often thought it would be marvellous to have a gelding as brave as Lucy, but I cannot bear the idea of Thor going through life on his own, the old fool just would not survive.

A patch of grass attracted the attention of the ponies and I let them graze while I sat on a boulder and looked down the way we had come to the deep cleft below the Sinclair Hut, where the Allt Druidh hurried on its way to link up with the many streams pouring off the hills that combine to swell the mighty Spey at Aviemore. Some say that the name 'Lairig Ghru' is taken from the Allt Druidh, but as usual other scholars disagree and offer their own interpretation. They range from 'Lairig Cruidh' (Cattle Pass) to 'Lairig Ruadh' (Red Pass) and one reverend gentleman calls it Learg Ghrumach (Savage Pass). It was this name that captured the imagination of the early map-makers and they dropped the 'Ghru' in favour of 'Ghruamach', 'for which,' wrote one critic, 'they apparently had not the slightest authority.'

In the days before railways came to alter drastically the way of life in the Highlands, the Lairig Ghru was one of the highways used by drovers moving cattle and sheep from the North to the markets of Deeside and Falkirk. In 1842 the Reverend Charles Grant wrote that the Lairig Ghru was made fit for the passing of cattle with 'much trouble by the removal of immense blocks of granite'. Apart from the drovers and shepherds using the Pass to take their stock to market, the women of Rothiemurchus used to walk through in groups carrying baskets of fresh eggs to sell in Braemar. What an incredible feat, walking a total of fifty-six miles and climbing twice to almost 3,000 feet to sell a few eggs. There was a time when one of the more selfish lairds chose to ignore the establishment of this ancient right of way and closed the Pass. It was only through the persistence of the Scottish Rights of Way Society that it was opened up again.

It is not surprising to learn that that formidable lady, the Honourable Mrs Murray, also tackled the Lairig Ghru, but on horseback rather than in her coach. The ghillie who was leading her pony was busy describing the view when the pony sank deep into a bog and struggled furiously to free himself and, she says, 'in an instant threw me over his tail. I fortunately fell on soft peat moss and had the presence of mind to roll myself out of the way of the heels of the struggling pony and got up without hurt.' We can only guess what she said to the unfortunate ghillie.

Looking down the wild and beautiful Pass to the forests of Rothiemurchus, I found it difficult to believe that serious suggestions have been put forward in recent years for building a motor road through the Lairig Ghru and other remote glens of the Cairngorms. What sort of people are they who think up these ideas? Are they so greedy and insensitive that they would destroy the very country in which they live in order to line their pockets? The wilderness areas of Scotland must be preserved at all costs, not just for the benefit of a handful of hikers who come to enjoy the peace and quiet, but in order to maintain a balance between the earth as nature intended it and man's attempts to change it. The dividing line between development and desecration is perilously thin. Unquestionably, Scotland must consider every means of strengthening its economy, but whether yet another motor road would attract more visitors or be an asset to the remote communities is doubtful. In any case, it would be poor compensation for an irreversible scar across the face of one of the best-known mountain regions in the country.

My resting-place was only a few yards from the summit of the Pass, two thousand seven hundred and thirty-three feet above sea level. Zephyrs of wind wafting down off Braeriach cooled the air and made me shiver. Gathering the ponies, I led the way through heaps of loose rock to a couple of shallow, almost insignificant pools of water, where by some mystical power the water nymphs fathered an infant rivulet that crawled unsteadily through the rocks, growing fast as he ran down to the floor of the glen to emerge into adulthood as the mighty River Dee.

The Braemar side of the Lairig Ghru was very different from the way we had climbed up. Instead of leaving a deep, narrow cleft, the receding glaciers had carved out a long glen between the massifs of Ben MacDhui and Cairn Toul. The view was marvellous and I looked down Glen Dee for a distance of eight or nine miles.

It was now mid afternoon and the gale that had raged all morning had blown itself out, leaving a warm sun to chase away the clouds. Lashing sweater and anorak to the saddle, I rolled up my shirt sleeves and felt the warmth of the sun soak into my arms as I led the ponies along a horribly churned-up path. Some very wet sections took a long time to negotiate and in bad weather the path would have been very hazardous. To shelter climbers and walkers, a refuge hut had been built in Glen Dee, under the lea of the towering rock face of Devil's Point. This part of the glen is wild and rugged country and anyone caught out in severe weather would surely perish if they failed to reach the hut.

Opposite the hut, the path for Braemar forked left and, contouring round the base of Carn a' Mhaim, descended to the edge of a river in Glen Luibeg. It was a different world from the bleak, barren wastes of Glen Derry and I lay in the grass by the river listening to finches flitting noisily among the branches of tall Scots pine. A flock of ptarmigan raced about overhead, landing in the heather high up the hillside, then swishing down again like a formation of aircraft. Thor and Lucy snatched hungrily at a patch of sweet grass and I let them get on with it while I stretched out in the sun.

The music of the shallow river splashing and gurgling over the rocks mingled with the chatter of finches. It was very peaceful and I hated taking the ponies away from their hard-earned meal, but evening was advancing and I had to find a campsite. I climbed into the saddle for the first time since starting up the Lairig Ghru. With Lucy close behind, Thor waded across the river and we followed a good track down to Derry Lodge.

By the time I had unloaded the ponies and pitched the tent darkness was falling and I sat by the river and watched a most beautiful sunset. It was a superb evening yet a wave of depression flooded over me. My journey was nearly over and though I desperately wanted to carry on I was almost out of food and money. Thor and Lucy were lying in the grass close to each other. I went over and sat with them. We had travelled over four hundred miles together and had built up a relationship between us that is almost impossible to describe, but has a lot to do with trust. It was a wonderful experience to journey with ponies day in day out, in good weather and bad, over mountains, through rivers and across bogs, never knowing what the day would bring or what lay over the next